# Changing Styles in Fashion

## Who, What, Why

# Changing Styles in Fashion

## Who, What, Why

### Maggie Pexton Murray

The Fashion Institute of Design & Merchandising
Los Angeles, California

Original Illustrations by
POLLY TRIBOLET

Fairchild Publications
New York

*for Kelly and J.G.*

*Changing Styles in Fashion: Who, What, Why* is a book, perhaps something of a primer, about fashion. It is designed to explain in simple, ordinary language what fashion is all about. It is also designed to give you a basic understanding of the great world of apparel, what motivates it, how it functions, where fashion comes from, and why.

The fashion industry throughout the world is enormous. Probably more people are involved in the buying, selling, production and execution of apparel and related industries than in any other business in the world. Fashion is as basic as steel, automobiles or power generation. It keeps entire economies functioning and interacts and responds to emotional and financial needs of most peoples of the world.

Fashion is not nearly as ephemeral as the word suggests, nor does it apply strictly to apparel. The word itself is defined in *Webster's New World Dictionary*: "Fashion—the make, form or shape of a thing. The way in which something is made or done, manner. The current style or mode of dress, speech, conduct; something, especially a garment, in the current style; to make a certain way. SYN: Fashion is the prevailing custom in dress, manners, speech, etc., of a particular place or time, esp. as established by the dominant section of society or the leaders in the fields of art, literature, etc. *Style*, often a close synonym for fashion in discriminating use suggests a distinctive fashion, esp. the way of dressing, living, etc., that distinguishes persons with money and taste; *Mode*, the French word expressing this idea, suggests the height of fashion in dress, behavior, etc., at any particular time; *Vogue* stresses the general acceptance or great popularity of a certain fashion. Fad stresses the impulsive enthusiasm with which a fashion is taken up for a short time. *Rage* and *craze* both stress an intense, sometimes irrational enthusiasm for passing fashion."

What wonderful words! Rage, craze, intense, irrational! But is fashion these things? Yes. In many instances, fashion becomes an overwhelming force that can, and sometimes does, take over our lives. It is interesting that the words rage and craze imply a certain level of insanity, and it is also interesting that fashion rages and crazes generally occur when a society or culture is emotionally under stress—in times of revolution, in times of rebellion, in times of protest when society itself becomes crazed. These are the times that fads sweep, not style. These are the times when one most easily can watch clothing mirror society. We might even call some of these fashions aberrational because they completely contradict ordinary costume cycles.

How fascinating these definitions are, especially the concept that fashion is not merely the custom in dress, but refers to manners, speech and lifestyle. We surely know that fashion exists on every level in the world: there are fashionable ways and places to travel, there are fashionable things to eat. There are fashions in flowers, slang, sizes of families, lifestyles, all subject to the continually evolving, changing moods of society and its needs. And further, all of these fashions arrive, become accepted, disappear into oblivion, only to reappear down stream once again to be recycled into new successes.

The most important lesson to learn about fashion is that it constantly repeats, sometimes in a slightly new way or with slightly different details, but when one least expects it, there it comes again. The little "Louis" heel is the legacy of the great Sun King, Louis XIV; high ruffled collars are descendants of Elizabethan ruffs; extended shoulders remind us of the forties, but also are reminiscent of Henry VIII and the German silhouette during the High Renaissance, when widened, extraordinary shoulder padding was the rage. Soft, ruffled jabots and collars come to us from gentlemen's shirts of the 18th and 19th centuries; separates and layering from the Middle Ages. All has been used before, worn before and adapted before. And will be again.

In this century, witness the mini of the 1960s. The hair, the attitudes, the clothing, all reflecting the protest of a large part of our society; the cutting edge in this case was the cult of the young and the disenfranchised. Fashion went up from the streets, rather than down from the elite. Witness an opposite in earlier times, when the Pilgrims and the Puritans, protesting the extravagance of the age in which they lived, changed their manners, their way of speaking, their dress and presented a different face to the world...subdued, somber, quiet.

So, even though we will skim through the history of costume, it is hoped that opening the door to the vast world of fashion will tantalize you into examining further the story of how clothing has evolved, how it changes and adapts to cultures, how important it has always been in the struggle for power, money and influence. For understanding where apparel fits into the scheme of our lives, where it comes from also means that one can begin to sense or predict where it is going next. And understanding how clothing represents the surface of our society, the iceberg with most of its size hidden, we can better understand our lives, our anxieties and our hopes.

1988                                              Maggie Pexton Murray
                                                   Los Angeles, California

In these notes of ackowledgments, the enormous contributions that so many people have made to this effort are in some measure noted. But it does seem a small way to say thank you for all that was done to help. A book could be written about those who help write a book, those who make any text of this sort possible, particularly those involved in research, fact checking, or digging-out of material.

But though this may be the small way, I mean to express in the largest sense my gratitude and appreciation to those who helped me through the process. First to those students at the Fashion Institute of Design and Merchandising in Los Angeles, who in a sense instigated this project. One young lady, one fine day, who was excited to find out that "Chanel was a person. I thought it was a perfume." That took courage. And another young woman, seemingly puzzled by the concept of stockings (something that went on, leg by leg), asked me to explain where stockings came from and how they were made. Such curiosity (and being up front enough to ask questions) triggered this effort to simplify and supply a framework for understanding fashion.

Of equal importance, the staff and teachers at the Fashion Institute of Design and Merchandising in Los Angeles. Charlotte Atkins, who struggled to help me master the word processor, and wept with me when that machine devoured an entire chapter, hiccuped a little, and died. Amy Gonzales, who calmly rescued Pierre Cardin, not once but twice, from the mysterious interior of the same dyspeptic computer. The devoted library staff, who were always ready to research and dig out facts, no matter how obscure. The encouragement first, of Sylvia Shephard, former Chair of the Merchandising/Communications Division; Barbara Bundy, Vice President, Education; BJ Shelton, Chair, Textiles and Manufacturing; the late Ron Lattinville, Chair, Liberal Arts. All helped me with enthusiasm and encouragement, in whatever I found mysterious and arcane.

Edward Maeder, Curator of Costumes and Textiles, Los Angeles County Museum of Art, and his entire department were never too busy to stop what they were doing to clarify a fact, check a date, research some obscure fashion. A particular thank you to Sandy Rosenbaum, Director of the Doris Stein Research and Design Center who patiently explored with me, century by century, the murk and mystery of the Middle Ages.

Bernard Kester, Acting Chairman of the Art Department of the University of California at Los Angeles, and Professor of Textile Arts, who lent me part of his personal library when I was unable to find reference books badly needed.

Lee Cass, Vice President and Fashion Director, Broadway Department Stores, Los Angeles, who helped me sort through the myserious highways and byways of European markets.

Merle Thomason, the secret weapon at Fairchild Publications, who can put her finger on almost anything, anytime, anywhere, with dispatch and serenity.

Polly Tribolet, my dear friend, who with great enthusiasm, not only cleanly and clearly illustrated all the fashions of obscure and distant times, but spent countless hours studying, checking, and redrawing each minute detail, until everything was perfect.

And finally, a very special thank you to Olga Kontzias, who edited this book, who struggled more than anyone, and had the patience to not only stick with it, but stick with me. She made it work.

# Contents

1. Covering the Body —————————— 1
2. Ancient Civilizations —————————— 19
3. From Barbarism to Baroque ————— 41
4. Revolution & Change —————————— 71
5. The 20th Century —————————— 95
6. The Great French Stars —————————— 121
7. How French Fashion Works ————— 149
8. The All-American Team —————————— 163
9. The Great American Stars —————— 185
10. How American Fashion Works ———— 205
11. The Story of Textiles —————————— 221
12. Summing It Up —————————— 235
    Bibliography —————————— 243
    Index —————————— 247

# CHAPTER ONE

# *Covering the Body*

No fashion is new. All costume has evolved from previous costume, every style has been seen, accepted and used before. Costume originated with simple geometric shapes: rectangles, squares, and triangles (folded squares and rectangles). These shapes were used in primitive times and are still being used. When a rain poncho is pulled over the head for protection, it is the same garment that was used for identical purposes during ancient civilizations. Primitive peoples created fabrics, possibly accidentally discovering the process while weaving baskets. The earliest textiles were simple rectangular shapes, woven on what are known as lap-looms, which produced a fabric by the most rudimentary form of interlacing spun fibers, one with another. The rectangles produced by this method were then fastened and draped about the body into what eventually became exquisite and intricate costumes.

*Slit-neck, side-fastened poncho, c. A.D. 1000–1500. Interlaced weave of cotton fibers. Los Angeles County Museum of Art.*

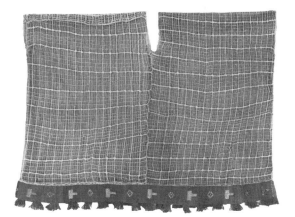

*Basic clothing categories:* above, left to right, *draped, pull-on, cut and sewn, artificial;* below, *close-fitting.*

In the history of costume, silhouettes are either natural or artificial, that is, they follow the lines of the body as in Greek dress, or disguise the body as in the fashions of the Renaissance. Clothing tends to fit into a certain number of basic categories. They are:

1. Draped apparel
2. Pull-on clothing; ponchos, etc.
3. Cut and sewn, semi-fitted clothing
4. Close-fitting; sheaths, body-clinging
5. Artificial; (hoops, padding, etc.)

As we examine the story of past and present fashion in the next few chapters, we will learn to identify apparel as belonging to one or another of these categories.

## WHAT IS FASHION?

If one uses the word in the strict sense of apparel, it implies covering the body with an article or some articles of clothing that have an acceptance in a recognized stratum of society. But perhaps if one starts with the basic concept that throughout the world, all people share the common impulse to cover, and/ or decorate the body, we can then understand that the Australian aborigine and the Beverly Hills sophisticate have something in common: both adorn themselves. And how the body is adorned creates fashion. Furs for Eskimos (but less and less in our day), and cotton gallabayas for the Egyptians have been achieved in response to climate and geography. The shared impulse is the same, however, for covering the body comes from a psychological need—the desire to alter our natural state. Strict students of the Bible tell us that covering the body comes from a sense of shame: but many fashion authorities maintain that body coverings are for exactly the opposite reason, to create an erotic appeal.

Evidence of forms of body adornment exists from prehistoric times. Cave paintings show us that primitive man was involved in decoration. The decoration might have been simply pretty stones that were strung about the neck and were believed to carry magic. Such magic stones are still worn, of course, but in different forms: once known as *amulets*, today they take the form of a St. Christopher medal, an Egyptian ankh, a Roman horn, a gold cross, a star of David. The motive, however, hasn't changed in thousands of years. These modern amulets give us the same sense of protection: they are guardians of the spirit. There is no doubt that in those distant ages, other items of apparel were used not only for psychological protection, but for physical protection as well. In the warm Mediterranean, man needed very little clothing, but as Ice Ages pushed cold down through Europe, furs and skins were needed to wrap about the body for warmth. Feet would also have been wrapped, creating shoes.

At whatever age mankind finds itself, the approval of society is desirable and necessary. Today, most people elect to follow the social and cultural mores that surround them, and that are believed to constitute accepted standards of fashion and behavior. In this instance, fashion is not confined simply to apparel: fashion exists in diverse forms and in countless manifestations. There is style in what we drink and eat. Chic people drink white wine rather than hard liquor. Others stick to Perrier. Light beers are invading the regular beer market. Fish is more "in" than beef. All of this marks our adaptability to change, and our readiness to accept new concepts and ideas. We can create fashions from need. For example, the fashion for fish comes from the recognition that it is healthier, and

*Fashion inspired by the street. Norma Kamali design complete with junk jewelry, bra-like bodice.*

today, society has grown tremendously interested not only in the healthy body, but in the protection of that body.

Fashion in this wider sense is everywhere, and deserves our attention, since it so often inter-relates with apparel. Food interconnects with body awareness, which, in turn is mirrored in clothing. In a wider, symbiotic sense, our eating habits affect fashion in other ways: less hides for leather if we reduce our consumption of beef. Less wool for apparel if sheep are reduced. Fashion surrounds us in every area of our lives. Automobiles have changed in a matter of a very few years from giant, long, chrome-streaked monsters to small, squared-off four cylinder cars. Has this any design relationship to the simpler, more pared down silhouette, or is it purely to conserve gasoline? Is the renewed interest in a larger, more luxurious car in the late 1980s a possible reflection of a renewed interest in fashions prevelant a generation ago? Or, is it part of a larger movement towards acceptance of luxury? We are too close to all of this to be objective: fifty years from now, these trends will be more easily understood. We learn quickly to accept change. An automobile from the 1950s or 1960s, with the heavy chrome trim and long sweeping fins, can cause spasms of delight, but just a very few years ago, the same spasms greeted the Volkswagon. The little stubby cars were the laugh riot of America when they were introduced, but today they don't rate a second glance.

Fashion is a most powerful force. One conforms, or one becomes an eccentric outcast. Fashion gives us not only an insight into the social structure of almost any society, but enables us to comprehend and understand the social and economic forces at work. For example, to the majority of us, *punkers* are considered to be fashion outcasts from the main stream of apparel, as are heavy-metal freaks. To one another, they are strictly costume conformists: they have created a concept of fashion which is not only comfortable to them, but is imbued with ultimate chic. In fact, the more antagonistic the attitude of mainstream society, the happier they are. The Mohawk-headed, pink-haired, strangely-clad young man or woman, loaded with chains, is delivering a message to us, and that message is understood. It is a message of rebellion and apartness. While it differs from the accepted norm for standard

*Evolution of fashion:* left, *string bikini, 1974. Contrast with the original Bloomer suit, scandalous in the 19th century, humorous today.*

society, it is delivering an alternative and powerful fashion statement, one that its adherents understand and enjoy. Further, some elements of these looks move up to different strata of society. One only has to see a press shot of the Princess von Thurn und Taxis, an internationally known beauty of European background, attending a ball with her hair standing straight up to understand that the fashion message from the streets is making progress. Certainly, jewelry and other accessories have been influenced by the ''heavy metal'' movement. One can also find similarities in the extraordinary hairstyles of the late 18th century, when hair piled high and lifted straight up into the air, was all the rage. These are not purely a 1980s phenomenon: the flower children of the 1960s exercised a strong influence on fashion, as did the street people of the French Revolution in 1789.

Almost all societies develop *counter-culture* movements, whose members establish some look that is different from that prevailing. Amelia Bloomer, as an example, rebelling against tight waists and hoops, introduced a whole new concept of clothing in the middle of the 19th century. Her rebellion is a fashion footnote, of course, but a significant one: it was a straw in the wind that would eventually blow away all such clothing restrictions. For most of the 20th century, children have dressed in miniature versions of adult apparel: the smash of the past few years is quite a different story—the fashions created by the San Francisco firm, *Esprit* with layering, fabric and color mixes, humor, and a light touch of madness. Young people adore it. Parents are puzzled, and thus the children adore it even more.

Clothing is worn for many reasons, and our selection of apparel unconsciously reflects that multitude of reasons. Basically, as Louis XIV said, "fashion is a mirror" and our acceptance of styles and changes in styles is a subconscious reaction to the society in which we live. The simplicity and elegance of Greek costume tells us a great deal about that civilization: conversely, the opulent, structured, dense-colored costume of the Victorian era reflects a totally different society. One can watch the changing mores of modern Japan as that nation gradually abandons its traditional, rigid, formalized costume for western dress, retaining, however, the rigid, traditional dress for formal occasions.

## THE FASHION SELECTION PROCESS

There are numerous reasons inherent in the selection of clothing, but those reasons can be grouped into certain categories and purposes. Implicit in the selection of these categories must be the understanding that each division can be broken down into hundreds of individual choices, created by the fact that we are all separate individuals and react individually to varying sets of circumstances.

*Why do people wear what they wear?* Choice of clothing represents combinations of reasons, psychological, geographic and historic, among others. Furs, for example, may be worn to show wealth, to protect against cold, or because they are part of traditional costume, such as a robe of state. Textiles can be chosen because they are comfortable, cotton or linen, as an instance, in hot climates: the same fabrics can be selected because they are fashionable, as in the casual, rumpled look. Psychologically, wearing rumpled clothing is communicating something else: the wearer has a sure sense of fashion and doesn't fear looking like a refugee from a rag bag.

Apparel reflects all of society. To quote James Laver, noted English costume historian, "in the perspective of costume history, it is plain that the dress of any given period is exactly suited to the actual climate of the time, and indeed bears a

close relation to such things as interior decoration and even architecture." In this context, compare the high, conical headdresses of medieval times with the high, Gothic arches of cathedral construction in the same period. As a further example, the spare, hard-edged silhouette of the 1960s in relationship to the glass-box skyscraper.

To return to the question of why people wear what they wear, the reasons can be broken down into certain basic motivations.

### Clothing as Protection

Clothing is most traditionally worn for protection. It is entirely possible that primitive humans covered their bodies to ward off insects, to protect against a harsh environment, or for simple warmth. However, we should not make the mistake of thinking that clothing is chosen purely as a protective device, it is simply one of the reasons. Cavemen, living in the great Ice Ages, would certainly have wrapped themselves with

*Extravagant furs with a primary thrust toward fashion:* left, *a fantasy Fendi fur design on the runway, 1978.* Right, *Christian Lacroix belted sable, 1988.*

animal skins, but today, throughout the civilized world, women and men also cover themselves with animal skins, not for protection in many cases, but for decorative purposes. If one accepts the theory that civilization began in the warm Mediterranean climate, where clothing was certainly not needed, one can see that the decorative purpose can outweigh the functional. Again, to refute the pure "clothing as protection" theory, we are reminded of the Indians of Tierra del Fuego, at the tip of South America, who lived in a freezing atmosphere and did not cover their bodies at all. It was simply not the custom. Conversely, in the heat of the Sahara desert, it is common to wear great, voluminous robes and head coverings of wool. Here, protection against the sun is certainly an element, but it has additionally become the custom to wear such clothing.

Nevertheless, a great deal of all clothing has a primarily functional purpose: boots and water-proof trenchcoats in the rain, brimmed hats to shade the sun, gloves and mittens in the snow and cold. In almost every case, however, these articles have the additional plus of fashion interest.

### Religious or Superstitious Selection
Why do people wear what they wear? For religious or superstitious reasons. It is plausible that some of the earliest forms of body coverings were inspired by just such motivations—to ward off evil spirits or demons. In primitive cultures everything not understood is frightening. We have briefly discussed the use and wearing of amulets, which are basically superstitious, but in carrying this concept further, we find that throughout history, people wore and still wear various articles of clothing for luck. In the early Renaissance, pointed-toed shoes were thought to keep witches away. Ancient Egyptians considered wool to be unlucky and it was rarely used. Bridal veils were originally worn to protect the bride from evil spirits that might be lurking in the vicinity (by hiding her face, the bride was able to fool the unsuspecting demon). Today's brides wear white, but in many cultures, white is unlucky, a sign of mourning . . . in those countries, brides often wear red. Every bride knows the adage, "something old, something new, something borrowed, something blue." Of course, it is pure superstition, as is the belief that it is unlucky for the groom to see his bride dressed in her wedding finery before the wedding.

Many of us secretly regard part of our wardrobes as "lucky" or "unlucky." We assure ourselves that some piece of clothing will bring us good luck if we wear it—or, conversely, we also have what we believe to be "unlucky" clothing: clothing that spots, or tears, or rips—bad things constantly happen. We have good times in some apparel, and bad times in others. A large part of the world imbues clothing with dimensions other than ordinary qualities, believing sincerely that some part of their costume carries magic.

Religious principles are often at work in selecting apparel. Religion dictates face coverings in many Islamic nations. In the Mormon religion, the truly devout wear long undergarments that cover the body at all times. The Shakers, Amish and "Plain" people wear clothing that has not changed in over a hundred years, dark, simple, and quaint. It is based on the costume of the Pilgrims and Puritans, whose clothing was based, in turn, on that of the gallant Cavalier. Orthodox Hebrew men wear hats in the temple, but their wives and daughters sit with uncovered heads. In reverse form, in the Roman Catholic Church, men bare their heads, and until recently, women always wore either a hat or a veil to cover the head, a fashion remnant of medieval times, when women's heads were always covered. The clothing of almost all people in religious life is, of course, different from apparel worn by the rest of society.

### Psychological Clothing

Why do people wear what they wear? For psychological reasons. If one were to survey a group to find out the varying processes by which clothing is selected, or to discover the multiplicity of reasons for the individuality expressed in apparel, one response would be repeated over and over. "I like the way it makes me look." In other words, some pieces of clothing are perceived as an enhancement. Clothing establishes a sense of self: it communicates moods and personal attitudes.

When we set out each day to face the world, we dress ourselves in garments that affect us psychologically though, in most cases, the selection process that goes into this choice of apparel occurs without a conscious rationale. Certain colors, certain styles, certain pieces of jewelry, favorite shoes, all are organized, assembled, and worn together to enhance some

*Stephen Sprouse finds inspiration from the street in his widely publicized graffiti collection.*

secret personal image. When one considers that at best our lives are spent in a hostile world, both in the narrow neighborhood sense, and in the broader, global sense, it is easy to understand that clothing, and the way it covers us, has many deep, inner meanings. Clothing becomes our security blanket.

Away from the protection of our homes, away from the shelter that covers us and the family and friends that love us, is that threatening "other" world, an environment in which we feel instinctively uneasy. To face that insecurity, we help ourselves by literally arming our bodies with costume. If what we wear gives us courage we can conquer the world. If what we wear creates a sense of insecurity, and is not protective, we break. It is that tiny crack in the daily armor that does us in: the over-run heel, the stocking with a hole, the drooping hem, the spot on the tie. Each miniature disaster takes its toll, leaving behind a vulnerable, unhappy human. Clothing is psychological armor; it not only covers us, it gives us the spirit to function. When we feel festive, we glitter—evening clothes sparkle and crackle with design excitement. When we are sad, we tend to retreat into dark colors and somber apparel. In the western world, black is the color of mourning: black, the absence of all color. The effect of clothing on our psyche is so profound that the subject has been covered at length by many famous analysts, both of the costume and the medical worlds. It is enough here to recognize the fact that clothing in itself represents deep personal wants, yearnings, and needs, and is so closely tied into our emotional and psychological lives that it is difficult to separate one from the other. Our clothing communicates our moods when we cannot. Our clothing is the image of our personality.

### Clothing as Identification

Why do we wear what we wear? Certainly for identification and decoration. What we wear is a banner. It tells others about us, just as we identify others from what they wear. The three piece Brooks Brothers suit is both identification and decoration: it represents a slice of our society: it tells us that the wearer is involved with work in certain industries, and even, often, gives us clues as to the financial means of that person. It certainly identifies a set of mind. On the other hand, jeans and t-shirts communicate a different message. The same young

*Establishment sportswear separates with a broad nod to both ethnic and country influences by Ralph Lauren, 1983.*

man might wear both, but in different situations and for different reasons. Additionally, attitudes are changed by the clothing we wear. Behaviour is constricted in the three-piece suit, and much freer in uncomplicated clothing.

The woman in the floor-length sable coat certainly sends a message, loud and clear; she is communicating wealth, for sables are synonomous with riches. The kilt on a Scot is instant identification, and if one knows plaids, the pattern will additionally tell us the man's name, the district in which he lives, and a great deal of his family history.

Many costume words have found their way into our daily vocabulary as identification: words such as ''blue collar'', ''white collar'', and ''hard hat'' quickly identify and stratify elements of our society. The elite once lived in ''silk stocking'' districts, signifying richness and quality. ''Shirttail'' relatives were poor. ''Lace-curtain Irish'' were uppity. ''Blue-stockings'' are prudes. Men in ''black-tie'' are identified with galas, and men in full morning dress are just as obviously identified with a wedding, and an upscale wedding, to boot. Black hats identify the villain in a cowboy movie while the white-hatted character is the hero. The woman on the street late at night in orange hot pants with high heels and a sequinned bodice identifies with yet another trade. Clothing is our badge. It is the continual, silent message that we transmit as clearly and succinctly as a radio signal, and the astute observer learns to tune in to that signal and understand it. Dress is an open book that informs others about attitudes, social position, and finanical status.

### Clothing for Sexual Attraction

Why do we wear what we wear? For sexual attraction. Most of mankind has always assumed that clothing was a sort of invention to cover the naked body, which is often considered shameful. The Bible tells us that it wasn't until Eve had the encounter with the snake-devil and ate the apple of wisdom that both Adam and Eve, in shame, covered their nakedness with leaves and left the Garden of Eden. (Incidentally, this is one of the earliest written records of clothing—leaves.)

Fashion is clearly selected on occasion to deliver a message to one's own kind—at other times, the choice is made to primarily attract the opposite sex. Many psychologists maintain that much of fashion is governed by the erotic principle, and they further maintain that fashion changes can be explained by what is known as the theory of the "shifting erogenous zone." In this approach to apparel, it is said that the function of clothing is to increase the appeal of the female by constantly shifting emphasis from one part of the body to another. At one time, the bosom is emphasized, at another, the buttocks by means of an attached bustle, for example. At times, bodices are cut low to expose the breasts, at other times ankles are allowed to peek from under a skirt. Fashion, therefore, follows a pattern of constantly varying allurements.

Throughout history, both men and women have considered different parts of the body to be extremely erotic. In some cultures, the foot was a sensual turn-on, as in the China of the recent past. In Victorian times legs were considered to be so provocative, that any careless exposure (or mention) of those particular limbs was enough to cast an otherwise quite proper young woman outside the pale of society. At its most extreme,

piano legs were covered with tiny ruffled pantaloons so that even that structural support—legs—could be hidden discreetly. Baring part of the body is, in most cases, infinitely more provocative than baring all of it, and the part that is bared constantly changes. Long skirts hiding the leg will give way to short skirts that flaunt them. The bosom will be accented, and then in a few years, will disappear under tight wrappings. Corseted waists will swell the hip and bust, but will alter in

*Selling sexual attraction:* left, *Givenchy's bare-bosomed evening gown, 1978.* Right, *Ungaro gives a mermaid shape to his evening separates, 1986.*

time to a bare midriff with no waist constriction. Soon, the cycle will repeat itself. Short, long, narrow, wide, a constant evolution of silhouettes.

In some societies, covering the body creates shame—in others, uncovering it has the same effect. It is all in the attitude of the culture and the historical concepts that govern that society or culture. Faces are veiled and bellies are bared in some Islamic nations. Monokinis are worn on the beaches in the south of France, but the same young woman would not think of appearing on the street with that much skin uncovered. It is generally considered to be true that clothing enhances erotic appeal rather than detracts from it. Covering or veiling parts of bodies is much more sexually attractive than nakedness: the body becomes more mysterious, involving the imagination. It has been said that the least sexually arousing experience in the world is a visit to a nudist camp.

### Hieratic Clothing

Why do we wear what we wear? Dress symbolizes achievement. This form of apparel is also known as *hieratic* dress, which indicates the rank of the wearer. The original meaning of the word is "priestly," or a "leader of sacred rites," but today the word refers to apparel which is stratified by custom. Kings and queens, with scarlet and purple robes and ermine furs, topped with glittering crowns, epitomize hieratic dress. It is worn on certain, special occasions, it is worn *only* by those entitled to wear it, and it is not at all worn by others, except perhaps at costume balls. While this form of apparel is not seen as much in our world, we are surrounded by hieratic dress in other forms.

A general of the army, for example, is immediately ranked by the number of stars worn across the shoulder, and is further identified by the various ribbons and decorations worn on his or her uniform. Indeed, some insignia marks all military apparel and identifies the wearer as to position and level of authority. The ribbons and decorations can also be easily read by other military people who can capsulize combat histories and various geographic locations with one glance.

It is no accident that the Pope wears white, or that Cardinals wear scarlet. Each level of the hierarchy of the church is precisely in color order and recognizably ranked. A Supreme

*Fashion borrowing from hieratic clothing: Lagerfeld mimics the French gendarme in his 1984–85 collection.*

Court Justice in his black robe (which comes to us straight from the Middle Ages) carries judicial majesty about his person, but it is the clothing that carries that majesty. In England, justices, barristers and solicitors still wear powdered wigs. Archaic, certainly, but carrying a message of accomplishment, achievement, and station in life.

It is interesting to note that throughout history, the hierarchy went to great effort to keep others from copying their clothing. This effort persists to this day, but in different forms. In the past, many laws were passed to prevent so-called common people from aping their betters. These laws were known as *sumptuary* laws. Even in our own early colonial days, certain laces and linens could not be worn by "common" people or those, in other words, who did not have sufficient wealth to allow them to wear certain fashions. Today, traces persist. It is against the law, for example, to wear a policeman's uniform. This law, of course, is designed to protect society, but it is in the nature of our understanding of that society that these laws exist. In societies past, the ruling class felt that *their* sumptuary laws also served as a protection for their society.

*INDUSTRY PROTECTION*   It is fascinating that fashion has been the subject of so much legal attention. Laws have been passed throughout time to protect the fashion industries of most countries, whether it was apparel, textiles, furs or leathers. England, for example, would refuse to accept French textiles, thus ensuring the prosperity of their own mills. The French, in turn, refused to accept textile imports from Italy and other countries. The Chinese zealously guarded for many centuries the secret of silk because, with a monopoly on its manufacture, China was guaranteed vast revenues. Export of any knowledge of silk, or silkworms was punished by death. Similar legal protectionism is rampant in our world. For example, Russia meticulously and successfully guards her sable production. South Africa controls diamond mining rigidly, thus keeping the price of the gems very high. Quotas are established to protect our American fashion industries. Cotton imports are limited and various tariffs and taxes are levied on leather goods, finished garments, laces, jewelry and other items of apparel. To be in the business of importing fashion merchandise, for example, is to weave through a minefield of intricate protectionism. Indeed, the ILGWU (International Ladies Garment Workers Union) presents an impassioned case for limiting all kinds of finished apparel shipped to this country from foreign nations. "Made in America" is the rallying cry: trade tariffs protect jobs. In a free-trade world, however, such exclusionary laws become a burden on all levels of society, and while restrictions on imported goods are found in most developed nations, outright protectionism and total bans are rarely in effect.

In any given period of history, including our own, many styles of clothing are worn. Not everyone in the world is fashionable, and indeed, not everyone is even interested, but none of us can be totally indifferent to prevailing style. We all must wear clothing, and as long as we cover our bodies with *something*, we cannot ignore what that something is. Once, fashion was purely the province of the very rich and, of course, in some respects that is still true. However, in this age, we can all clothe ourselves in style by presenting our own individual and personal concept of fashion. Fake fur may be the mink in some wardrobes, and rhinestones play the role of diamonds, but nothing is forbidden as it once was. What is too rich for the pocket can indeed be out of reach, but at least it is legal. We can adapt a Paris original and change it to present our version of that fashion to society on whatever economic level is supportable. Indeed, much of fashion is copied, nothing is patented or trademarked. The extraordinarily rich of today, for example, are the only supporters of the French couture, for no one else can afford the cost. But we can all wear the adaptations that are rampant. We are not restricted.

*IS FASHION ART?* A question constantly asked, and not always successfully answered. But it would certainly seem so, if the collections in highly respected museums are any criteria. Many fine artists today work with clothing or textiles as their medium, producing exquisite and unusual works of art. Textiles, in particular, have become an increasingly successful medium for artistic expression, the surfaces turned into highly unusual tactile art pieces. Clothing, however, is not a static surface—it is a moving, changing aesthetic form, dependent to a large degree on the manner in which it moves and changes. But as more and more superbly talented creative people turn to this discipline to express their emotional and artistic explorations, the answer to the "is fashion art" question will be apparent. Yes, it is.

When we look back at costume throughout history, we realize that what we are seeing in most cases is a distillation of an age. Today, the fashion press presents in most cases, the epitome of high chic. Alas, it is the rare person that hasn't at one time or another, taken a stricken look at a fashion magazine, and wondered what *that* was all about. Two hundred years from today, however, *that* image may be the

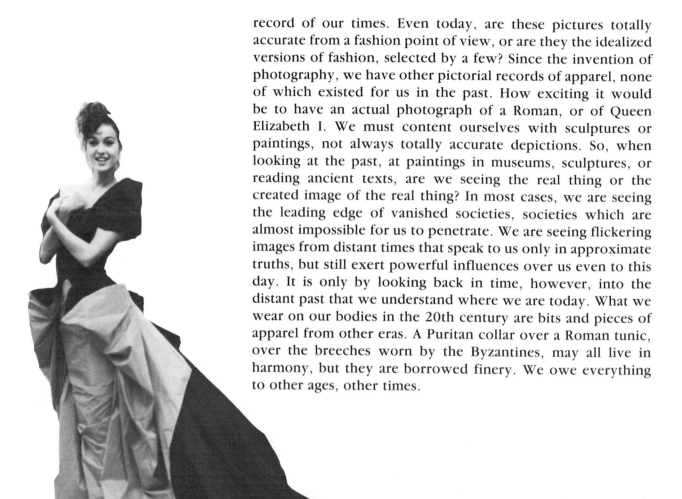

record of our times. Even today, are these pictures totally accurate from a fashion point of view, or are they the idealized versions of fashion, selected by a few? Since the invention of photography, we have other pictorial records of apparel, none of which existed for us in the past. How exciting it would be to have an actual photograph of a Roman, or of Queen Elizabeth I. We must content ourselves with sculptures or paintings, not always totally accurate depictions. So, when looking at the past, at paintings in museums, sculptures, or reading ancient texts, are we seeing the real thing or the created image of the real thing? In most cases, we are seeing the leading edge of vanished societies, societies which are almost impossible for us to penetrate. We are seeing flickering images from distant times that speak to us only in approximate truths, but still exert powerful influences over us even to this day. It is only by looking back in time, however, into the distant past that we understand where we are today. What we wear on our bodies in the 20th century are bits and pieces of apparel from other eras. A Puritan collar over a Roman tunic, over the breeches worn by the Byzantines, may all live in harmony, but they are borrowed finery. We owe everything to other ages, other times.

*Norma Kamali carves a sculptural shape from fabric, an artist working in the medium which displays her considerable talents. Is this art? Is this how people wull remember 1988? In this century, when all art can be so controversial, who will make the judgment? The eyes of the future, looking back at us.*

# CHAPTER TWO

# Ancient Civilizations

The human body has a singular construction—a head, a torso, two legs, and two arms. There are just so many ways to cover that body, and while the coverings constantly evolve and change, in the final analysis, there is no totally new way to do anything. In some instances, items of clothing have not changed in the slightest throughout many thousands of years—sandals, for example. One of the most interesting recent fashions is the so-called "gladiator" sandal, an identical revival after some 2,000 years.

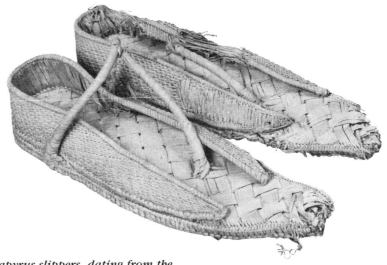

*Papyrus slippers, dating from the New Kingdom (c. 1580–1085 B.C.).*
*Courtesy Barakat Gallery, Rodeo Collection.*

*Indian sari, example of draped clothing. Archaic costume still in wide use to this day.*

## EARLY BODY COVERINGS

Humans probably first decorated the body itself, perhaps inadvertently. This might have occurred after a battle with a wild animal which left scars, in turn leading to the respect and admiration of other tribe members. In Germany during the 20th century, facial scars were much admired because they resulted from duels—and were considered a mark of courage. Many societies resort to the process of body scarring and tattooing, or other alterations of the body as a form of decoration. While we may be stunned with an African custom of extending lips into giant plates, or stretching the neck with brass and copper disks, both practices are regarded as signs of beauty. For generations, the Chinese bound feet into tiny stumps and found them irresistible. We find it grotesque. In our own society many women (and men) routinely pierce their ears, but other cultures find this practice abhorrent. Ear piercing is ages-old, and while at first flash, we think of this as a woman's accessory, what self-respecting pirate ever appeared without a gold hoop? There is a revived interest again in tattooing, totally unacceptable to many people, but highly regarded by others.

For many, marking the body or changing the proportions of the body are unthinkable customs, however, both are common practices all over the world, and have been for many thousands of years. We find traces of these body-altering customs reflected in our society, bras and girdles as an instance, which modify the figure, in some cases, substantially. We must therefore accept as a concept that perhaps even before clothing, body marking and distortion might have been the first body covering.

## PREHISTORIC APPAREL

Apparel was developed very early by mankind. Iron Age costume, thousands of years before Christ, has been discovered in peat bogs, the pitchlike substance preserving the garments in an almost intact condition. We see simple garments, shaped from squares of textiles, fastened across the shoulders and belted in quite a sophisticated fashion. The fabric was woven and somewhat coarse, but it does show that prehistoric man had a sense of style. Further archaeological finds have produced treasures in jewelry which show a high

Ancient costume as interpreted twenty years ago: left, Balenciaga's exotic silver brocade gown wrapped about the body à la sari, 1964. Right, design based on traditional costume of Indian dancing girl, bare waist and diaper-wrapped pantaloons.

degree of skill and a sense of beauty. Jewelry, made of metal and stone, obviously has a far better chance of surviving than does apparel made of fabric, which is subject to destruction from the ravages of age and climate. It is through these early finds, in both northern Europe and the Mediterranean basin, that we see the artistic and intellectual level of these vanished peoples.

Archaic costume certainly still exists in daily life throughout many parts of the world. Ethnic costume in particular tends to remain unchanged, principally because it is how people cling to their past. One notable example is in the daily dress of India, where women in *saris* are still draping rectangles of fabric about their bodies even as the Greeks and Romans did. Men wrap, diaper fashion, a small square about their loins. This piece of apparel is called a *dhoti* (dough-tee). Women wear a much larger rectangle, wrapped and draped about the body and worn over a simple, sliplike shift. Just as in the past, the appeal is in the textile itself, the beauty of the weaving, the artistry of the decoration, and the grace and skill with which the garment is worn. The sari, of course, is a version of ancient drapings and is derivative of ancient costume. It is possible to see traces of these civilizations in the beauty of the national dress of India. Most apparel from early cultures, while simpler in its approach to body-covering than today's cut and sewn clothing, was extraordinarily beautiful.

## THE EGYPTIANS

In the ancient world, many civilizations preceded or paralleled in time that of the Egyptians, but somehow we find that the Assyrians, the Medes, the Babylonians, and the Sumerians, for example, seem more foreign and distant. Egypt relates to our cultural background, perhaps not to the extent that we relate to Greece and Rome, but with some feeling of communication, at least in a fashion sense. Whenever we wrap and tie a garment to our waist a-la-sarong, we are emulating a trick that Cleopatra might have used. Again, when we wear a dress with a waistline lifted up to the bosom, we are wearing Egyptian costume, just as the French did after the French Revolution at the end of the 18th century. Details have changed, but the over-all effect is very similar.

Our somewhat slanted view of Egypt probably comes to us from Bible stories as well as from motion pictures. That view is not terribly accurate. The Egyptians, as a race, survived almost intact for many thousands of years, enjoying a stable, prosperous, and structured society. The Egyptians built vast monuments, enjoyed tremendous wealth, and were an industrious and practical people. Additionally, they were a fun-loving people, who told ribald stories, played games (many of which are still played), and loved to party. We learn these things from tombs, where wall paintings and papyrus rolls have left a meticulous record of daily life, some of the records dating back four thousand years. We read stories about ghosts, tales of a Cinderella-like character, sagas of wandering sailors, and learn about primitive forms of hopscotch, dice, and checkers. They were a sophisticated civilization with a sophisticated attitude towards style, fashion, art, and sculpture.

Because the society was so stable, the costume remained relatively stable as well. Not totally static, of course, because changes obviously occurred throughout the thousands of years that spanned this civilization, but more or less with a cohesiveness that remained unchanged throughout the many kingdoms. Men wore a garment called a *schenti*, which was a sort of wrapped loincloth—a slightly skirtlike garment. Versions of this garment are worn all over the world today, primarily in primitive societies. Women wore a garment known as a *kalasiris*, which was a long, rather clinging skirt, which usually covered the body from under the breasts to the ankle, held up with one, and occasionally two, shoulder straps. These were basic garments, but tomb paintings and other records show us myriad costumes based on these particular foundations. Pleating was often used in both mens' and womens' apparel, fine, exquisite pleating, often radiating into sunburst effects. White was regarded as sacred and was worn predominantly throughout the society, but brilliance was added with jewelling and occasionally by bright dyes.

The height of Egyptian fashion technology appeared in textiles, which were sheer, delicate and beautifully woven of flax (linen), a principal crop along the banks of the Nile.

Linen was woven from at least 3000 B.C., and it has been said that the favorite textile of these ancients was of the delicacy and fragility of one of the finest handkerchiefs. It is interesting that although they understood and knew how to loom wool, occasionally using it for warmth, it was at varying times considered unlucky. Such fashion superstitions appear and disappear in history. In this particular case perhaps the Egyptians feared wool because marauding, wool-wearing tribes surrounded their borders.

It is also interesting that the ideal of the Egyptians was not dissimilar to our own image of body perfection. Temple paintings show us tall, slender, elongated figures, and there is no

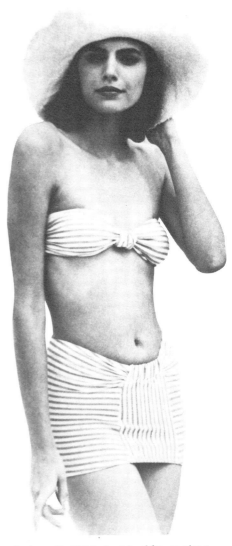

*Swimsuit, 1988. Inspired by ancient Egyptian male apparel: kilt, complete with tiny apron detail is a reflection of front pleating in original costume.*

*Egyptian wig (similar to today's cornrows) with banded gold crown. Reign of Thut-Mose III (1501–1447 B.C.). The Metropolitan Museum of Art, Gift of George F. Baker and Mr. and Mrs. V. Everit Macy, 1920.*

question but that they were also deeply involved in the care and maintenance of their bodies, just as we are. Archeologists constantly discover, in one dig after another, the elaborate equipment which was used to maintain their appearance—cosmetic jars, combs, razors, highly polished mirrors, and incredible wigs. Wigs were a common accessory because the Egyptians usually shaved all the hair on their bodies, perhaps because of the heat, perhaps for hygienic reasons, or perhaps simply because they liked the smooth, shiny, well-oiled body surface it presented.

While generally the Egyptians went without shoes, we know that they wore sandals—sometimes of gold and other precious metals—but seldom inside the house. They were for outside use usually. Their jewelry was incredible, exotic, brilliant, and enormous in size. In later Egyptian kingdoms, apparel included vast collars of jewelling (a fashion which reappeared in the Byzantine culture later) and when we see necklines banded and beaded in sequins, paillettes or embroidery, we are seeing repeats of fashion details that were prevalent in this civilization.

We see these people from a great distance so we are more easily able to understand how their apparel reflected their society. The basic items, generally unchanged throughout many thousands of years, reaffirms the stability of Egyptian life. Their clothing was originally of great simplicity and purity, but the garments gathered fashion steam as the kingdoms became wealthier. Simple clothing became more complex and more decorated. Embroideries and ornamentation became a passion with all classes, and the decoration became more elaborate as the wealth of the individual grew. We may think of the Egypt of those times as a distant and lost civilization to us, but in actual fact, they and we have a great deal in common. Egyptian women sat at dressing tables just as we do, with polished mirrors and a multitude of cosmetics and lotions to choose from. She outlined her eyes, with kohl, heightened the color of her cheeks, and scented and carefully cared for her body. Clothing for formal occasions and that worn for everyday life varied, even as ours does. Egyptians loved parties, liked to gamble, enjoyed visiting with friends and, of course, those of wealth lived a carefree and happy life.

## THE MINOANS

Prospering at the same time as the Middle Kingdom of Egypt (2000 to 1000 B.C.) the great Greek civilizations began to thrive. One of the earliest kingdoms was the Minoan, or Cretan civilization, and it was here that one of the most unusual and highly stylized approaches to fashion appeared, almost aberrational for that time.

It was a totally artificial costume, unlike the naturalistic approaches of other societies. Both men and women bound their waists tightly with wide belts—and wore skirts that tiered. Women's skirts tiered and flounced in gradually increasing rings almost to the ground, while men's costume, tiered in a similar way, usually stopped above the knee. (In any discussion of apparel, we should bear in mind that throughout costume history, unisex clothing has been more the norm than the oddity.) It is not odd, of course, for men to wear skirts even today. The Scottish kilt is but one example of a wrapped skirt. Men in traditional apparel in the Near East wear what is to all intents and purposes a long dress, and in current Paris prêt collections, skirts for men often appear on the runway.

Left, *tight-waisted Minoan costume worn by both sexes, usually bare above the waist. Elaborate headdress and skirt detail for male apparel. Bolero-like shoulder covering over tiered, flounced and stiffened skirt on woman's dress. Compare the 1869 Victorian ballgown by Worth featuring similar flounces, apron detail and bound waist.* The Metropolitan Museum of Art, Gift of Mrs. Philip K. Rhinelander, 1946.

Hair on Minoan women was bound and lifted into long, corkscrew curls, á la Shirley Temple, and was often wrapped and tied with ribbons and lacings. (Men's hair was also coiffed into formalized ringlets.) Perhaps the fashions of later times that most closely resemble those of the Minoans, would be costume worn by elegant women of Queen Victoria's time (A.D. 19th century) and although the Minoans bared their breasts, and women did not follow that practice in the 19th century, it is true that evening clothes of this period were often cut so low across the bosom that the tops of the breasts were completely exposed.

Apparel was usually made of linen, wool or both. Brilliant colors were prevalent and their textiles were often heavily patterned. Elaborate embroideries were also an integral part of their costume. Still, the most interesting aspect of their clothing was the tiered, stiffened skirt, which, though it resembled skirts later worn over hoops, was probably widened and held rigid by bands that were sewn right into the garment.

*Modern men still wear skirts: opposite page, left, Malcolm Forbes in Scottish kilt photographed with Elizabeth Taylor (almost Minoan in her costume). Right, unisex in feeling, Jean-Paul Gaultier's wide pajama-legged pant for him, long, apron front skirt for her, 1985. Greek soldiers in pleated, starched military skirts, ethnic costume still worn in the late 20th century.*

While breasts were usually bared, quite often a brief little bolero of some kind completed the bodice of the costume and covered the shoulders. Boleros that are worn today are almost exact duplicates of those that were part of the Minoan costume thousands of years ago.

These forerunners of the Greeks also wore hats of varying styles, and were frequently shown with one kind or another in paintings which have survived from that time. Much of what we know of the Minoan culture is learned from these paintings. It would seem that they, like the Egyptians, made up their eyes rather heavily, ringing them with black to make their appearance more intense. There is also no question that they were a hedonistic civilization, full of gaiety and extremely advanced. For instance, in the ruins of the Great Palace of Knossos, capitol of Crete, archeologists have found sophisticated plumbing systems, including flush toilets and running water. Both of these refinements would disappear for many centuries throughout later more advanced societies.

## THE GREEKS

Left, *open-sided and belted peplos caught with fibulae at the shoulder, over banded chiton seamed at the sides.* Center, *man's one-shoulder short chiton, girdled at waist, dark short cape.* Right, *banded cloak, wrapped himation-style over the chiton.*

In the Greek civilization which evolved from these earlier peoples, while many different styles of costumes were in common use, we are most interested in those garments and fashion apparel that we identify with what we call Classic Greek. Both men and women wore a garment known as a *chiton* (key-ton) a forerunner of the tunic that is still worn to this day. The chiton was two lengths of fabric, rectangular in shape, simply fastened at the shoulders, usually with fibulae. *Fibulae*, sometimes made of precious metals and jewelled, were the original safety pins and were in common use throughout the ancient world. By pinning the two rectangles together at the shoulders, a costume was created. Sometimes the created garment was belted at the waist, often not. Sometimes one shoulder was left bare and the garment was caught together at only one shoulder, at other times, sides hung open, revealing the body. Greek women wore a more sophisticated version of the chiton, known as a *peplos*, which required either an extra long length of textile, caught and bloused up at the waist, or two pieces, one smaller than the other which created the effect of an overblouse. All kinds of combinations of styles and effects were possible by judicious use of ties, belts, and pin fastenings. The peplos was perhaps the earliest version of what we now call a *blouson*, and while our blousons are cut and sewn into shape, the draping and blousing of the classic Grecian costume achieved quite a similar effect. The name itself—peplos—comes down to us as *peplum*, and while our peplums are totally different from the original, it is ancient language still in common use. The blousons of both the 1950s and the 1980s are quite similar in silhouette and feeling to early Greek costume.

While these early garments were of linen or wool, by the time of Alexander the Great (220 B.C.) the Greeks, as well as other contemporary civilizations, were importing silk from China. The method by which silk was created was unknown to western civilizations, and these shimmering, beautiful textiles were highly valued. Cotton was also introduced from India, and both of these fabrics were perfect for Greek costume, which required soft, clinging draping to achieve perfection in silhouette. It was as if these new fabrics were made to order for Greek costume. The Greeks were so in love with delicate, transparent textiles that they even re-wove silk imports, by slowly and painfully taking the cloth apart thread by thread, and respinning the threads into even more delicate yardage.

One of the myths about ancient Greece is that the people wore white. They did, of course, but certainly not to the extent that we believe. We have gained this impression from what is left to us—the temples and statuary of the time. However, it is the passage of time that has rearranged the truth. Greeks wore brilliant color—scarlet, purple, mustard yellow, indigo, and bright green. Further, they ornamented their garments with embroideries, usually at the hem, just as the French did after the revolution in the late 18th century. In many cases, French costume directly copied classic Greek apparel. The French made the same mistake of believing the fashions of antiquity were white, and wore a great deal of white in their effort to repeat the styles of ancient Greece. The original statues and temples, however, were ablaze with color, painted over every inch of their surfaces. The originals have long since faded, but a trip to almost any museum with Grecian sculpture will show faint traces of paint here and there on the marble.

*Various ways of forming Greek costume,* top to bottom: *A long rectangle, folded down, pinned at shoulder and worn open-sided. A short chiton pinned at both shoulders, to be belted or left loose. Woman's chiton, with many fibulae to form draping (see Mariano Fortuny "Delphos" dress). Squares with dropped triangle fold pinned at one shoulder.*

*Contemporary version of ancient Greek costume: peplos-like blouson over narrow skirt.*

How wonderful to have seen the original Acropolis, brilliant in the Athenian sun, filled with hundreds of people in ravishing costumes of deep-dyed intensity.

To fully understand Greek costume, we must also understand that they felt a deep reverence for the human body. While clothing was certainly worn by all adults, nakedness caused no particular concern. It was not uncommon for garments to be simply removed if they interfered with some activity. This was also fairly common in the Egyptian society. Clothing was merely an adjunct, an enhancement to that body which was so much admired. Clothing was meant to move gracefully and to add to the beauty and dignity of man. Fussiness and ostentation were frowned on, it was the other side of the coin that was admired—elegance and simplicity.

The Greeks also originated fine, delicate draping, and added the first "twist" to the fashion world. Garments of sheer linen were washed, starched and twisted tightly to achieve fine, crystalline pleating. While this technique is not in common use today (incidentally, as we will see, it still works just fine) crystal pleating created by other methods certainly appears and reappears throughout current fashion collections.

Designers lean heavily on Greece for inspiration. Our looks may be achieved with cutting, sewing and shaping, but the origin of what we put on our bodies comes to us from the past. Designers who use Grecian costume as inspiration include the famous Mme. Grès of Parisian fame, who designs entire collections with Greek draping and pleating. In America, Mary McFadden produces garments of exquisite workmanship, traceable in many instances to Ionic or Doric origins, and also reminiscent of the early 20th century designs of Mariano Fortuny.

*MARIANO FORTUNY* No discussion of Greek influence on costume would be complete without noting the incredible adaptations of original Greek costume designed by Mariano Fortuny in the 20th century. An architect, inventor, and above all fashion creator, he was born in Spain in 1871 and lived until 1949. Fortuny's style was totally classic in its approach to dressmaking. He made almost direct copies of Hellenistic apparel, even naming his designs after the originals. He used

*Mariano Fortuny pleated "Delphos"*
*gown, caught with jewelled pins at*
*the shoulders (see pinning on*
*previous page).* The Fashion Institute of
Technology, New York.
*Mary McFadden tissue-pleated*
*evening gown with irregular hem,*
*1976.*

titles such as "Delphos" (a reference to an ancient Greek community) for his creations, and these designs, just like the originals, were exquisitely created of tissue-thin silk. Rolled into tiny balls, "Fortuny's" were (and are) stored and kept in miniature hatboxes, coiled and ready to be shaken out at a moment's notice into stunning evening wear. Even the delicacy of these creations reflect ancient Greece. The gowns usually simply slipped over the head, and sometimes—not always—tied with a cord, or cording either at the waist or where the owner fancied. He also produced magnificent stencilled velvets, often in gold and silver patterns. The Fortuny factory is still in existence in Venice, Italy, where it is primarily involved in producing textiles of splendid quality for the home decorating market. While the original Fortuny's were worn throughout most of the twenties and thirties, their beauty is timeless: owned and still worn by fashion literati, they have become almost a cult. These tissue-thin silks in opalescent colors (sometimes known as wedding ring silks because it is said they can be pulled through a ring) are worth their weight in gold. When a Fortuny turns up from time to time at auction, it is snapped up immediately, at prices starting at $5,000. The process by which this talented man created these garments is quite lost to us—it was his secret. Some believe the textiles were woven under water, but truly, the technique is unknown.

Pleatings are not new. Pleats appear and reappear through costume history. The Indians of the American Southwest twisted cottons around sticks and allowed the textiles to dry—a similiar method to that used by the Greeks. The result? Fine, crisp pleating. In the 1940s, California designers made the look popular once again with *broomstick* skirts, which were, in the same way, wrapped sopping wet around broom handles and left to dry.

The clothing of ancient Greece was unique. As is true in most societies, apparel reflected their belief in a larger harmony, where costume, philosophy, architecture, artifacts, jewelry and sculpture all were mirror reflections of one another. They were also blessed with a friendly climate, and had an open attitude about health similar to ours. The Greeks loved beauty and deeply admired both the intellect and the idealized human body.

## THE ROMANS

By 200 B.C., however, Greece had fallen to the Republic of Rome, but the Romans respected Greek culture, and adopted their fashions enthusiastically. Although the Romans were busily engaged in enslaving subjugated peoples, which happened wherever their armies went (indeed at the same time, the Romans sold 10,000 Greeks into slavery), they held Greek society in great esteem. The Romans were quite aware of the superior intellect, philosophy and attitude towards the arts inherent in Grecian culture, and held a healthy regard for their knowledge and sophistication. Indeed, while many Greeks were enslaved, they usually held high positions of great trust in Roman households. Actually, Rome looked to Greece as a center of taste, even as we look to Paris for creative ideas. Greece was the font, the source of inspiration for the Romans. All that was desirable and wonderful was traced to the Grecian civilization, but in most cases, added to and aggrandized by the Romans. As an example, most statuary of the Romans was merely a copy of the best of the Grecian sculptors.

The principal Roman garment was the *toga*, which, though draped and wrapped, was considerably different from the

Left: *Roman matron with veiled elaborate hair, stola (Roman version of chiton) with pleated hem. Over it, the palla, rectangular length of fabric, usually brightly colored worn as cloak or outer wrapping.* Right: *male costume of toga, draped and wrapped over the tunica, which usually carried decorative banding.*

*Drawings of details on skirt (known as Greek Key design) and sandals worn after the French Revolution, both inspired by ancient classic cultures. Below: revival in 1984 of shoes adapted from 2000 year old designs.*

earlier Greek chiton. A toga, the principal garment of men, but worn in an earlier version by women and children, was almost always made of wool. At its full size, a toga was approximately eighteen feet long by five and a half feet in width at its widest part, for it was, in fact, a giant semi-circle or arc. This garment was carefully wrapped around the body, not unlike a sari, carried around and draped up over one shoulder and brought around the body again to fasten at the rear. In most cases, the right arm was left free, partially because it was the fighting arm, and partially because it became the custom. The manner in which the garment was draped, the way in which the folds hung in place with tiny weights, all told a story. Each fold had a name, and each toga identified its wearer by the manner, or style, in which the garment was worn. Togas were not usually worn in the home—but were considered more or less a "public" piece of apparel. The toga was an extremely heavy garment, of vast size, which may explain the aversion the Romans had to dropping costume during strenuous activities, as the Greeks were wont to do.

If we believe that "clothes make the man" the toga certainly contributed to the making of the Roman. Or, at least, contributed a great deal to the manner in which the Roman carried himself. Romans wore their togas with dignity, and the toga, in turn bestowed dignity upon the wearer. The toga always identified a citizen of Rome: all others were known as "barbarians." To be a citizen was a tremendous and much to be desired privilege. To lose one's right to wear a toga was to lose all rights. Those stripped of their toga, usually because of crime, were outcasts and banished from society. In almost the same way, a dishonorable discharge from the armed services means the stripping of uniform, rank and privilege.

Women draped themselves in a *stola* which was a large, loose robe, attached with fibulae and belted or girdled at the waist. In the house, a simple garment known as a *tunica* was worn, which corresponded to a Grecian chiton. (Our word "tunic" is of Latin derivation.) These tunics were also often worn under men's togas, and were a simply cut garment something like a shift, with two holes for arms (they were occasionally sleeved) ranging in length from above the knee to the floor. Often, they were belted and bloused at the waist. According to the weather, several might be worn, one on top of the other—very early "layering." Just as the togas indicated rank or status, so, too did the tunica by decorative striping and bordering. While men's and women's tunics were almost identical, women's were usually of a lighter weight material. Tunics were occasionally banded with color, or embroidered with wool embellished with gold.

The Romans used color as well as borders for hieratic insignia. Senators, for example, wore red shoes. Priests showed their calling with purple bordered togas. Gold embroidery was an identification for magistrates or generals. Citizens wore white. Purple eventually became the traditional color for the costume of the Emperor. The origin of the word "purple" is

*Indian saris: worn and wrapped as they have been for over a thousand years, many believe inspired by the toga. The sari is a rectangular, wrapped and draped fashion, up to four feet in width, and ten yards in length. It can be embroidered or printed and is draped according to personal preference. (Photo by Brian Hagiwara.)*

the Latin word "purpura" which refers to the shellfish which yielded the famous dye so loved in the ancient world. The phrase "wearing of the purple", referring to royalty, has its origin in this Latin word.

In the Imperial Rome which followed the Republic, fashions became more lavish. Gold and jewelry, which had been frowned on in earlier, more austere years, were highly desired, as were gems of all kinds. Women's garments were woven of softer, more delicate textiles, for by A.D. 200, the Romans were importing and wearing silk, and also looming linens and cottons into lovely, gossamer fabrics. Silk, carried to the west via the exotic Great Silk Route from China, was worth its weight in gold. Throughout this period until well past the Renaissance in the 14th and 15th centuries, silk was used as a medium of exchange between kingdoms. Silk was the great passion of the rich, and the more delicate and sheer, the more desirable. To quote from Michael and Ariana Batterberry's book, *Mirror, Mirror*:

Try to imagine Roman women of means as they must have looked in the second century A.D.; butterfly creatures, their gossamer silks billowing in jewel-like shades of reds, purples, yellows and greens, gems twinkling from head to foot, skin radiantly pink and white, lips red, and on the head, piles of curls streaked blond. A trailing scarf or kerchief, a fan in hand and a sunshade carried by a slave who walked behind completed the effulgent image, which was seen always in the brilliant light of day. The Romans rose at sunrise and began their evening entertainments at four in the afternoon in order to avoid the dangers of returning home after dark.

This description would quite adequately describe any Mediterranean resort with the exception of the slave with the sunshade, and getting home before dark. Thieves, muggers and robbers have always been with us—actually, we are much more free in our abilities to move about than were peoples of other times.

Roman women (and men) were extremely partial to cosmetics, and various coloring agents and lotions were always at hand. Faces were whitened with a lead compound, an extremely dangerous substance. Rouge and lip brighteners were in constant use, as was kohl, for darkening eyelids and lashes. The word "cosmetic" is of ancient origin, coming to us from the Greek word meaning "I adorn." Roman women were also among the early believers that "blonds have more fun" and bleached and dyed their hair with all sorts of agents, most of them quite primitive by our standards and detrimental to health. In addition to bleaching, women coaxed the Roman armies, who were conquering the barbarians of the north, to buy and bring back the thick blond hair God had so favored the savages with. In turn, this hair was turned into splendid wigs, with tortuous curls and masses of ringlets. Some women, bored with the tedious bleaching methods and unable to find enough blond hair to buy, simply powdered their hair with pure gold dust.

Romans were also enamored of jewelry. No expense was spared in adorning the body with precious metals and stones. Pliny, a writer of the times, noted that on no part of the costume of Roman women was more money spent than on earrings. This particular item of jewelry ranked as one of their truly great extravagances.

Another Roman writer, Seneca, pointed out that "there is nothing a woman will not allow herself, nothing she holds disgraceful, when she has encircled her neck with emeralds and inserted earrings of great price in her ears, stretched with their weight." Roman goldsmiths set precious stones into earrings by a process known as *en cabochon* which simply means polished, but not faceted. Pearls were extremely popular, but in most cases, whatever the jewels worn, the Romans were more interested in the size of the piece than the workmanship.

The splendid Roman civilization slowly disintegrated into excesses of one kind or another, and by the early 4th century Rome was coming under the influence of the more austere Christians. When the Emperor Constantine himself embraced Christianity in A.D. 312, he not only made it the official religion of the civilized world, but decided to move his capital east to a city then named Byzantium. This new city, to be renamed Constantinople after himself, would be the most powerful influence on costume for the next one thousand years, but the Romans left us a vast fashion heritage. Tunics, wide belts, laced sandals, wrapped and enveloping capes, elaborate hairstyles, and heavy, chunky jewelry, among other fashion, reflect their society in our everyday life.

*Calvin Klein borrows from Ancient Rome as inspiration for this tunic, slightly bloused and belted.*

## THE BYZANTINES

Constantine evidently believed that the fresh beginnings of the first Christian empire required a fresh start in a new city. There, in Byzantium which straddled the east and the west geographically, costume gradually osmosed into a different silhouette and appearance, merging the influences of Asian societies with those of Rome. In the early days of this new empire, Roman influence remained, but fashion moved rather quickly from the folds and draperies of the west to a stiffer, more rigid and eastern look, which also involved the wearing of pants by both men and women. It is one of the earliest periods in costume history showing both sexes wearing pants. The wearing of pants by women is, of course, of eastern origin: pants have been worn in Asiatic countries for many thousands of years. It is only in our so-called advanced western civilization that this fashion was so late being accepted. This period also marked the beginning of trousers into the western world for men. While the Roman legions had found both the English barbarians, the Celts and the Teutons wearing a primitive, short, rough-spun sort of trouser, pants were regarded as only fit for savages for indeed, that is who wore them.

The Byzantine pants were covered with straight-cut tunics, usually knee-length for men, and floor-length for women and this tunic was usually girdled at the waist. Generally, arms were covered, and sleeves extended to the wrist. A garment known as a *dalmatica* was worn until the 6th century, which resembled nothing so much as a long nightshirt, banded vertically with stripes of color or embroidery known as *clavi*. This garment—the dalmatica—had been worn in Imperial Rome, as well, but was in more common use in the Byzantine Empire. Dalmatics still appear in the modern world, particularly in priest's vestments and robes. A visit to a Catholic Church or a Russian Orthodox Church on any Holy Day will give one a fairly accurate picture of the costume of that time, and the sort of garments that were worn daily. Clerical dress owes a great deal of its costume language to the Byzantines as well. We use

*Typically Byzantine, simple, straight garments of richly woven textiles, ankle-length tunics under dalmatics. Woman's costume includes elaborate stole-like scarf, usually jewelled, fastened about the body. Man's costume will eventually evolve into caftan.*

the same names for the same article of clothing—words such as *chasuble*, *cope*, and *alb* refer to garments that can be seen in the brilliant mosaics which document the costume of this civilization so well. These churchly garments are direct descendants of the robes worn a thousand years ago. In the Byzantine originals, they were elegant, splendid garments of richly brocaded fabric. The simple shape and cut is what remains, but the incredibly rich, dense and weighted textiles in common use then, have all but disappeared.

Actually, the most significant inheritance we enjoy from the Byzantines is in the textile arts. Elegant brocades and heavily woven silks, shot through with metallic threads (although pale imitations of the originals) come to us from this period. By the 3rd century, the knowledge of how to loom these textiles had been acquired, and by the 6th century, the then Emperor Justinian had begun to manufacture silk, breaking the monopoly of the Chinese.

Other current fashions derived from the Byzantines are dresses and coats designed with what we call *princess* lines, shoes that look like short boots, and floating panels. Caftans, still common costume throughout a great part of the world, originated in Asia, and were one of the most fashionable costumes in the Byzantine culture. Usually a simple garment, it was coat like, in most cases crossing at the front where it

Left, *religious dalmatic*, A.D. *1570. Elaborately embroidered tapestry weave, the richness of the textile based on Byzantine designs.* Los Angeles County Museum of Art. Right, *Michael Novarese "Dalmatic" dress, the loose, floating front and back panels caught at the sides. 1967. Fashion Institute of Design and Merchandising, Los Angeles.*

*Orientalia swept the early 1900s. Left, drawings from Poiret costume sketches, 1913. Right: Ronaldus Shamask, harem trousers and loose, caftan-like, overlapped top, 1981.*

fastened. While many versions existed then, and do today, it probably marked the beginning of the jacket and the coat to our modern world. Again, it was the Byzantines that introduced this piece of apparel to the west.

As time went on, this society became more and more Oriental in its attitudes and apparel, and while the Byzantines remained a strong influence on the slowly developing European world, a totally different sort of clothing was evolving there. Western apparel had become a mixture of traces of Greco-Roman costume, Byzantine richness in color and textile, and body-concealing fashions inspired by the teachings of the Catholic Church. In 1453, Byzantium, like Rome, collapsed, and from that time, costume lines were clearly drawn between the east and the west.

# CHAPTER THREE

# *From Barbarism to Baroque*

Over one thousand years. What enormous changes occurred during this tremendous span of time. How can one capsulize so many centuries in just a few thousand words? Not very easily. During these centuries, just to hit a few of the highlights, the barbaric tribes of Northern Europe were civilized, the Roman Empire fell, Byzantium disappeared: later, the Renaissance flowered, bringing a rebirth of the pursuit of intellectual freedom, the collapse of royalty and the Divine Right of Kings, and the even more important collapse of the singular authority of the Roman Catholic Church facing the onslaught of the Reformation. The Americas were discovered. Printing was invented. The Industrial Revolution was born. The world was discovered to be round. The arts flourished, producing some of the greatest works known to man, created by some of the greatest artists known to mankind. Shakespeare, Rembrandt, Dante, Michelangelo, are only a few of those towering geniuses.

While this book deals primarily with fashion, we know by now that *everything* that happens in the world shapes fashion, and affects the coverings of our bodies. So, what *did* happen to fashion during this one thousand years—those long, long centuries known by so many names; the Dark Ages, the Middle Ages, the Gothic Ages (Early, Middle and High), the Moyen Age, the Renaissance, the Baroque, the Cavalier, Rococo? What happened was the slow but inevitable advance from the draped clothing worn by the ancient civilizations, combined with the laced, skin and hide clothing worn by the barbarians, to apparel that we now identify with and recognize. Commonly, references to the earlier years of this extraordinary span of time place events as happening during the *Dark Ages*. But how strange that reference. It is from these *Dark Ages* that we conjure up images of the glorious days when knighthood was in flower, when wandering minstrels sang of chivalry and love, when gallant men gathered at the Round Table in Camelot. All damsels were fair, all hearts were pure, and the environment charming. The truth, alas, isn't even close. Most of the early part of this one thousand years we are discussing was miserable, not at all full of romance and beauty, even for the very rich. In contrast to the splendor of ancient Rome and Constantinople where luxury abounded, medieval and early Gothic Europe represented a truly ferocious and barbaric age, when the mortality was less than thirty years, and life on every level was a continual and difficult struggle for survival.

The earlier centuries before the Renaissance are not superbly documented, especially in fashion history. Additionally, fashion apparel throughout Europe moved in varying time frames, advancing quickly in some countries, more slowly in others. While generally, costume evolved through the stages discussed in this chapter, there are overlapping periods when more advanced clothing had already been accepted in one country, but had not yet appeared in others. The thrust, however, during this long period of time, was a slow but steady evolution from ancient, unstructured clothing to the tailored, cut and sewn clothing we wear.

To keep this long period of time in some sort of historical perspective, however, let us break down these centuries into more manageable time frames, discuss them one by one, and trace the evolution of fashion as it became more sophisticated and worldly. (Note here that you will find overlapping dates and eras. Some fashion movements existed in one part of Europe and had not yet been taken up in others. Further, the Renaissance, for example, did not suddenly arrive one morning, as the Gothic Age disappeared. (See Time-Line.)

- Barbarism and Carolingian, A.D. 350–1150
- Middle Ages, Gothic, A.D. 1000–1300
- Early Renaissance, A.D. 1300–1450
- High Renaissance, A.D. 1450–1600
- Cavalier and Baroque, A.D. 1600–1700
- Louis XIV, A.D. 1644–1715

While these are extremely arbitrary divisions of time (indeed, each one of these historical periods is divided more correctly into all kinds of sub-divisions), it will give us a general framework and easier point of reference. Certainly, costume and apparel didn't stop and start at any one of these dates, but a quick glance at even this simple time-line will tell us that America was discovered during the Renaissance, that knights in armor flourished during the Carolingian and Gothic years, and that Pilgrims were landing in New England while the Cavalier reigned supreme in Europe.

## BARBARISM & CAROLINGIAN

Rome collapsed early in the 5th century under the onslaught of the barbarians—the Goths, the Visigoths and the Gauls—ferocious tribes with little taste for the niceties of life. They did, indeed, wear horned headdresses, occasionally dripping with seaweed, over hair that was greased with rancid oils and butter. They also wore one of the earliest versions of pants instead of the wrappings of the (until then) more civilized world. Their apparel heritage depended on animal skins, rather than cloth. The skins were laced together and shaped to the body. Weaving was known, but it was coarse, with little artistry in the finished product. Early European costume seems to merge these barbaric laced and tied garments with the wrapped and draped garments of Rome. As slowly but surely these savage people were brought under the control and influence of the Roman Catholic Church, they gradually evolved into the Europeans we know. In those times, the Church was the repository of all knowledge and learning and it, further, exercised rigid control over the lives, manners, customs and certainly the costume of these tribes as they emerged from barbarism into civilization.

*Early Christian apparel, based on the dalmatic and tunic. Essentially unisex, except for length. Both wear large mantles for warmth. His clothing shows wrapped and tied leggings, an early forerunner of pants. She has covered head with caul, linen band and fluted cap.*

*Modern version of cotehardie, this Marc Jacobs design, 1986, is reminiscent of the fitted princess-line dress prevalent in the 13th century.*

### Early Christian Dress

From a fashion point of view, apparel of early Christianity was a composite of influences, borrowing the dalmatic from the Byzantines, the tunic from the Romans, the cloaks, breeches and laced garments from the barbarians. The first ruler of any particular fashion interest from one of these quarreling feudal kingdoms was named Pepin, A.D. 751–768, whose claim to fame lies principally in the fact that he was the father of Charlemagne, the first Holy Roman Emperor, but also in the fact that he ran rather a dressy kingdom for that time. While this all took place during the 8th and 9th centuries, those peoples were just as interested in costume and fashion as we are. Even in those dim and distant days, Pepin and his court were concerned with apparel and, though by later standards that apparel was quite primitive, the nobles shone in brilliant silks, linens, and woolens dyed in showy colors. They wore lavish jewelry—an affectation borrowed from the Byzantines—and if they couldn't afford the real thing, they made do with large lumps of colored glass.

Charlemagne, A.D. 742–814, whose aim was to re-establish the concept and might of the Roman Empire, thought of himself as a devout Christian. However, he enjoyed five wives and four mistresses, all of whom, it is said, dressed exquisitely. Because of the cold, and lack of central heating, most garments of what is known as the *Carolingian Age* were of wool, and brilliant color was always favored. On occasion, Charlemagne wrapped himself in the Roman toga as a symbol of rank, but seemed to prefer the simpler clothing of peasants and frequently covered himself with sheep hides, apparently keeping a foot in both fashion camps. Costume is not terribly well documented during this period, but we do have many depictions of men wearing versions of trousers and other leg coverings. Both sexes wore tunics, usually as an undergarment of one sort or another, over which another tunic or, in the case of women a gown, was worn that was designed with shorter sleeves. Women's heads were invariably covered, and large, loose mantles or cloaks made the final layering. Actually, clothing of that time shares some of the common characteristics we associate with contemporary ecclesiastic apparel: the tunic and dalmatic worn by men, and the women's costume

resembling a nun's habit, which is still worn in many parts of the world. It was extremely simple clothing, and had not yet developed much individualistic style.

Actually, we cannot bestow on any of these feudal kingdoms the sophistication of a word such as *civilization*. Quite the contrary, they more closely resembled those barbarians which were their progenitors and were still in the process of being tamed, somewhat like the wild animals they resembled in many ways. Their clothing was worn in various layerings; pieces were added in the cold and removed in the heat, even as we add and subtract layers. They lived, however, more in the cold than in the heat, for there was very little warmth then except from open fires. Floors were of dirt, and furniture consisted primarily of a bed-pallet. Rich and poor didn't differ so much in the style of their apparel, as they did in the fabric and decoration of the garments that were worn. As we noted, this is not a well-documented period, but we can learn from histo-

*Wrapped and hooded heads, typical of the Middle Ages, as is the enveloping apparel, loose and body-concealing.* Left, *Missoni, 1978.* Right, *Ronaldus Shamask, 1982.*

rians of that time and from archaeologists some of what was covering bodies. As one fashion oddity of these murky years, it would seem that both women and men wore early versions of what we call plaids, a totally different textile look than any before. It would also, of course, be the antecedent of the Scottish plaids and kilts. The plaid effect might first have been achieved by interweaving animal skins of contrasting colors, and recent discoveries indicate that plaids of wool were woven as early as 600 B.C. Both sexes wore a simple undergarment; men, a kind of diaper-type underwear, over which they pulled cut and sewn pieces of clothing known as breeches, which were drawn up onto the leg and fastened to the waist. These were usually separate legs, similar to women's hosiery which still existed in the first half of the 20th century. Over these breeches came an outer wrapping they knew as hose, which were more like leggings. Different classes wore them at different heights and with different decorations, so that it was quite simple to rank the wearer.

### Carolingian Dress

By the 10th century, women still wore a simple under tunic, but the outer tunic or gown was now richly embroidered, and was occasionally bloused over a low set girdle, or belt, an early version of the blouson. The wide leather girdle dropping low across the hips, gathering the fabric to the body, was also similar to our modern, hip-slung belts. Garments of a slightly later date, during the 12th century, began to be laced either at the sides or down the back to give the appearance of a tighter fit. Often, the skirt was beginning to widen, adding dimension to the hem. By the 11th century, these garments, known as *bliauts* (blee-awt) were the basic apparel for men and women and were to remain so for at least two hundred years. Our version of this fashion would be a princess dress, which appears and reappears from time to time in the course of fashion history.

The bliaut, as noted, was worn by both men and women as an outer garment. The male version was a close-fitting tunic, laced up the sides, and in length, ranging from the knee to the ground. Remember, men were still wearing versions of what we think of as a dress. Priest's robes are similar to that prevailing costume silhouette. Occasionally, the garment was split up the side, which showed the heavy hosed leg. The beginnings of chain mail are in evidence, although mail was almost always worn only by nobility.

Women by A.D. 1150 had embellished the bliaut, wearing a more elegant version, known as a *court bliaut*. It was much more elaborate, had very wide sleeves, and was belted, often with jewels or chains. It was usually worn over a shift called a *chemise*, a common fashion word. A simpler version, known as a *cote* was also widely worn in the 12th century.

The Europe we know was far different a thousand years ago. It was composed of dozens of warring principalities which formed the feudal political system, allegiances between the nobility and the serfs, in which the Lord of the manor offered protection to the peasants in return for work. The only brightness on the horizon of these people at this time was to die and escape to heaven. It had been commonly believed that the world would end at A.D. 1000, and when that ominous date passed with no signs of destruction, it brought new hope to those devout people, it seemed possible that there might be a brighter future. It also marked the beginning of the long road out of feudalism to the flowering of the 12th century Gothic Age.

## THE GOTHIC AGE

The time period known as *Gothic* lasted from about the middle of the 12th century until the Renaissance. Europeans were beginning to form nations with recognized borders, which owed a wider allegiance to a king, rather than to a petty feudal lord. During these centuries, we find all sorts of varying costume, differentiated by time subdivisions: Early, Middle, Late, and Flamboyant Gothic describe not only a particular period in time, but also relate to all the other arts and artifacts prevalent. The center of life was shifting from the countryside to the embryonic cities, and the cities centered on the soaring Gothic cathedrals, which represented the peak of the religious experience. Soon, the new humanism founded by the cities would appear across Europe. The vast cathedrals which stamped the Gothic ages, epitomized by Notre Dame in Paris, were reflected in costume, which lightened, lifted, and soared, even as the flying buttresses lightened and lifted into soaring height in the new churches.

*Paco Rabanne in 1966 worked with gilded plastic rectangles and squares joined with metal links to create his vision of the future; however, the design owes a great deal to medieval armor.*

Man's shirt of linen and lace. Venetian, 1500. *Los Angeles County Museum of Art.*
Below, *sideless, laced bliaut. Underrobe showing at sides, richly embroidered sleeves and mantle lining. Wimple and veil.*

In the early part of the 12th century, two basic garments appeared, a *surcoat*, copied after the covering worn by knights over their armor, and the *cotte*. Both pieces of apparel were, once again, worn by both sexes. The cotte, even then a sort of undergarment, turned into a petticoat, and the surcoat finally evolved (for women) into a dress. The man's surcoat also developed into what was known as the *cotehardie*, which became a garment for both men and women.

One of the great fashion pace-setters of the Middle Ages (the early Gothic age) was Eleanor of Aquitaine, A.D. 1122–1204, who during her lifetime first reigned as Queen of France, and after a divorce (a scandalous proceeding for that age) married Henry II, King of England. In her own name she controlled vast estates in the south of France so she was, indeed, considered a great marital prize. Eleanor was responsible for the lavish Courts of Love which bloomed during those times and many of the images of that period that have come down to us. She engaged minstrels to compose love songs at her court; troubadours not only sang and performed, but also carried gossip and news from her court to others. She wore garments of specially woven silk covered with pearls, and draped delicate veils over her head. She travelled on the Crusades with her first husband, Louis VI of France, but that was not totally unacceptable: many women accompanied knights on these journeys, some of them wearing armor and riding astride. It would appear that women enjoyed occasional freedoms even then, although basically they were considered to be no more nor less than simple property. Travelling to the east, even with

*Bonnie Cashin looks to the Middle Ages as inspiration for her loose and layered fashions in the 1960s. These loose, pullover garments created a new classic look at that time. Below, crusader in bliaut with dagging trim, leg wrappings and mantle, is also wearing layers.*

an army, was certainly one way to escape the stupefying boredom of the times and in the process, do some visiting, some sightseeing and a little shopping, just as tourists still do.

### The Crusades

The surcoat, mentioned earlier, was one of the fashions spawned by those vast travelling armies marching towards the Near East and the Middle East. It was an open sided garment, cut like a tunic and dropped over the head. Its primary function was to serve as protection for armored men from the heat and glare of the sun. In effect, it was a sort of poncho that began to sport symbols and identifying colors, which led in turn to the complicated insignia of heraldry, a legacy left to us in banners, shields and flags. It also introduced men to wearing parti-colored garments which became so fashionable in the later Middle Ages, and preceded the use of brilliant color during the Renaissance.

The armor that was worn gradually advanced from simple chain mail to the more spectacular articulated armor that the nobility and men of wealth wore. Simple fighting men, the foot soldiers of the time, wore heavy cloth padding for protection. Armored knights wore padding as well, but the purpose was to protect their skin from the metal of their armor which heated in the sun; over this came the surcoat. The surcoat was also taken up by women and by the 13th century was the preferred costume for both sexes. The man's reached just below the knees, the woman's, longer and fuller, touched the floor and was usually belted. Another interesting style preva-

lent at that time was the wearing of long, fantastic, and totally fake sleeves, a fashion detail that remained well into the 16th century.

The brilliantly garbed armies, swarming with camp followers and rabble, crossed Europe in ten mighty Crusades over a period of two hundred years, starting in the 11th century. While their motives were pure, the rescue of Jerusalem from the infidels whom the Europeans considered to be barbarians, in many cases these so-called barbarians they set out to conquer exposed the Crusaders to a civilization that was extremely advanced. Just like travellers of all times, the armies brought back souvenirs, spices, perfumes, woven carpets, exquisite textiles, mirrors of glass (new to Europe, where polished metal was used) and the refinement of the bath. The heavy woolens and simple fashions of the Europeans began to take on a more oriental look. Shirts, turbans, gowns woven with silk and glittering gold threads, and embossed slippers for feet became the rage. Similar to the craze for all things Chinese that swept the 18th century, a craze for all things Arabian swept Europe in the 13th century. The spartan life of Europe began to soften, and while the Church raged at the acceptance of these earthly delights, it was a losing battle.

The last battle of the Crusades was lost to the infidels at Acre in 1291. But the long range effect was to influence European history for many, many centuries. Not only did it open the west to new ideas and concepts, but it helped advance the cause of monarchy in Europe by reducing the influence of the Pope. It further opened new and vast trade routes through the hitherto unexplored world of the east. Most of our concepts of chivalry come to us from the Crusades, a heritage left us in familiar, everyday customs as simple as a man tipping his hat.

From the middle of the 13th into the early 15th centuries, sumptuary laws were rampant. The size of a cloak, the manner in which it was trimmed and even the cut of the hood were carefully proscribed by law. Even the shoe was not exempt from attention. While the footwear of a prince could sport toes as long as two feet, common people had to be content with just six inches of pointed toes. The exaggerated shoes were called *poulaines* (poo-lain). People struggled to walk in them, indeed, the shoe was so difficult to manage that the wearer

*Double-horned hennin and veil, worn with cotehardie under sideless, fur-edged surcoat.*

usually fastened the pointed toe to the knee with a tiny chain. A fashion remnant exists from time to time in pointed-toe shoes. Other incredible accessories of the time included the *codpiece* (14th to early 17th century) attached to skin-tight hose, cloaks that trailed on the ground (picking up substantial filth and mud in the process), and heavy, gold chain jewelry. Women wore very low-cut bodices and created a craze for sleeves so tight they had to be fastened on at each wearing.

During the late 14th century, the beautiful, soaring Gothic arch was not only reflected in costume, but in headdresses turned into high, spiked, conical cones as *hennins*, from which long, delicate veils usually floated. The only costume reference today to this style is the peaked hat always worn when portraying a witch. It was a period of unusual interest in head coverings, including the double-horned hennin, cauls and snoods (which were net-like coverings), all unusually ugly fashions, giant ear-puffs and turbans. Another vogue of the time was to affect a high forehead, and in some cases, hairlines were plucked to increase the illusion of a long, narrow face. The *wimple* was everywhere. A somewhat generic word, a wimple referred to any one of several pieces, a head-wrapping, a chin-band, a linen scarf that floated about the face, or a loose, throat band that covered the neck. It was usually topped with a circlet or tiny crown of some sort. (Crowns did not necessarily equate with royalty at that time, but were simply a commonly worn fashion accessory.) Often the wimple was topped with a tiny, pillbox-like hat, quite like the one Jackie Kennedy wore on the occasion of her husband's inauguration in 1961.

Bodices clung and belts were lifted high, just under the bosom, a style repeated during the Napoleonic era of the late 18th and early 19th centuries. As the styles of the garments changed, so did the name of the garment. The tunic gave way to the *doublet* (worn between the 14th and 17th centuries only by men), which was the beginning of the jacket, and the surcoats eventually gave way to the *cotehardie*. While the cotehardie was worn by both men and women, in general appearance it varied. For women, it was a very tight fitting dress-like garment with a widened, flared skirt. For men, it was shorter, often buttoned down the front (fastening with

*Cotehardie, tightly fitting, padded sleeves over multicolored tights. Wooden platforms on his feet were known as "pattens," structured to lift his pointed toe shoes out of the dirt.*

| BARBARISM & CAROLINGIAN (350–1000) | | MIDDLE AGES/ GOTHIC (1000–1300) |
|---|---|---|
| *Significant Dates, People & Events* | Fall of Rome to Barbarians<br>Age of Feudalism<br>Pepin<br>Charlemagne<br>Holy Roman Empire | Crusades<br>Heraldry<br>Eleanor of Aquitane<br>Byzantium collapses<br>Guns invented<br>Norman invasion of England<br>Great cathedrals of Europe are built (Chartres, Winchester, Notre Dame)<br>Magna Carta, first Rights of Man |
| *Key Apparel for Men & Women* | Tunics (based on Rome and Byzantium)<br>Laced and tied clothing<br>Mantles and capes<br>Plaids | Bliaut (variation of tunic) later evolves into cotehardie<br>Mantles and cloaks<br>Surcoats, cottes<br>Long-pointed sleeves |
| *Key Apparel for Men* | Leg coverings (origin of pants)<br>Breeches | Armor<br>Leg coverings<br>Breeches<br>Pockets |
| *Key Apparel for Women* | Head coverings<br>Elaborate girdles and belts | Sideless bliaut or surcoat<br>Head coverings, coifs, wimples, hoods, veils, chin straps<br>Cotehardie, fitted bodice, gored skirt |

*This Time-Line Chart uses very arbitrary divisions of centuries in an effort to simplify prevailing apparel during various periods. Understand that modes of costume did not suddenly appear on any date, or disappear on another. For example, the Spanish clung to the farthingale long after the rest of Europe had discarded it. Older generations also tended*

## EARLY RENAISSANCE 1300–1450

Rise of Spain and Venice as
world powers
City-states of Europe
gradually become
kingdoms

Beginning of cut and sewn
to fit clothing
Pourpoint (replaces tunics)
Shorter mantles and capes
Pointed-toe shoes
(poulaines, cracows)
Pattens

Codpieces
Cut and sewn hose
and tights
Parti-colored apparel
Hoods
Fur trims
Dagging

Stiffened underbodice
Extraordinary headdresses,
caul, turban, hennins,
wimples
Robes, gowns (women's
pourpoint)
Chopines

*to hold on to clothing traditions they were accustomed to. Some
countries, e.g., France, were often ahead of other European nations in
accepting new fashions. This Chart, therefore, is to be used only as an
aid in following the evolution of styles.*

| | HIGH RENAISSANCE 1450–1600 | CAVALIER & BAROQUE (1600–1700) |
|---|---|---|
| *Significant Dates, People & Events* | Printing invented<br>The Medicis<br>Henry VIII<br>Field of Cloth of Gold<br>Columbus discovers America<br>Elizabethan Age<br>Shakespeare<br>Rise of Protestantism<br>Michelangelo and Leonardo da Vinci | American colonies<br>Globe is circumnavigated<br>English throne overturned by Cromwell<br>Religious Reformation, Puritans and Pilgrims |
| *Key Apparel for Men & Women* | Extraordinary textiles<br>Slashing<br>Ruffs<br>Masks | Extravagent lace collars and cuffs<br>Ribbon trims<br>Softer silhouette |
| *Key Apparel for Men* | Padded doublets<br>Trunk hose<br>Codpieces<br>Tights<br>Short capes<br>Beginning of shirt<br>Caps | Doublet evolves into waistcoat with sleeves<br>Beginning of cravat, or tie<br>Pantaloons tied with ribbons<br>Boots, capes, plumed hats, rosettes |
| *Key Apparel for Women* | Farthingale<br>Boned and pointed bodice<br>Deep, open necklines<br>Elegant sleeve details<br>Stiff, shaped headdresses<br>Chopines | Smaller skirt extension<br>Softer silhouette<br>More normal waistline<br>Lingerie collars and cuffs<br>Pumps |

## LOUIS XIV
## (1644–1715)

Great palace at Versailles
French textile industry
    pre-eminent
European trade with India
    and the Orient

Elaborate wigs, powdered
    wigs
Muffs, canes
First costume (artificial)
    jewelry
Jewelled buttons and
    buckles
Heeled shoes

End of the doublet
Coat lengthens
Petticoat breeches
Knee breeches
Embroidered silk stockings
Ruffles, ribbon trims
Beginning of modern suit

Softer silhouette
Dress gradually returns to
    rigidness
Boned bodice
Low necklines
Beginning of modern
    couturier or
    dressmaker
Heavier textiles
Extravagant cosmetics
Wide use of real and
    artificial pearls

buttons was a novelty, for buttons were invented only in the 13th century), sometimes flaring slightly over the hips. Brief capes usually finished the ensemble for men, long, trailing robes for women. Occasionally a surcoat was worn over this garment, open at the sides and showing wide, jewelled belts fastening the under-dress.

Fashions during the late 13th and early 14th centuries gradually became more delineated in the separation between male and female apparel. Both sexes until this time still dressed in somewhat similar garments which had either the same name, or served the same purpose. However, little by little this began to disappear. Women's clothing became more seductive: gowns were shaped to the body, necklines dropped, skirts widened and sported numerous gores and sleeves were still emphasized. Men began to identify themselves and their families with various crests and colors, and as marriages occurred between families, the bride's colors and crests were added, creating brilliant, parti-colored decorative effects. Scalloping, known as *dagging* added even more detail to these fashionable garments.

### EARLY RENAISSANCE

By the beginning of the 15th century, as the Renaissance blossomed, the doublet became the all-purpose man's garment. While women still wore the cotehardie, it was slowly turning into a garment known as a *robe*, a much more elaborate style, with a snug, short-waisted bodice, heralding the return of corset-like underclothing. The early days of the Renaissance marked the true beginning of cutting and shaping to fit. Before this time in apparel history, clothing was basically a one-piece, dress-like garment. The one-piece dress disappeared for hundreds of years, as Renaissance fashions became more sophisticated and complex. Actually, the one-piece dress did not truly return until the 20th century; for almost four hundred years, women lived in separate pieces, even as we do.

The Renaissance owed a tremendous debt to the textile industry. Not only did dress and its composition indicate wealth and rank, but the import and manufacture of fabrics laid the foundations of many of the great fortunes. It would be fair to say that the single most important feature of early

Renaissance dress is in the magnificent textiles. Italy, of course, was not only the center of the Renaissance but was also the main center of the silk industry. Both Venice and Genoa were great shipping cities and had substantial ties to the east, and their textile mills employed many thousands of workers, for we are still centuries away from power looms and the Industrial Revolution. All of these magnificent textiles were handwoven, the workers earning little, the owners amassing vast fortunes.

Europe was in an intellectual ferment. It was a time of flowering in all the arts, painting, sculpture, literature and of course, fashion. The invention of moveable type in the mid-15th century began to disseminate knowledge to all peoples, and the establishment of printing made possible the transmission of fashion information from one country to another. Interestingly, some of the earliest publications were devoted to information about fashion. It was an age of incredible explorations. The Americas were discovered, sea lanes to the Orient were finally opened, vessels circled the world. The vast treasures and knowledge that had always existed in other geographical areas of the globe were now en route to Europe.

### Spanish Fashion

If Italy was the birthplace of the Renaissance, Spain was certainly the dominant leader of the newly emerging interest in fashion. Spain had been under the occupation of the Moors for over eight hundred years, but the Spanish had gradually regained control of their kingdom. By the 16th century the Moors were totally expelled from Spain, but they left a legacy of their superior culture that lasts to this day. One fashion item, for example, introduced by the Moors for which we can all be grateful, was the steel needle. Another inheritance in Spain was the use of metallic threads and the technique known as "Spanish blackwork," delicate, black embroidery.

As the Spanish grew wealthier and became more powerful, reaping the riches of the New World which was under their dominance, fashion, in turn, was launched by that country. The hoop, the ruff, puffed and padded doublets, for example, were Spanish innovations. Spain also contributed the chic of wearing black, another fashion very much with us to this day.

*Doublet and trunk hose with canions of silk velvet. Italian, late 16th century. The full breeches are laced to the inside waist of the doublet. It is thought that this fine Renaissance suit belonged to James I.* Victoria & Albert Museum.

*Velázquez painting of the full court dress worn by a Spanish princess. This version of the farthingale was known as the ''guardinfanta.''*
Prado Museum.

By the middle of the 16th century, women were wearing a garment known as a *farthingale*, which was a skirt stiffened and extended by the use of gradually widening hoops of pliable wood. Rumor has it that the farthingale was invented to hide pregnancies: perhaps, but it also allowed the wearer to show off the magnificence of the textiles worn at court simply by spreading the skirt, which revealed the incredible richness of the fabric. Originally, the structure of the farthingale was quite obvious, but the clever French sewed the wooden strips inside a sort of canvas petticoat, which hid the underpinnings. Bodices were heavily corseted and confined, and usually came to deep points in front. Spanish gowns were often of the ubiquitous black, trimmed and festooned with gold and embroidery. The effect of the stiffened bodice and the rigid, bell-shaped hoop resembled nothing so much as two ice cream cones point to point. Any trace of the human body was quite lost. The Spanish farthingale swept western Europe, but took different forms in other countries. The farthingale in France and England, for example, was shaped differently, and was known as a *drum* or *wheel* farthingale, which tended to be less conical, and stood away at the waist.

Men wore elaborately embroidered doublets cut from glorious textiles, and the fashion for showing a little of the undershirt, edged with lace and trimmings, grew into the ruff, eventually to be worn by both sexes. The peeking undershirt also evolved into today's shirt. Sleeves were very full and puffed, and under their short doublets men wore *trunk hose*, which were often padded to give the effect of a more shapely leg, even as 20th century women wear padded bras. Other interesting accessories of the period included the first heeled shoe, introduced by Catherine de Medici, the fashion for wearing black velvet face masks (both men and women), a lavish display of jewelry, and an extraordinary use of cosmetics, again by both men and women.

While Spanish fashions swept part of Europe, in France and England the taste was for much richer textiles in weave and design. Lace edgings appeared on everything, for lace making had just been perfected. Versions of lace had been known in ancient times, but lace of the mid-16th century, originating in Italy was totally different, using flax as its raw material. The fashion for lace immediately swept Europe. (Incidentally, the famous Catherine de Medici introduced lace to France.) So, in addition to the beautiful embroideries, lace ribboning and ruffles began to be added. In some cases, the starched and stiffened ruff widened into what was known as a *cartwheel* ruff (for obvious reasons) which extended across the shoulders. Another ruff fashion was for a standing-up, fan-shaped sheer collar which rose up behind the head, and framed the face. How uncomfortable these enormous, heavily starched collars must have been, but when we wear ruching or elaborately ruffled collars, we see their fashion roots in the 16th century.

## LATE RENAISSANCE

The fortunes of Spain waned, the destinies of France and England waxed. Henry VIII (1491–1547), the great Tudor king represented all that was fashion in England, and in France, Frances I (1494–1547) was the man of the age. The peak of Renaissance splendor is said to have been reached when the two sovereigns met at the famous Field of the Cloth of Gold in 1520. Each monarch, determined to outshine the other, brought thousands of retainers with them to Calais, where they lived in tents of silk and gold with imitation palaces of painted canvas and velvet. Each king sported his personal colors: Henry's were green with gold spangles, and Francis' were royal blue and violet. Both rulers were handsome young men at the peak of their powers and their rivalry was intense. Interestingly enough, it was at this famous meeting that we see the origin of some of the military uniforms that still exist: the Beef Eaters of England who guard the Tower of London, and the soldiers who accompanied the French, and still patrol the Vatican as Swiss Guards.

Henry was devoured with the pursuit of fashion. He was a handsome young man over six feet tall with great good looks and flaming red hair. He set the styles for much of Europe, although some of his apparel was influenced by the Germans. As he grew older, and so did his paunch, he took to the enormously padded, widened shoulders that he believed distracted eyes from his expanding girth. When we add shoulder pads to our garments we are after the same effect— the appearance of a more slender waist and hipline. He was also proud of his sexual prowess and took to wearing the then famous (or infamous, by our standards) *codpiece*, which was an attachment to tights designed to accentuate the male organ. In some cases, codpieces were padded for extra allurement; in others, they were a convenient place to tuck a handkerchief.

Among the more exotic fashions that swept the Renaissance were *chopines*, shoes lifted up on wooden soles that became a tremendous fad, particularly in Italy. Some chopines lifted the wearer by as much as twelve inches, necessitating the helping hand of a servant, suitor or husband to enable the woman to walk. While we also wear platform shoes from time to time,

*Elizabethan dress, elaborately padded sleeves. Bodice and skirt separate, worn with hip-roll and narrow farthingale.*

the fashion being the same to a degree, the extremity of height has disappeared. Another rage that occurred during the Renaissance, was the fashion for wearing hair that had been tightly braided, unwound after setting, and then combed into a gigantic frizz, rather like some of our hairstyles of the late 1980s. Incidentally, if that hair was also blond, it was supremely chic, for the women of the time, once again, fell prey to the "blonds have more fun" syndrome. It would be difficult in some instances to separate a Renaissance woman of the 16th century from many young women of fashion today. Our young women are tan, those young women found that pale skins were *it* achieved with even more intensity by the use of whitened lead or flour: but attitudes about cosmetics, hair, and the allurement of provocative fashions would be quite similar.

It is curious that people of this time understood the concept of separates in somewhat the same way we do, although their components were quite different: a writer of the time noted that:

Italian women were far thriftier than the French or Spanish, for with only two dresses and ten pairs of sleeves, they could make numerous combinations at very little cost.

In a world of costume which had included for some time an emphasis on, and constant, sleeve-changing to alter the appearance of a garment, one can easily see that with a sleeve selection of ten different sets, one could indeed make a multitude of costumes. Clothing was severely restricted by sumptuary laws in the 15th century: just two garments could be owned. However, with sleeves, which were often jewelled or richly embroidered, it was possible to circumvent the law. Incidentally, sleeves were usually pinned on, for straight pins had been invented by this time.

Particularly in Italy, the Renaissance woman emerged, at least for a time, from centuries of second place. She became the leader of salons, she wrote books, she entertained the intellectuals of the day, and in some cases, ran the country. An educated Renaissance woman spoke several languages and could converse fluently with foreign visitors. Many wrote and

*Elizabethan man's costume. Doublet with trunk hose and canions. Ruff and padded sleeves.*

spoke in Latin, which was still the universal language. Women played musical instruments and on occasion even wrote the music. Needlework was, of course, a great hobby, and generally, the upperclass woman of Italy, and England and France as well, was widely admired for her grace, charm and intellect.

Catherine de Medici (1519–1589), from the great Florentine family, married Henry II of France in 1533, and brought much of the brilliance of her country to Paris. While she was not a particularly attractive woman, she did introduce France to a great deal of the sophistication which we still believe to be of French origin. She brought superb chefs in her retinue who originated French cuisine. She initiated dancing. She rode side-saddle to show off her one good feature—her legs. She introduced the heeled shoe, and it is also said that she made fashionable the wearing of underdrawers, since to that time, they were considered to be proper wear only for courtesans. Catherine was an intense rival of the fascinating Diane de Poitiers, who was the official mistress of the king, and an elegant fashion plate in her own right. It is hard for us to completely understand the manners and morals of the time. Kings regularly kept mistresses, who in most cases were accepted, enjoyed great privileges, and in effect, established their own courts. Most marriages were arranged by families for political reasons; in many cases, the bride and groom had never met. It was not uncommon for both protagonists to dislike one another intensely. However, distaste was overcome long enough to father children, ensuring the stability of the regime, and then, off to greener pastures.

## HIGH RENAISSANCE
## (The Elizabethan Era)

In England, after Henry VIII died and Elizabeth eventually inherited the throne in 1558, another powerful figure introduced a new great age and became another great fashion influence. During her reign England became a dominant world power. Her ships ruled the seas, wealth was flowing into the country from all over the world, and a truly brilliant, iron-willed young woman was in charge. Elizabeth I was even more enamored of fashion than her father. A slender, erudite young woman, also with the Tudor red hair, she avenged herself for

the many privations of her youth. As a child she had literally no place to lay her head and nothing to call her own, but when she was crowned, she embarked with a vengeance on a path to the most scintillating court in Europe. During her reign, which lasted for forty five years, this extraordinary, enigmatic woman dominated the century as she dominated fashion.

There is an interesting document of that time, written in the early 1600s by a traveller to her court. It gives an idea of the sumptuousness in which she, and her entourage moved.

First went Gentlemen, Barons, Earls, Knights of the Garter, all richly dressed and bare headed; next came the Chancellor, bearing the Seals in a red silk purse, between two, one of which carried the Royal Sceptre, the other the Sword of State, in a red scabbard, studded with golden Fleurs de Lis, the point upwards: Next came the Queen, in the sixty fifth year of her age, as we were told, very majestic, her face oblong, fair, but wrinkled: her eyes small, yet black and pleasant. Her nose a little hooked; her lips narrow and her teeth black (a defect the English seem subject to, for their too great use of sugar); she had in her ears two pearls, with very rich drops; she wore false hair, and that red; upon her head she had a small crown, reported to be made of some of the gold of the celebrated Lunebourg Table. Her bosom

*Portrait believed to be Queen Elizabeth I painted by an unknown artist, 16th century. Note elaborate wired whisk ruff, spendid textile and lavish jewels.* The Metropolitan Museum of Art, Gift of J. Pierpont Morgan, 1911.

*By the early 17th century, the silhouette had softened. This gown of brocaded Italian silk is slashed and features a standing, lace-edged collar. We will see a similar soft style return in the 18th century.*
Victoria & Albert Museum.

was uncovered, as all the English Ladies have it, till they marry; and she had on a necklace of exceeding fine jewels, her hands were small, her fingers long, and her stature neither tall nor low; her air was stately, her manner of speaking mild and obliging. That day she was dressed in white silk, bordered with pearls of the size of beans, and over it a mantle of black silk shot with silver; her train was very long, the end of it borne by a marchioness; instead of a chain, she had an oblong collar of gold and jewels. As she went along in all this state and magnificence, she spoke very graciously, first to one, then to another, whether foreign ministers, or those who attended for different reasons, in English, French and Italian; for besides being well skilled in Greek, Latin and the languages I have mentioned, she is mistress of Spanish, Scotch and Dutch . . . She, after pulling off her glove, gave him her right hand to kiss, sparkling with rings and jewels, a mark of particular favor, and as she was going along, everybody fell down on their knees. The Ladies of the Court followed next to her, very handsome and well-shaped, and for the most part dressed in white; she was guarded on each side by the Gentlemen Pensioners, fifty in number, with gilt battleaxes.

What a glittering procession, but not changed much in several hundred years. Queen Elizabeth II is surrounded on state occasions with just as much pomp and ceremony. It would be unusual, however, for her to be accompanied by such a splendid procession while on her way to church—which is what Elizabeth I was doing in the passage described above.

Elizabeth and her court wore little heeled slippers, the important new fashion. The original pump was a delicately soled shoe, with a slightly lifted heel to add height. Incidentally, this is the first use of the word *pump*, and this was also the beginning of the low-cut shoe.

It was during this time that silk knitted stockings were introduced to fashion. Before this, what were known as hose, or stockings, were simply cut and sewn from fabric, although there are records of knitted woolen stockings from earlier ages. Elizabeth's stockings, which she adored, were a gift from Spain. It probably required about a week to knit a pair of ordinary hose, and for the elegant fine stocking worn by nobility, it might take as long as six months to finish one pair. Silk stockings were valued highly by their owners, because for the first time in history, stockings fit, and clung to the leg. A machine for knitting hosiery was invented by an Englishman during Elizabeth's reign, but she refused to have anything to do with it, fearing it would eliminate jobs for her subjects. The invention was later taken to France, which became the center for knitted hosiery.

Another curious fashion fad of the Renaissance in the late 15th and early 16th centuries was known as *slashing*. Many apocryphal stories are told of its origin, such as slits made by marauding soldiers, and so forth. In actual fact, slashing developed from the peeking-through of under fabrics when sleeves were pinned to garments. This turned into a fashion, which in turn became a rage. An early example of conspicuous consumption, slashing was simply a show-off that indicated to others that the wearer was so rich it was possible to wear one expensive silk over another—and in addition, cut it up a bit. Clothing for both men and women was slit and cut over and over again in complicated patterns with other colors and textiles showing through, layer upon layer. Eventually, in addition to the slashing, puffing came into style, which simply meant that the under fabrics were pulled through the slits to form tiny puffs on the outer surface. Puffing, starting from these tiny slits, turned into gigantic explosive surfaces on garments: even armor, which by now had become almost totally obsolete was influenced by puffing. Late articulated armor shows quite giant, extended "puffs" at shoulders and elbows. Incidentally, armor is still with us. Police wear body armor from time to time and soldiers wear steel helmets and other body protection similar in concept to medieval and Renaissance protective armor.

Personal cleanliness was not considered terribly important;

remember, forks had only recently been introduced, along with napkins. Before this time, most food was eaten with the fingers, a personal dagger, or, on occasion, a spoon, which was often shared by several people, as were cups and drinking vessels. Hands were wiped on the edge of the tablecloth, and inedible bits of food and bones were tossed on the floor. So much for delicacy. Bathing was literally unknown, and perfumes and spices were used to disguise the fact that clothing was seldom changed or cleaned. Indeed, the growing use of undergarments as we know them, started from an effort to protect the rich and expensive textiles from the soiled body. Undergarments were particularly worn in the Meditteranean countries, Italy, in particular: the upperclasses changed linens daily.

## CAVALIER & BAROQUE (includes Louis XIV)

During the first half of the 17th century, new sumptuary laws, particularly in France, appeared. Some examples, no person other than of royal birth could wear crimson, except perhaps on undergarments. A farthingale's dimensions were rigidly circumscribed. The wearing of gold and silk was prohibited. Black and "tawny" velvet were reserved for the aristocracy, as were silver and gold buttons and jewels for the hair. If you were middle class, and with some wealth, it was permissible to use silk, but only for false sleeves, a border or lining; it was not otherwise to be seen. All this was in vain. Sumptuary laws were particularly flouted in England where a rapidly growing and wealthy merchant class was becoming even richer with the expansion of international trade, much of it in textiles. The distinction between the classes was breaking down, and if it could be afforded, it was bought and worn.

The pomp and ceremony of the courts of Europe were in contrast to the religious reformation which was sweeping across Europe. And, with the beginning of the movement away from the domination of the Catholic Church, many people began to join what were called Protestant sects. In strict fact, they were indeed protesting in other ways than in their

religious beliefs: our American ancestors, the Puritans and Pilgrims were Protestants, and their somber clothing was in stunning contrast to the extravagant costume that surrounded them. They came to America to escape religious persecution and brought with them the quaint clothing which marked them as a distinct breed. While it was the Spanish that discovered The New World and conquered much of what is now Central and South America, it was the English who dominated the northern part of this hemisphere. The Puritans and Pilgrims who are so identified with much of our early American history wore simple adaptations of costume prevalent in the early 17th century, but modified to an extreme by its gray and black simplicity.

In direct counterpoint to the clothing of the reformers was the apparel of the gallant Cavalier, whose styles reigned during the 17th century. (In actual fact, Puritan and Pilgrim clothing was a pared-down, somber version of the Cavalier.) The epitome of the Cavalier was Charles I, of England, who ascended the throne in 1625. Charles represented the most

*The Cavalier. A superb example from 1630, doublet, breeches, and cloak of slashed satin. Wide lace is used not only for collar and cuffs but is also added to cuffs of soft boots. Plumed hat completes costume.* Victoria & Albert Museum.

extreme appearance of the Cavalier Age. One has only to think of the "Three Musketeers" with their wide-brimmed, drooping hats flaunting giant plumes, long ringlets of hair, leather boots with floppy cuffs trimmed with rosettes, to see the image of the dashing Cavalier. Not for them the stiff ruff, or the tight doublet; they wore wide lace collars, puffed sleeves and decorative ribbon garters, topped off with swirling cloaks. It was a look of abandonment, or at best, a sort of "throw-away" chic in fashion attitude. Women caught the fever. The giant, super-structures that had extended their skirts vanished; the waist lifted once again, and skirts fell in deep, graceful folds of soft, shimmering silk. Women wore soft plumed hats just like the men, and also sported wonderful, wide, lace collars.

### Age of Louis XIV
The Cavaliers gave way to what is known as the *Baroque* period in costume which was exemplified by the most famous of all French kings, Louis XIV (1638–1715), known as the "Sun King", who was to rule France for most of the 17th century—and part of the 18th—and who remains to this day the epitome of French royalty.

Louis XIV was astute. Not only was he personally interested in all that was fashionable and decorative, he knew that the fashion industry itself was important to France, as it certainly is to this day. The revenues from the famed silk mills at Lyons, for one example, supplied the tax funds for a great deal of his ostentatious court. In addition to personally having an affinity for the fashionable, Louis decided to make fashion serve his political needs. He brought all the quarrelsome courtiers and members of the nobility together to live under the same roof with him at Versailles, the better to keep an eye on them. In addition, he set a dazzling fashion pace that kept them all literally hopping to keep up. He built the Palace at Versailles to house in its vast splendor some forty thousand people, all of whom had to comport themselves in exactly the manner he decided.

To care for this enormous throng required a staff of thousands. For example, there were over five hundred people on the kitchen staff, and one hundred wardrobe workers who kept the clothing in order. These people washed, ironed, starched, and spent their long working days organizing the clothing of the nobility. Fashion was all, and French brilliance in dress, furniture, textiles, architecture, and furnishings was recognized throughout Europe. The courts of the entire continent were mesmerized by Louis, and copied *what* he did and *how* he did it, with slavish attention to detail.

Men's costume during this period was of particular interest. It was an extraordinary combination of lace, rosettes, cuffs, wigs, canes, sashes, silk stockings, brocades and satins, and let's not forget the high-heeled shoe, the Louis pump, known to this day by his name. The king added inches to his stature with a square-toed, high-heeled pump, fastened across the instep of the foot with jewelled buckles. A stunning but extreme fashion rampant during his reign was known as *petticoat breeches* which resembled nothing so much as a divided skirt, or culotte, decorated with tiered ruffles and gigantic swirls of ribbon. Louis absolutely adored the look, for he adored fashion. He also adored seeing all of his women precisely and superbly dressed, glittering with diamonds and other important jewelry.

The etiquette at his court was stiff; even though he took one mistress after another, he was quite puritanical in how he wanted people to behave. This rigidness was mirrored in women's clothing; back came the stiffened, widened skirts, back came the boned bodice, back came heavy, rich and elaborate textiles. As the 17th century wore on, Louis became more autocratic and demanded more and more attention. The entire court revolved around his every wish and whim. They danced attendance on him, and his, literally. Much of their day was spent simply standing (it was not possible to sit in the presence of a king without express permission, which was rarely granted), waiting for a sign or an indication of what the King's pleasure might be. Clothing was changed constantly during the day. The court of the great Sun King may have been the most dazzling in Europe, but it also must have been the most incredibly boring life possible to those unfortunate enough to live it.

Towards the end of the 17th century, the fashion of powdering wigs developed, and of course, Louis' were powdered. Preceding this time, the practice had begun of cutting *en suite*, or matching all the various pieces of men's

*Man's handbag from Spain, 1568. Made of cream-colored leather, it bears a steel frame, clasp and belt carrier. It could be an evening bag from the 1980s. Los Angeles County Museum of Art.*

clothing. This marks the true beginnings of a modern suit as it is still worn, a vest, jacket and breeches, worn with a decorative shirt. It was also during this time that the word (and the concept) *suit* became popular. The word has the same meaning for us that it had for them, but suits in that time were made of elaborate silks, satins and brocades, not only extremely costly, but supremely showy. The height of *peacockery* in male fashions.

Women's skirts were still extended over caning, but a sort of bustle began to appear, with some of the fullness either swept to the back or designed with the illusion of back fullness. A favorite accessory was the folded and pleated fan used by both men and women. Tiny parasols held by pages shielded women. Jewelled buttons, often the real thing, glittered on men's jackets. The square-heeled, square-toed pump, caught and fastened with buckles, was worn by all, and walking canes were an affectation indulged in, again, by both men and women. Women's fashions, of course, were a feminine version of the male's. Elaborate, heavy, and be-ruffled, although a hint of things to come appeared in the growing delight in gossamer weight Indian calicos and cottons, which were being taken up by the aristocracy for informal wear. These textiles were introduced to Europe as a result of the expanding Indian trade from the Far East.

At the end of his life, Louis XIV, with his morganatic wife, Mme. de Montespan, epitomized the Baroque. He wore giant, powdered, towering, curled wigs which reached incredible heights. His clothing was of silk and satin, elaborately jewelled, his fingers were adorned with rings, his hand trailed lace squares, and perfume filled the air around him. His death in 1715 was greeted with a vast sigh of relief. His reign had become totally oppressive, not only to the aristocracy but to much of the emerging middle class and certainly to the poor, who struggled to pay the taxes that supported this most fashionable and lavish of courts.

His successor, Louis XV changed everything. He opened the door to the 18th century and to the exquisite, lighter Rococo period. But the door was opening as well to revolutions and modern times.

# CHAPTER FOUR

# *Revolution & Change*

The 18th century was a time of extraordinary change. Not only did the reign of total aristocracy begin to crumble, but doors slowly opened to the world as we know it. And, of course, as these changes occurred, changes in fashions followed.

The manners, mores, and modes of this period in history were unusual. In the middle of booming development, both in industry and in trade that was rapidly expanding throughout the world, most of the privileged and the aristocracy still moved in total artificiality. Both costume and society became even more set and were totally circumscribed both as to rank and position. In the 18th century, before the American and French revolutions, you *were* what you wore. And *what* you wore more often than not was splendid, elaborate, and costly.

At a time when manufacturing was beginning to flex its muscles, creating slowly but surely a new class of industrialists, the nobility of Europe discovered that often the members of the once lower class possessed more money than they did. Social lines and long-established castes began to blur, and the court, particularly in France, soon discovered that intermarriage with these new entreprenurial fortunes often saved the old family name from ruin.

## *WHAT THE COURT WORE*

This softening of distinction between the classes was reflected in costume. Typical of the loosening of tradition at the court of the new King of France, Louis XV, was the

*The sacque returns* (above and opposite page), *Balenciaga chemise with the typical curving back, 1953.*

lovely *sacque* which was soft, flowing and made of lighter more delicate textiles. The sacque was to evolve into fashions that we associate almost totally with the 18th century, although many, many versions of this style still appear. The silhouette was known by many different names, all, however, had certain details in common: the bodice was tight fitting, usually with an inset known as a *stomacher*, which was a triangular piece of textile matching the robe, covering the stays or corset boning. The gown had long sleeves, tight to the elbow, bursting into beautiful ruffles, and all versions featured a floating back panel with loose, set-in pleats or soft folds that hung from the nape of the neck to the ground. Occasionally, this panel trailed into a slight train. It is also referred to as a *Watteau gown*—not because it was invented by that famed artist—but because he painted so many beauties of the time wearing this particular style. Some called it a *robe volante* (robe vo-lawnt) or flying robe. It was also called a *robe du chambre* (robe du shom-bruh), *robe d'Anglaise* (robe donglaze) or after the English style, or *robe à la Française* . . . for obvious reasons.

Eventually, the sacque began to be worn over a skirt extension and unlike the farthingale of earlier times, the skirt was lifted into width at the sides. This fullness to the side was held out by a device called a *panier* (pan-ee-yay), usually of whalebone or cane. The word panier literally means "a bread basket." Eventually this skirt extender became collapsible, and could be picked up and folded into one's sides, rather like closing a fan. This was extremely important, because in full court dress, paniers sometimes extended for five feet on each side, which meant that for all practical purposes, one was set apart rather like a ship under full sail. When this fashion reached its peak, it was necessary to widen doors, reconstruct carriages, and redesign chairs and tables so that the width of the skirt could be accommodated. The fashion was, however, quite charming and beautiful, and while it must have been extremely difficult to move about in it with any grace, it was certainly the predominant costume.

Another fashion rage—or craze—of the 18th century was *powdering one's hair* or *wearing powdered wigs*. The powder was no more nor less than plain old flour, and it was blown

Left, *French sacque, c. 1750. Structure of design can be easily seen, with hip extension and soft, pleated back falling to slight train. Prevailing silhouette of middle to late 18th century.* Los Angeles County Museum of Art.
Right, *similar shape returns in Ungaro's collection, 1986.*

*Satirical drawing from 18th-century magazine showing ridiculous coiffeurs extant before the Revolution. These monuments were not easily maintained.*

up into the air so that as it floated down and settled, it landed evenly on the coiffure. The custom was also common during this period in our own country, where the term "powder room" was used for a special, tiny closet where the powdering took place, obviously to keep the flour from soiling the rooms that were public, or lived in. Of course, we still have powder rooms, but the original meaning of the word has changed. Now, it is simply where faces are powdered, but once it carried more significance, referring to one of the elaborate conceits of the 18th century.

It was during the unhappy regime of Marie Antoinette that the powdered wig reached its most extreme form, towering high into the air and sporting all kinds of strange devices. One lady of the court appeared with an entire bird cage set into her hair, complete with live birds. Others crowned their skyscraper coiffures with hunting scenes, ships or strange creations bearing titles like "New England" or "Asia." Fine ladies fought to outdo one another. The hair was usually partly one's own and partly false, but the elaborate styles became a nightmare for the owner. Once constructed, they were kept in place sometimes for weeks at a time, inviting all kinds of unattractive living residents. Most of the aristocracy carried

*Skirts in the 18th century were extended with panniers: this is an authentic side hoop of that time.*
Victoria & Albert Museum.

tiny scratchers which were always at the ready to enable the elegants to reach down inside these monuments.

Actually, during the 18th century, one passion merged into another. Fashions, of course, were merely keeping pace with the growing instability of the times and reflecting the increasing insecurity of people of wealth. In addition to powdered wigs, men and women (mostly women) sported the fad of *patching*, which meant sticking pieces of black plaster paper about the face. We would call them beauty spots, and at that time they were thought of in the same way, but instead of a tiny dot of black, a beauty patch of the 18th century could cover one's entire forehead. One fashionable sported a frigate pasted across her brow. We can only make a comparison by conjuring up a vision of a young lady of today sporting the battleship Iowa on her face.

*Fans* were used everywhere and at all times. The pleated, folding fan had replaced the feather fans of an earlier era, and many of them were painted with Chinese scenes which reflected yet another passion of the times. *Chinoiserie* (shin-wos-eree) swept through France and all of Europe, and the beautifully decorated home not only featured Oriental lacquers and painted objects, but textiles reflecting the mania. Chinese names were given to stylized fabric patterns, and what were considered to be Chinese colors conquered the world of fashion. Tea became the "in" drink, as did delicate tea services. One can easily date many of the exquisite textiles of this period by the tiny parasols, pagodas and other Chinese motifs scattered throughout.

The two most famous fashion leaders and trend setters of the 18th century—before the French Revolution in 1789—were the Marquise (also known as Mme) de Pompadour, mistress of Louis XV, and the other, Marie Antoinette, the Queen of France, wife to Louis XVI. Although a generation separated them, both women totally charmed their contemporaries, and were endowed with a rare and elusive beauty that was difficult even for the superb artists of the time to capture. And, both set the fashions and styles for all the courts of Europe. The

Marquise de Pompadour left her stamp on French architecture, design, artifacts and literature that is still remembered to this day. It was at her direction that the porcelain works at Sèvres, still one of the finest trademarks in the world, were founded. Although she was not a member of nobility, she had impeccable taste and helped create the reputation that Paris still enjoys as a great fashion center.

Marie Antoinette, the Austrian princess who became Queen of France in 1774, was young, pretty and innocent when she arrived in Paris to marry the future King Louis XVI. She was also enamored of fashion and soon set the styles for most of Europe. When she put her stamp of approval on a color or a detail, it was copied instantly by the other ladies at her court. She was also the first celebrity we know of to bestow recognition on one of her dressmakers—Rose Bertin—who became not only her seamstress, but her friend and often her advisor.

Marie longed to retreat from the rigidity of court life, and created the lovely Petit Trianon, a miniature marble palace on the grounds of Versailles, in which she pretended to be a simple country girl. Here, children's games were played, and peasant costumes were affected in pretty cottons, sashed usually in white, and often covered with embroidered aprons of silk or satin. Simple clothing, indeed, but made of luxurious fabrics and involving great sums of money. The French, who didn't like her one bit to begin with, were even more distressed with this behaviour, for they felt that she was deliberately humiliating the poor. It only added to the antagonisms that were being built up slowly against the royal family. But her little aprons swept aristocratic Europe, and were worn commonly as a charming accessory.

We may find silk aprons for the nobility odd, but this was a time for odd, strange and unusual practices. For example, one of the extraordinary curiosities of the French Court was that all French were welcome—rather as if any citizen of the United States could wander at will through the White House, or an Englishman drop in at a moment's notice for tea at Buckingham Palace. It was possible for any French person to attend balls and other court divertisements if his or her dress was correct.

*Silk brocade sacque from England, 1780, with pannier extension and stomacher. Los Angeles County Museum of Art.*

All was fashion: all was vanity. Costume, and dressing for occasions, was one of the principal occupations of the time. The tremendous expense of engaging in this pastime became crippling. It was not unusual to spend the equivalent of seven to eight thousand dollars on a dress. Men's clothing was every bit as extravagant. For example, one noted garment made for the Marquis de Stainville, embroidered in pure gold on silver cloth and lined with sable, cost twenty five thousand pounds. While these seem to be staggering figures, we must bear in mind that eyes seldom blink even today over a beaded evening gown from the Paris couture costing anywhere from twenty to thirty thousand dollars.

Left, *the Duchess of Windsor in Mainbocher design derivative of 18th-century styles, as pictured in the late 1930s. Compare with the Lacroix, 1988, which once again turned to the 18th century for design inspiration.*

Most modern women (and some men) use makeup; it is part of our daily toilette. However, during the 18th century, overwhelming amounts of cosmetics and paints of one sort or another were used commonly by both men and women. Lipstick and rouges, darkened eyebrows, shockingly white skins. Unfortunately, these cosmetics were made with extremely dangerous ingredients—the effect was important, the content was not. It was still not considered particularly a pleasant habit to bathe: it was thought to cure certain diseases, but was of little value for any other reason. It was during the latter part of this 18th century that cologne was invented. Originally, this simply meant that water from the city of

Designers tend to repeat themselves: Yves Saint Laurent returns to a loose, flowing silhouette time and time again. Both are not only reminiscent of the Balenciaga sacque, but also borrow from the loose, voluminous gowns of the Middle Ages. Two piece (right) is from 1975, one piece (left) from 1981.

Cologne, Eau de Cologne, was infused with various spices and scents. It was used to mask body odors, but was also thought to be of medicinal value.

*FASHION DOLLS* This was also the period of fashion dolls— one of the interesting ways in which the designs of France were disseminated. Although fashion dolls were not new—they had been known in Europe for several centuries—they became much more important at this time. The dolls, also known as *Pandoras*, were predominantly of miniature size, but in some cases, grew to almost human proportions. They were shipped everywhere wearing the latest Parisian costumes, and were used as a sort of fashion information service. Not that fashion magazines were not available. As a matter of fact, they were in common use. The *Mercure Galant* had been published since the end of the 17th century, and by the middle of the 18th, had been joined by many others. However, it was the dolls that carried the excitement, even to the Americas, which were still English colonies. Here, the somewhat extreme fashions brought to the country both by the publications and Pandoras of Europe were modified: even at that time, in this country, many women worked side by side with men and this physical activity made the wearing of artificial and exaggerated costume impossible. Still, French fashions reigned supreme, and other European countries, as well as the colonists in America, were usually content to follow the leader.

A style which originated in the 18th century still with us in a modified form, is the *redingote* which started life as a caped, fitted overcoat. The word is derived from ''riding coat.'' The English were addicted to riding, as they are to this day, and this style has been adapted and changed over the intervening years until it has become one of the ubiquitous costumes of the 20th century. Another fashion legacy from 18th century England is lightweight cotton. The English were also addicted to Indian cottons, perhaps flaunting the imports of their rapidly growing empire. A great deal of chintz and calicos (both are words of Indian derivation) was worn, imported from the new colonies. English textile mills were becoming extraordinarily important. In addition to the fact that the manufacturing industry was growing, England enjoyed the expertise of many of the French Huguenots who had fled to England in 1685 to escape religious persecution in their own country. They came with enormous background in textile manufacturing, and established an important industry in their country of refuge. As textiles gradually assumed importance in Great Britain, the effort to establish international trade led to a chapter in that country's history that is still regarded with shame.

In the latter part of the 18th century, the trade known as the infamous ''Golden Triangle'' contributed to the wealth that England was accumulating, and also contributed to that terrible period in America's history involving slavery. Printed cloth was shipped from the great industrial cities of England to Africa, where it was traded for slaves. From there, the slaves were shipped to the American colonies, where raw cotton was grown. The cotton, in turn, was shipped back to England to be made into finished textiles. A sad period in the histories of

*Painted wooden doll, complete with human hair wig, which was also carefully constructed to show prevailing modes, 1770. Los Angeles County Museum of Art.*

*A late 18th-century dandy, known as a "Macaroni," which explains the phrase in our song Yankee Doodle. Dandies "stuck a feather in their hats" and pretended to be fashion leaders. Cream silk brocade waistcoat over knee breeches.*
Los Angeles County Museum of Art.

all involved, but a telling footnote on the importance of fashion on world history.

Fashion played a large part in the economics of the 18th century, and helped trigger the French Revolution. When the leaders of the country finally prevailed on Louis XVI to call the Estates General into session in 1789, Louis made an enormous tactical error. The Estates General was a sort of loose parliamentary body that had not met in two hundred years. It was composed of the nobility, the clergy and the towns, or commons. (Interestingly, we still refer to the press as the "Fourth Estate".) The King made the mistake of seeking to enforce the sumptuary laws that had been in effect at that previous meeting, over two hundred years earlier. These sumptuary laws rigidly proscribed exactly what each estate could wear: this proscription was greeted not only with great contempt by intellectuals and liberals of the day, but it served to illuminate the distance that separated the monarchy from the people. The king had lost touch with his own.

In America, a successful revolution had already been fought and the United States had been formed. Indeed, the American Revolution was fought with a great deal of help from the French nobility, one of whom, the Marquis de la Fayette, is still remembered by us with great affection. It is curious that it did not seem to occur to the French court that it could face a similar uprising. The French nobility was totally fascinated by the American revolutionaries, and copied them in many ways. Benjamin Franklin, who represented this infant country at the court of Louis and Marie, wearing his simple, dark, Quaker costume, was regarded with enormous affection. But when the revolution in France finally erupted, it was much different than ours, of course, for it brought about a reign of terror that caused thousands of lives to be lost (among them the hapless King and Queen), totally devastated the country, and brought an immediate and bloody end to a system of society that had lasted for centuries.

When society undergoes any drastic change, so does costume. Satins and brocades vanished. Hoops and paniers disappeared, All jewelry was whisked out of sight. One of the most bizarre accessories of the time was the wearing of a bright red ribbon about the throat—a reminder of the guillotine.

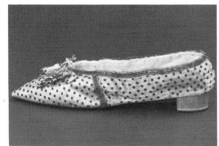

## DIRECTOIRE & EMPIRE PERIODS

The costumes which evolved and prevailed for approximately twenty five years after the revolution were known by two names: Directoire (direct-twor) and Empire (om-peer). The first of these was named after the Directory, the name given to the ruling junta of Paris during and immediately following the Revolution. The second owes its name to the period after the Directory was dissolved, and Napoleon proclaimed himself Emperor of France. Both styles resembled one another, with, of course, many modifying changes during the twenty five year period. Basically, both of these charming new fashions erased the rigid corsets and widened skirts which marked most of the costume of the 18th century. In their place came a natural body, lovely high-waisted gowns, usually of lightweight textiles, which dropped in a long, slim line from a seam placed above the normal waistline. Usually, the narrow skirt started at a point placed just under the bust, emphasizing the bosom. Vanished also, the high-heeled brocade or satin slipper fastened with glittering buckles. Instead, a simple little flat, very much like those worn today. The other favorite shoe

*Women's shoes of the 18th century.* Above right and below, *the pre-Revolutionary, curved and thick-heeled Louis pump which would have been fastened with jewelled buckles. Above left, the radical change to the soft little flat, similar to a 20th-century shoe. Footwear changed as dramatically as the silhouette after the French Revolution. All shoes are of silk or silk brocade.* Los Angeles County Museum of Art.

*Mantua (another name for dress with pannier-extended skirts) in elaborate brocaded silk, England, c. 1750. Los Angeles County Museum of Art.*

was a sandal, copied as closely as possible from those worn by the ancients. Actually, the sandal was just one expression of a renewed fashion interest in what was believed at the time to reflect a return to a simpler, classical life. Skirts were bordered with tiny Grecian motifs, and embroideries felt to be Grecian or Roman in origin sprouted everywhere. It was the first time in many hundreds of years that fashion did not either constrict or restrict. Women moved freely under the slim lines of the clothing and occasionally the textiles were so sheer that the body showed through. This was considered very chic and quite

seductive. Sometimes the body was lightly oiled, and in the most extreme version, the dress was wet through so that it clung to the figure. Coats were not worn so much as giant shawls, which were wrapped about the body in faint imitation of the once well-known himations or pallas of ancient times.

The Empress Josephine, the fashion leader of the late 18th and the beginning of the 19th centuries, wore the elegant, high-waisted, slender fashions beautifully. Once again, all Paris and all Europe watched and copied another French woman of style. Napoleon's reign, and the fashion domination of Josephine did

Left, *costume prevailing after the Revolution—the Directoire, a much more natural body shape. White embroidered muslin—even the fabrics were simplified.* Los Angeles County Museum of Art.

Right, *Christian Lacroix borrows from the Directoire period for this high-waisted gown in this 1986 collection for Patou.*

not last too long, but the fashion imprint of this historic period is still felt. This lovely silhouette appears and reappears in apparel. In our times, the word *Empire* is more commonly used than *Directoire*, but every revival is greeted with fashion enthusiasm, as though it were totally new.

The astute Napoleon, aware that a great deal of the tax revenues in France depended on the luxurious textiles which were famous throughout the world, made a tremendous effort to revive the factories which the revolution had left in ruin. One of the devious devices he used to get them functioning again was as simple as dictating that no woman could appear at court wearing the same gown twice. Another trick which forced women out of the delicate, clinging (less expensive) fabrics that fashion demanded, was boarding up all the fireplaces. The cold required heavier, more luxurious, costly textiles. And, since Paris then, as it had been for several centuries, was the leader of fashion, the approach to women's costume throughout the Western world once again began to change.

### Men's Clothing

Men's clothing throughout the 18th century foreshadowed the styles that are still worn and accepted in the late 20th century. As in women's costume, satins and brocades had been discarded after the French Revolution. In their stead appeared more somber cloth. And while a long tailed waistcoat, and a shorter vest were still worn with knee breeches, following the Revolution, trousers came into fashion, for by wearing pants, one was identified with the lower classes, a much safer social stratum. These rather loose trousers evolved gradually into a long, tight-to-the-leg pant. Many of these pants were fastened under the instep with cloth, even as ski pants and other fashion pants are designed currently for women. The idea behind this, of course, (then as now) was to give the appearance of a lengthened, slender leg. Indeed, some suits of clothing came with two sets of pants; one was designed for standing, the other for walking. These late 18th and early 19th century styles, with many variations, were to set the pattern of men's clothing through the 20th century.

Men's fashions centered in London. After the defeat of Napoleon, and his exile to Elba by the British, Englishmen became the arbiters of male costume. (To this day, the meticulous tailoring and exquisitely fresh-starched linen epitomized by that period are the hallmarks of a gentleman of style.) A great deal of this fashion was set by a famous Londoner known as "Beau" Brummell. A friend of the Prince Regent of England, he was a hopeless snob endowed with a caustic wit. This extremely difficult, effete man set the fashion pace for the next one hundred and fifty years. Beau Brummell made daily bathing acceptable. He stopped the practice of hair-powdering. He shaved facial hair and Presto! beards and mustaches disappeared. But it was his devotion to tailoring that is his lasting legacy.

Another Brummell inheritance in common use is the *stock*, or *cravat*, the wrapped square of material that fills in the throat line instead of a tie. It is an interesting aside, that distinguished gentlemen all over Europe sent their laundry to England to be washed and starched, for it was only there, they believed, that it would be correctly handled.

The fact that Brummell went quite mad, and ended up in exile and poverty in Paris are merely footnotes to his life. He reigned for a time as the supreme arbiter of male taste, and modern grooming dates from this time.

Other fashions set in the early 19th century still in common use are men's formal clothes—*white tie* and *tails*, for example, with the starched, stiff *wing collar*. Another fashion inheritance is the *greatcoat*; although it has been borrowed extensively by women during the late 19th and the 20th centuries, it is still the typical man's overcoat.

## THE SECOND EMPIRE 1852–1870

In France, Napoleon was finally defeated in 1815, and the Hapsburgs (the royal family of France) were restored to the throne. Women's fashion once again began to stand away from the body. The skirt still started above the normal waistline, but did not rise up to just under the bosom. Skirt extenders made a modest return, sleeves widened and puffed, and boning to narrow the body returned. Then, in another twist of fate, the Hapsburgs were overthrown to make way for a return of a republic, followed by a reappearance of the Bonaparte family, and what was known as the Second Empire began in France in 1852.

*19th-century drawing showing a definite unisex slant to fashions. The hats are almost identical, curls and sideburns mimic one another, the silhouette is rigidly corseted (or appears to be in the man's case). He is wearing stock and very narrow trousers. Contemporary male apparel can clearly be seen emerging in this apparel.*

## THE EMPRESS EUGÉNIE
## & THE AGE OF WORTH

*A 1980 revival by Frank Olive of the "Empress Eugènie" hat, which was also all the rage in the 1930s.*

On the fashion scene, the first great leader of the 19th century was the Empress Eugénie (wife of Napoleon III), a woman of Spanish and Scottish descent, with tremendous flair and style. Interestingly, she lived well into the 20th century. (There was a millinery style rampant during the 1930s known as an Empress Eugenie hat—which dipped over one eyebrow, and flaunted a feather.) Concurrently with the arrival of this dazzling Empress came the man who is known as the first true couturier of France, Charles Frederick Worth, founder of the House of Worth, which is still in existence. He was the progenitor of that long line of designers who enjoy fame and fortune. To be dressed by Worth was a sign of arrival in society. He created designs not only for the Empress, but most of the ladies of her court. In addition, wealthy women from all over Europe and England flocked to his atelier in Paris.

Worth's arrival came at the peak of the giant hoop. This new excess in extending skirts differed from the farthingale in many ways. Farthingales and paniers tended to widen toward the side—hoops were circles. Originally, skirt width was achieved with petticoats, which were layered one on the other. To further that width, heavy padding was added to lift and broaden. To achieve the most extreme skirt size, the whalebone or lightweight steel hoop arrived, which enabled the wearer to extend a skirt for several yards in every direction. On occasion, the hoop was so enormous in circumference, it had to be dropped from a hook on the ceiling onto the body, for it was impossible to either step into it, or for anyone to come close enough to help one into it. In a strange way, men's apparel echoed this costume. Male fashions also added rounded shape to jackets with padding, and pants were curved into peg tops. In extreme cases, men wore corsets to achieve the fashionable slim waist. The overall effect was of a rounder, softer line.

By the middle of the 19th century, skirts had widened to such an extreme that it was becoming impossible to move with any freedom whatsoever. Indeed, there are many stories told of tragedies caused by these extraordinary skirts. Women on shipboard were caught by winds and swept off the decks to

FARTHINGALE    DRUM FARTHINGALE    PANNIERS    HOOP    DIOR PETTICOAT

Above, *the progression of major skirt extenders during the past 500 years. In between these widened silhouettes, a more natural body line reappeared.* Left, *illustration in the mid-1800s of women in extended hoops.*

sea, the incredible size of the hoop acting rather like a parachute. There was a news article of the time that told the story of a young woman jumping from the third floor of her home in a fit of pique after an argument: it is said she landed gently upright on her feet, totally uninjured, because of the protection of her giant hoops which slowly lowered her to the ground. The word *crinoline*, still used to describe petticoats that widen a skirt, dates from this period. *Crin* is the French word for horsehair, and originally, petticoats were made of horsehair.

Also, by the middle of the 19th century, the Industrial Revolution was in full swing. The sewing machine had been perfected in 1846 by an American, Elias Howe, followed in rapid succession by the introduction of standard patterns,

The construction of a wire hoop is depicted in this 19th-century drawing. Also, note pantaloons peeking from under petticoat.

buttonholing machines, and pressing equipment. Men accepted "ready made" garments more readily than women did at first, but it was simply a matter of time before the garment factories democratized the clothing industry. Fashion became more readily available because it was possible through machinery for even people of modest means to dress in current styles. The cost in human suffering was great; a work day of seventeen hours was not uncommon and work continued for seven days of the week. In many factories, children as young as six years of age toiled these long and incredible hours. The Industrial Revolution indeed changed the entire face and distribution of fashion, but at tremendous human cost.

Back in Paris, Worth, tiring of the giant hoop, introduced an entirely new fashion. He swept the fullness of the skirt to the back of the dress. This fullness at the back was known as a *bustle*. Dresses were now flat across the front and the sides,

but lifted over a boned cage at the back. Bustles were originally set at a rather low point, several inches under the waist with the skirt trailing over. Later, the bustle was set squarely on the buttocks, fastened high at the waistline, and grew to such gigantic proportions that it rather resembled a perpendicular shelf. To the eye, it appeared that the wearer might indeed possess four legs, a second pair trotting behind the front. Waists were rigidly boned, the smaller the span of a woman's middle the better. Textiles were also stiff and rigid, heavy in feeling. Garments were swagged with braid and festooned with lace. Colors were intense, deep and rich, in many cases because chemical aniline dyes had been discovered, and more exotic, violent colors were possible. Quite often, the bodice of the dress—still a separate piece—dropped down over the stomach à la 18th century French costume. The skirt was swagged to the back and lifted into formalized shapes.

Left, *Dior's famous New Look, tight-waisted, voluminous petticoated skirt, 1947. Fashion Institute of Design and Merchandising, Los Angeles.*
Right, *a Lacroix look-alike forty years later, in 1987.*

## THE VICTORIAN ERA

The "S" curve at the turn of the 20th century—the pecular mono-bosom and strange posture was quite elegant at the time. This period also marks the beginning of the shirtwaist dress, or the skirt and shirt to American fashion.

Costume in the last half of the 18th century to a large extent reflected the reign of Queen Victoria of England, who occupied the throne from 1837 to 1901, one of the longest rules in history. She set manners and morals, certainly for her own country but also for America and many parts of Europe. She was a woman of somewhat dour disposition, tiny, indomitable, and arbitrary. Men and women were to behave correctly and with respectability according to her vision of the world, which was extremely narrow. Class distinctions were drawn with great clarity and Victorian society above all was to behave. It is small wonder that costume was also rigid and artificial—it reflected a society that was vanishing slowly but surely as the turn of the 20th century neared, a period known as the "Fin de Siecle."

Between the 1890s and the 1900s, simpler fashions began to peak through. Women were approaching a more sensible attitude towards clothing: Charles Dana Gibson created the charming "Gibson" girl, and incidentally also created one of the lasting fashions of the 20th century. The Gibson girl was the all-engaging American beauty, and in her simple skirt and shirt, we see the origin of the shirtwaist dress. The *shirtwaist* is undoubtedly the most enduring, endearing, and longest lived fashion in American costume history.

Women were beginning to work, and they were also tentatively engaging in sporting activities such as bicycling and croquet. Tennis and swimming were acceptable, although clothing for these activities still was voluminous.

Men had begun to wear clothing that was generally adapted to specific occasions. Business suits, evening suits and casual suits arrived, the casual clothing often sporting knickerbockers, a pant which was full to below the knee and was then cut short and cuffed at that point. These were worn with heavy woolen stockings. Curiously, trousers had been pressed with the crease to the side until this time. Now the crease began to appear with the edge down the front and back of the trouser leg.

The 19th century represented an era of almost total fashion excess. Costume evolved from one extreme to another. Skirts became huge, narrowed, and became huge again. Sleeves

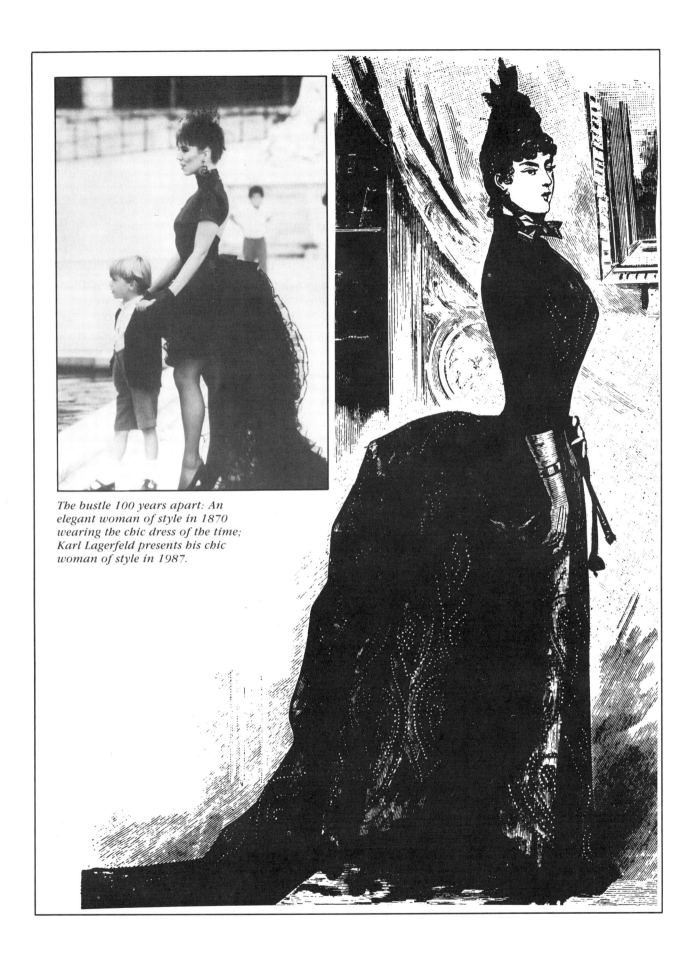

*The bustle 100 years apart: An elegant woman of style in 1870 wearing the chic dress of the time; Karl Lagerfeld presents his chic woman of style in 1987.*

puffed into gigantic shapes, diminished, and blew up yet another time. Fullness swept to the sides, to the back, retreated, then reappeared. Interiors of homes reflected all of this. They were generally a riot of bad taste and over-decoration, as was fashion. Swags, tassels, embroideries, feathers, and brilliants covered everything, what was worn, what was sat on and what was lived in. But technical progress was making headway: giant steps to the modern world were being taken. The first department stores, which had indeed originated in the late 18th century, were now growing in size and number. Harrods in London, the Bon Marché in Paris, Macy's and Wanamaker's in America, for example, were all filled with inexpensive, ready to wear clothing. Department stores originated "one-stop" shopping, for, at long last, under a single roof, it was possible to buy merchandise not only for the entire family, but for the home. Indeed, original department stores also did a thriving business in foods and groceries, a practice followed to this day, particularly in continental department stores, and enjoying a renaissance in American stores, where food and gourmet shops seem to crop up on a daily basis.

The death of Queen Victoria in 1901 finally brought an end to the Victorian Age. The stamp she left on the manners and morals of the time did not die with her, but times were changing. Attitudes were changing. Society was changing. Making way for the 20th century and freedom.

# CHAPTER FIVE

# *The 20th Century*

This is our century. Everything's up to date in this century—free, modern, today, "with it." In just a few years, though, this century will have slipped away, we will be living quite happily in the 21st century, and we will be looking back nostalgically at the quaint world that people lived in in those "good old days." The 20th century is stamped with many radical changes in fashion and the perception of fashion. Not so much fashion novelty—we are still recycling all those old looks—but in how fashion is approached. It marks the arrival of mass merchandising, the appearance of the designer cult, and the slow, but steady, trend to an ease in apparel not seen since ancient days. There has been a remarkable growth in universal literacy: television has changed the transmittal of information as radically as the printing press did, five hundred years ago. And finally, we live in a steadily shrinking world in which we have come to realize our interdependency, one to another. All this has changed our attitudes about apparel, and the way clothing fits into our lives.

Fashion, in our modern perception dates from about A.D. 1300, when in the western world people began to slowly discard the loose, often wrapped or draped, simple shapes of ancient civilizations and began to cut, sew, and shape to fit the body. While both sexes in Greece and Rome wore similar garments with similar names, those peoples had no more trouble telling clothing apart than we do. There were many, many differences—it is the passage of time that has rearranged our thinking. It is vital to keep in mind that both sexes have always been very involved in fashion and appearance, and that distinguishable characteristics have always separated the costume of men and women. A look back at the Byzantine culture would have us believe that men and women of these distant times looked more alike in their apparel than we do, for the untrained eye sees almost identical clothing. However, now, both men and women wear tailored suits and pants, crop their hair short, and carry bags or briefcases. Society, five hundred years from today, will see us, also, seeming to wear identical clothing.

Fashion in this age is the province of all—unlike the manner in which clothing was approached in the past. Additionally, fashion in previous ages originated with the wealthy and titled, and only slowly worked its way down to the other classes. In the 20th century, fashion germinates everywhere: it can rise from the streets, as it also did during the French Revolution or slowly work its way down the ladder from the most aristocratic salon. It is provocative that this century parallels in many ways those distant days of the early Renaissance, for the fashion changes have been as profound during the past ninety years as those which occurred five hundred years ago.

## LA BELLE EPOQUE

At the beginning of the 20th century, it took a great deal of money to indulge in fashion, as indeed it has throughout history. Paris, at the dawn of the 1900s was celebrating an era known as "La Belle Epoque" (the beautiful time) and was at the height of sophistication and luxury. Paris was the magnet for the creative mind, it was the home of painting, the ballet, theater, design and literature. In London, the restrictions of the Victorian era had exploded into the splendid and elegant reign of King Edward and the "Edwardian Age." In America, wealthy young women, heiresses to great fortunes, were literally resupplying European titles with much needed cash, as they crossed and re-crossed the Atlantic seeking husbands among the aristocracy. In this process, the beginnings of

*American evening dress, 1894,
features the extraordinary puffed
sleeves popular at that time.* Victoria
& Albert Museum.
*Such details return again and
again: above, Bill Blass, 1982;
below, Lacroix for Patou, 1986.*

today's jet-setters formed, for in addition to the young women, families and friends also took to travelling. An international set was born that accepted similar fashions and styles, for their lives became similar, the countries of origin mattering less and less.

During the early part of the 20th century, women of money and taste changed their costumes constantly, sometimes as often as six or seven times a day. Wealthy women had, in actual fact, little else to do, for it was still possible to have large households of well-trained servants. (The perfect picture of an upper class household of the day was the popular and long-running BBC series, *Upstairs, Downstairs.*) Every function needed a specific costume. A trip across the Atlantic might require several steamer trunks: a weekend in the English countryside might possibly be undertaken with just one. No truly elegant lady was ever at a loss for the correct apparel for any occasion. When a fashionable and elegant woman went to a ball, her evening dress was complex and magnificent, bound with garlands of ribbons, etched with beading, and frothed with lace. Women wore one sort of dress to go calling on friends; some gowns went only to lunch, while others were held in reserve for tea time. Indeed, the exquisite fashion of the "tea dress" reached its zenith during this period, and these delicate, ruffled, luxurious designs were among the loveliest of all apparel. They were also the forerunner of what today we know as "at-home" fashions, the practice of wearing a distinctly different look for presiding over the house, or entertaining at home.

Under it—and all of the fashions of the time—was a figure, stance and pose known as the "S" curve, a rigidly corseted body which pushed out the bosom and compressed it into one smooth shape, minimized the waist, and emphasized the buttocks, so that the wearer appeared to be in the general shape or form of a giant letter "S." It is curious how posture and bearing have changed throughout costume history: from languid to erect, from rigidity to looseness, from freedom to constraint, each change in costume and attitude requiring another new posture, another new shaping of the body.

Opposite page: *While the "S" curve presented a totally artificial figure, designers still flirt with fashions of the past as inspiration for current collections. Right, Lagerfeld for Chloe, 1982.*

*The already ubiquitous shirtwaist, c. 1900. White linen with embroidery trim, and a straw boater, which reappeared in 1988.*

### EARLY 20TH CENTURY

In America the ready-to-wear industry began to blossom. "Cash-and-carry" general stores had evolved into department stores, where a variety of fashion merchandise was becoming available. Five and a half million women had left the home and were already employed in the work force, buying, not making, apparel, principally skirts and shirts, or the Gibson Girl look. Fashion magazines, both *Vogue* and *Harper's Bazaar* had been in distribution for many years, and were spreading the news of fashion trends, thus creating a larger demand for new fashion apparel. A huge wave of immigration

supplied a vast labor pool, particularly in New York City, and these arriving needleworkers and tailors, already highly skilled, made their way rapidly into manufacturing, creating the garment district, which still supplies the bulk of all American ready-to-wear. While the clothing industry was flexing its muscles, rayon, the first man-made technological miracle began to be used by the lusty infant. Rayon, invented in France at the end of the 19th century was the first of the synthetics, and also made its contribution to the growing apparel business. Known as "artificial silk," it was not originally greeted with great enthusiasm by the fashion industry, but by 1910 was being turned out in quantities both in France and America. This new, low-cost fiber, also helped bring down the cost of apparel. Rayon, of course, was only the first in a long line of textiles introduced in the 20th century, and while it eventually fell into disfavor, being regarded as "second rate", it is enjoying a return to fashion acceptance in the late 1980s.

In France, where the art of dressmaking reached its height, a great impetus to fashion, in the modern sense, was the

Vogue *Magazine in 1914, captioned drawing: "A flare of footlights, a moment of silence, the curtains part, and—America passes judgment on what America can do."*

meteoric ascent of the talented Parisian designer, *Paul Poiret* (pwor-ay). While other designer names were also becoming known, it was Poiret who recognized the changing manners, modes, and attitudes of women and swept away most of the restrictive design of the time. He cracked open the door to body freedom, which had been in decline since the end of the Empire period in the early 19th century. While designer names had yet to become familiar household words in the United States, Paris and even London were busily creating the couture salon. In America, copies of French fashions were seen everywhere—in a sense, stolen from the couture in Paris. Poiret, on a visit to New York, discovered exact copies of some of his designs selling for as little as $15. Enraged, he returned to Paris and established the forerunner of the Chambre Syndicale (see Chapter 7) to protect his, and his friends', creations. But by 1914, buyers from American stores were still crossing the Atlantic constantly, serving up French creativity to their customers.

## THE WAR TO END ALL WARS

Hostilities broke out in 1914, and the "war to end all wars" as it was known, devastated France, but the French couture continued to function in a modest way. Many of the couturiers joined the armed forces and left their establishments. It was felt, at first, that French inspiration had vanished. American stores and some manufacturers, nervous about a loss of their traditional source of fashion, joined with *Vogue* to present a collection of American designs. This was the first fashion show ever held in the United States, and with the support of wealthy New York matrons, and a good cause, European War Relief, the show was a smash. It was a tremendous coup, and showcased American talent for the first time.

In Europe, millions of men disappeared into the military and women, for the first time, "manned" the home front. For many, it was a liberating and exhilarating experience. For most, it marked the first time that women dressed in tailored clothing, and the outbreak of war in Europe radically sped the arrival of simpler and more functional clothing. With women replacing men in heretofore traditional male roles, costume altered to enable them to perform these new functions with

*Women's clothing inspired by the uniforms of World War I. Brown cotton twill jacket and jodhpurs (derived from costume of India turned up in the late 1980s in Ralph Lauren's collections).*

some degree of efficiency. On the home front, those women who had for years depended on a well-trained staff, to not only keep their homes in order, but their wardrobes, as well, lost their household help. Those young women, who had automatically gone "into service" as working in a home was called, now earned more money working in factories. In addition to the larger paychecks, women reveled in their new freedom of choice. By the end of World War I, women had acquired some freedom in other areas of life as well. Not only had many left the home to work in war factories, but a widespread suffragette movement for the right to vote was in full swing. We take this voting privilege for granted, but in our grandmother's time, women did not vote. They were not allowed to. This struggle for freedom, the right to work, the right to leave home, the right to vote, made its mark on fashion. Clothing began to reflect this struggle with less restrictive fashions, and as the 1920s arrived, the body also began to move more freely. In Europe, Poiret had already decreed the death of the corset, and natural waistlines and busts appeared. Even ankles were peeking out from under shortening skirts.

*The Chanel suit as it appeared in the 1920s, complete with striped jersey pullover, pleated skirt, and masses of costume jewelry. The Chanel suit as it appeared in 1985, the easy, classic lines still powerful after 60 years.*

## THE 1920S

The war ended in 1919, and fashion moved in an entirely new direction. For the first time, women showed their legs, and the first wave of short skirts to hit during this century appeared. Actually, it was the first time in costume history that women had shown their legs. Undergarments vanished overnight, and a slim, tubular silhouette was in vogue. The 1920s were a period of tremendous fashion change, and, perhaps as a further affirmation of the changing role of women, it also introduced the rise of women into the couture, such as the Callot sisters, Vionnet, Grés, Schiaparelli, and of course the queen of them all at that time, Coco Chanel. More and more fashion began to be borrowed from men: jackets cut like blazers, sweaters copied from men's pullovers, and horror of horrors, even pants. Women liked the simplicity of men's clothing, and the easy tailoring and comfort that the average man enjoyed.

Hair was cropped short—inspired perhaps by Poiret's sleek-headed look, but more probably by the fact that Chanel had bobbed hers. The hat worn over bobbed hair was the ubiquitous *cloche*, which was an absolutely necessary fashion accessory. The word "cloche" means bell in French, and indeed it

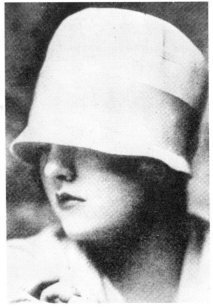

resembled a deep bell, drawn down over the head. Tea dancing became an international rage, as did the *Marcel*, a new method of waving hair invented by a Frenchman. Something called a *cocktail* dress achieved instant success, designed in exquisite lamés and beaded chiffons, the designs often sporting pointed hemlines, known as "handkerchief" hems. The shoe of the 1920s was the elegant T-strap, also executed in brocade, satin and lamé. Black stockings vanished: beige and tan were the new fashion, made of both silk and rayon. Elizabeth Arden and Helena Rubenstein worked endlessly to supply cosmetics to women who, after a makeup rest since the 18th century, were painting and powdering their faces. And finally, white skins were replaced with tans as women stopped protecting their complexions and bared their bodies to the sun.

Men in the 1920s copied the young Prince of Wales, whose every move was followed with close attention. He was the heir to the British throne, and an engaging, attractive young man. He not only enjoyed fashion, but set a great deal of it, notably *Plus Fours* which were baggy knickers fastened just below the knee. But men's clothing was also in the process of becoming simpler, paralleling women's costume. Soft shirts were gaining acceptance, and the oxford shoe was worn in place of high-buttons. Both knickers and the so-called "flapper" look didn't last too long, but both looks epitomize the decade of the 1920s.

*The cloche of the 1920s, here, resembling nothing so much as an upturned flower pot, but the depth of the crown representing ultimate chic. Left, chic women of Paris in the 1920s in their Chanel costumes and deep-crowned clothes.*

Above, *the early 1930s capsulized: bias-cut, deep, plunging back, liquid crepe. A Vionnet design.* Right, *Marlene Dietrich during the same period, wearing her totally scandalous pantsuit.*

## THE 1930s

If the bare-legged flapper dancing the Charleston represents the 1920s, perhaps the 1930s are best represented by glamorous movie stars. People sought relief from the somberness of the Great Depression, which started in 1929, as it swept across the world and left millions of people desperate for simple food and shelter. Many turned from the despair of their lives to the glamor of the movie screen. Garbo, Dietrich, Crawford, Astaire and Rogers were the pace-setters that were slavishly copied. Marlene Dietrich wore man-tailored pantsuits on the street and to nightclubs and was greeted with giggles and amusement, but it started a trend. Katharine Hepburn also took up the fashion and wore loose, baggy, men's trousers. Adrian, who designed for most of the great MGM stars, introduced widened shoulders on Joan Crawford, as well as the little pillbox hat, copied from a medieval headdress. While a great deal of fashion was set by motion-picture designers, the French couture was still all-powerful.

In Paris, Vionnet (vee-on-nay) epitomized the temper of the times with her famous bias cut, which clung softly to the body and was extremely feminine. The long, cling-to-the-body silhouette was *the* silhouette of the 1930s. Halter and cowl necklines were seen everywhere. Deep, scooped-back gowns were one of the innovations of the 1930s, the preferred accessory, a trailing, chiffon handkerchief. The ultimate chic was smoking. Nice women, of course, didn't smoke, but *sophisticated* women did. Hair softened and grew longer. While fashion was still the play thing of the wealthy, the wealthy were borrowing new looks from the poor. Little slivers of dresses made in jersey, for example, a fabric until then not considered fashionable, and striped pullovers, which turned into our t-shirts, were launched by Chanel, as the "poor" look. She also replaced real jewels with fakes, starting the fashion of "throw-away chic" by showing them in vast cascades: this added impetus to the costume jewelry industry. Bras and girdles were reintroduced to keep the clinging lines of the clothing in order. A platform shoe appeared towards the end of the decade, a 20th century version of the *chopine* of Renaissance fame, but differing in the thickness of its sole and heel.

From the late 1890s to the 1930s, America had changed from a basically rural society to one centered in cities. Department stores were growing rapidly, and the ready-to-wear industry was by now a gigantic business centered in New York. The techniques of the assembly line had been transferred from heavy industry to clothing manufacturing, and specialized machinery had been invented that made the growth of inexpensive clothing even more rapid. Cross-country railroads and the growing circulation of women's magazines were spreading an increasing body of fashion information from one end of the country to the other. While multiple and branch stores were still thirty years in the future, vast retailing empires were being established, and smaller specialty stores were becoming more important.

## WORLD WAR II

In 1939, World War II broke out in Europe. In 1941, the United States was drawn into the conflict when Japan bombed Pearl Harbor. The fighting raged until 1945, when the atomic bomb was dropped on Japan and the tragic war finally came to an end. In Europe, Germany had earlier surrendered

*Mme. Schiaparelli wearing her famous snood in the 1940s. Based on medieval cauls, smart women in the early 1940s wore them for every occasion.*

to the Allies, and the war-torn countries were starting the long climb back to some semblance of normality. But the war years were long, and left an indelible impression.

In our understanding of how fashion is affected by world events, it would be obvious that war would produce the most radical changes of all. When the Germans occupied France, most of the French couture ceased to function in any meaningful way. Not only was there very little market left anywhere for fashion, but there was no way for any fashion information to get out of France. Some of the great couturiers simply closed their doors: others struggled to stay open, but it was a sham effort. In the United States, cut off from Paris and that design source for the first time, American designers finally began to "star." At last, talents from both New York and Los Angeles were recognized and featured in the fashion press, and American women learned to accept these new fashion influences: Hattie Carnegie, Maurice Rentner and Pauline Trigère, for example, as well as Mainbocher, who had fled Europe at the outbreak of hostilities.

Fashion restrictions were drastic. Millions of men—and women—were serving in the military. While the enlistment of women was voluntary in the United States, it was compulsory in England. Even Queen Elizabeth II, then a young princess, served in the British army as a truck mechanic. In Russia, women fought side by side with men, as did thousands of partisans all over the world. Not much time for fashion. Pure function was the rule of the day.

### Apparel Controls

Governments controlled all apparel manufacture. In America, price controls were enacted in 1943, and prices were frozen at that level. Style restrictions and rigid measurements were also imposed. The War Production Board specified the amount of yardage used in clothing, achieving a 15 percent savings. Under L-85, as the law was known, there was a total ban on turned up cuffs, double yokes, sashes, patch pockets, attached hoods, etc. Skirts could be cut with just so many inches of circumference. Coupons were needed to buy shoes made of leather. Handbags and costume jewelry were heavily taxed. The fledgling nylon industry vanished overnight, and with it the adored hosiery that had replaced silk and rayon. Rubber disappeared and zippers were in short supply.

But, bereft of inspiration from abroad, American designers hit their stride, even with all of these edicts. Markets, other than New York, began to be created, and in California, particularly Los Angeles, sportswear and swimsuit manufacturing flourished (as we shall see in Chapter 9). All over the country, in Dallas, Chicago, Philadelphia, and St. Louis, clothing production soared.

Women's apparel during this time was naturally somewhat militaristic in feeling. Usually quite tailored, sporting the broadened shoulder made famous by Adrian, similar to the extended shoulder in fashions of the late 1980s. Skirts were narrow, styles were sensible. Most of the factories were, for the first time, run by women, who were doing heavy production work, usually wearing pants. "Rosie the Riveter" was the glamor girl of the war years. But the war years ended in 1945, the armies disbanded and, certainly at first, women were delighted to return to the home and start raising families. The famous era of "togetherness" was about to begin. At the same time, there was a pent up demand for everything that had been denied them during the war. People wanted it all . . . cars, refrigerators, children, marriage, houses, and perhaps secretly more than anything, women yearned for fashion.

## RETURN OF FRENCH COUTURE

French designers wasted little time in re-establishing their couture operations, and once again, fashion marched to the beat of Paris. The House of Christian Dior was new, but from it came the fashion revolution of the post-war era, which lasted from the late 1940s into the early 1950s. Christian Dior's first collection, launched on February 12, 1947, snatched the fashion crown back from America. Women plunged into his romantic fashion revival, called *The New Look*. Once again, petticoats arched skirts, the bosom was lifted and became rounder, the waist narrowed, and the same kind of boning devices used in centuries past reappeared: the shoulder pads vanished, leaving a sloping line. The waist cinch was everywhere (known as the Merry Widow) and women sucked in

*In the 1950s, the New Look evolved into another famous silhouette by Dior known as the "Trapeze," close to the body, with a floating back.*

their breath and allowed themselves to be laced tightly into clothing. Not only were wide, full skirts worn over petticoats, layer upon layer, but even the metal hoop showed up again. Heels on shoes went higher and higher and the toe and the tip of the heel came to spikey points. The whole look was female and sexy. Costume historians and psychologists maintain that after any cataclysmic event, fashions change radically, usually becoming more seductive, particularly after wars, or for example, after the deaths that decimated Europe during the Black Plague centuries earlier. They reason that this is nature's way of ensuring the continuity of the human race.

The New Look was the rage, but like all fashion, when the zenith of acceptance is reached, it begins to mutate and evolve. Skirts inched up the leg, fraction by fraction. The silhouette diminished year by year. Waists gradually eased into a more comfortable line. The world was getting ready for the next great design inspiration, this time created by another supremely talented couturier, Balenciaga. The fashion was known as the *chemise*—or *sacque*. The silhouette stood away from the body, and the body moved inside the garment. While incredible construction was necessary to create the true Balenciaga look, the inner workings were not apparent. The Balenciaga chemise was shaped into the body across the front, but stood slightly away from the body—cupping and curving out—across the back. It is indeed possible that the inspiration came from the sacque of the 18th century, which in its time, also molded the front of the bodice and floated free across the back.

This became the predominant fashion. Understand, *predominant* doesn't mean *only*. At the same time this fashion was first among fashions, other styles were certainly appearing and were being worn by women of all classes. While the men of America were rejecting the sack (or bag, as they scornfully called it) other fashions were being presented in showrooms all over America, notably in garments that were easier and less structured. Further, they were being featured in fashion magazines along with French designs. The unravelling of fashion authority dictating one look was taking place. American designers were making their presence felt more and more.

Other stand-away-from-the-body apparel gained favor. The

*The 1950s moved from the Trapeze into the chemise, here interpreted by Givenchy. Note shortening skirt.*

"A-line" from Dior was followed by the "trapeze" from the young Yves Saint Laurent, who inherited the design chores of the House of Dior on the untimely death of that great designer in 1957. Only twenty-one years old at the time, he is considered by many to be the great designing genius of the second half of the 20th century, as was Chanel during the first half. The designs of the late 1950s were generally clean and sculptured, an approach to fashion that was somewhat paralleled in men's wear.

For men, it was the period of the gray flannel suit, often worn with a bright pink shirt, which was considered to be very fashionable, and not a little startling. Button-down collars were de rigeur, and ties narrowed. Brooks Brothers, a firm originated in 1818 by a man named Henry Brooks, had grown into a men's clothing store that epitomized male fashion of the 1950s. Anything with the Brooks Brothers label on it was accepted eagerly and worn by men who were interested in fashion. While it was certainly conservative, it also was an extremely comfortable, totally safe uniform, and just as in women's apparel, somewhat less structured. The classic Brooks Brothers look hasn't changed a lot since the 1950s, but the pink shirt of that time has totally vanished.

### MAN-MADE TEXTILES

Certainly one of the most significant additions to costume history was the surge of new fabrics that were spawned in the test tube. Nylon, invented before World War II, returned with a vengeance, and in the late 1940s, women stood patiently in long lines to buy a single pair of nylon stockings. It took time, however, before enough fiber was available to service the ready-to-wear industry. The new textiles, although not as resilient and well constructed as they are today, added another push to the newer ease in fashion. Boasting proudly that "no ironing" was needed, that garments made from "miracle" fibers would wash and dry in minutes, some of the claims were exaggerated, and consumers on the whole were frustrated by these new textiles, and became somewhat reluctant to accept them. But time healed all wounds: as techniques were perfected, and the fiber qualities understood better, synthetics swept the apparel world. It was difficult to find either clothing, or items in the home furnishings field that were not composed entirely, or in part, of man-made fibers. They were the most desired textiles of the day—pure fibers took a second seat to the new inventions. It is only in the late 1970s and 1980s that natural fibers have made a tremendous comeback. The minimal care of the synthetics made them an article of joy to the busy homemaker and the working woman.

## FASHIONS OF THE 1960S

As the 1960s neared, the stand-away-from-the-body look mutated into another fashion trend: it became the hard-edged *mini*. Women in fashion, and women of wealth were among the first to appear in these straight little, tough-chic designs, many somewhat tubular in feeling, reminiscent of the 1920s. In this case, however, the revolutionary designs came from the hand of André Courrèges, who created an almost architectural silhouette in his designs. While some credit Mary Quant of London with creating the first minis (it was the beginning of design ferment in England), it was certainly Courrèges who propelled the look into a major fashion trend.

The mini of the 1960s was only part of the fashion revolution that was going on at that time. Young people around the world took to the streets, some rebelling against the war in Vietnam, others engaging in acts of defiance against any kind of authority. The revolutionary fashions of the 1960s reflected the attitude and attack on accepted societal values by the young. The emerging post-war "baby-boomers" rejected out of hand most of what they felt the establishment stood for, including style. Or at least what style meant to them. Why the revolution? Another war, this time slinking through the back door, catching us unaware, slithering quietly into the fabric of America, until to our surprise, hundreds of thousands of young Americans were fighting in Vietnam. But young people, selected to fight the war, erupted.

Anti-fashion took over, and it was not only a mark of distinction but highly desirable to stop bathing, to wear old, cast-off clothing, to go barefoot, to scorn material possessions, to stop combing hair, and above all, to grow it. As a matter of fact, any and all kinds of hair became chic—including the

*The shocker of the 1960s. . . . Courrèges over-the-knee mini and boots. As noted, this looks tame to us, but at the time the public was shocked.*

obligatory attendance at the musical by the same name. Beards, sideburns, mustaches, and long, lank locks were it! Hair on women who followed fashion once again resembled the towering styles of the 18th century. Known as "beehives," they topped faces covered with incredible amounts of

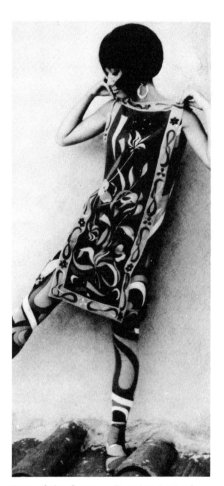

*One of the famous Pucci prints of the late 1960s, brilliant in psychedelic colors, topped with a beehive.*

cosmetics or other face paint. Along with this, young people began wearing cast-offs, army surplus, secondhand clothing, and jeans—the more faded and ragged, the better.

While the fashion revolution of young people was peaking, so was the mini. In a parallel to the Renaissance, when men's doublets shortened, it became necessary to fasten stocking legs together to avoid embarassing the wearer. The answer? Pantyhose, resembling nothing so much as the tights of six hundred years earlier. Pantyhose made it possible for women to sit and move with some measure of modesty. Men's tights reappearing as women's pantyhose is but one more example of fashion borrowing from the past. Pantyhose, which many consider one of the great fashion breakthroughs of the 20th century, replaced stockings which were fastened separately on the legs. They also replaced, in most cases, a girdle which suspended stockings so women's bodies immediately became much less restricted. To further the fashion interest, parti-colored and wildly embroidered designs recalling the Renaissance added additional zing to the new leg coverings.

Giant sunglasses shielded eyes and flat "Mary Jane shoes," banded across the instep, were dead ringers for the footwear worn by medieval scholars. A few minutes spent leafing through the pages of any fashion magazine of the late 1960s will quickly capsulize the extraordinary costume extant. Nothing was too wild or "far out." Fashion presented itself at the most extreme level: for example, the penultimate model was a young woman named Penelope Tree, who looked woebegone, hungry, wan, and humorless. A waif.

Men enjoyed a change almost as revolutionary. Gone, perhaps forever, felt and straw hats. Copying the young President John F. Kennedy, they were tossed to the ash heap. The men's hat industry scolded the President to no avail: that fashion disappeared into the past. Color blazed, not only in shirts, but in jackets and slacks. Neckties vanished, open collars became the rule, and chains and jewelry abounded, a male fashion accessory that had been unseen for two hundred years. The Nehru jacket enjoyed a brief span of attention (copied from clothing worn in India), but disappeared almost as rapidly as it appeared. Dress codes that had been set in concrete during the Victorian Age were simply erased.

All this anarchy was mirrored in design. The Paris couture, somewhat rattled by the gradual disintegration of elegant fashion, began to share the design throne with top Seventh Avenue designers, the young, avant-garde newcomers in London, and the thriving fashion inspiration from Italy. But, whatever the geographical source, all were presenting one mind-blowing collection after another. Mindful of the power of this young market, secondary lines appeared, and the first ready-to-wear from Europe began its assault on the enormous American industry.

A last abortive attempt at fashion dictatorship occurred in 1970 with the introduction of a lengthened skirt known at the time as the *midi* or the *maxi*. While most of the European couture, as well as top American ready-to-wear designers pushed it with great enthusiasm, spurred on by the fashion press, it died a rapid and unlamented death. It was no longer possible for any designer or group of designers, to order fashion: it is the province of society as a whole, and society's attitude about life. A few years later, when the temper of the times had changed, longer skirts did, indeed, return, but fashion cannot be forced. It can only change in response to conditions.

## THE 1970S

The 1970s can be summed up in one word—pants. In the confusion that erupted over the abortive midi, as opposed to the lingering short skirt, women found a simple solution: they covered the legs with pants. Pants were the perfect answer to the skirt length problem. It is hard to believe that so recently, the length of a skirt was the most important fashion consideration on the part of a vast majority of American women. It is only in the late 1980s, that length has become less significant, depending more on line and silhouette that any rigid formula. But at that time, with so much fashion confusion rampant, pants were the answer for all fashion insecurities. It is also hard to believe that in the early 1970s, women were not allowed to enter fine restaurants and clubs wearing pants. I remember taking an extraordinarily chic young French woman who represented the Yves Saint Laurent *Rive Gauche* collection to lunch at a smart restaurant. She was

*Thierry Mugler presents his wide-legged version of a pantsuit in 1985. Pants even in the late 1980s are still the perfect solution to any puzzle-ment over skirt lengths.*

wearing a version of his smashing *Le Smoking*, this particular style featuring a buttoned jacket over long, cuffed pants that literally dragged on the ground covering the shoes. The maitre d', recognizing me, and a little of my (then) anguish, seated us in a side room off the bar, where the condition of my guest couldn't be observed. How different today.

Pants appeared in every form imaginable, from divided skirts and culottes to the classic, pleated-front, tailored pant and the baggy "Fred Astaire" version. Pants widened into elegant evening pajamas, and top European and New York designers showed numerous versions in every collection. Of course, as with any fashion, there were horrors, but this particular category of apparel is definitely here to stay. The fact that women discovered they could avoid fashion dictates quite easily by turning to pants (but curiously, wearing exactly what the "new" pant look was), is one of the cornerstones of the new fashion freedom.

Starting in the middle of the 1970s, skirts began to lengthen again, but very slowly, and this gradual lengthening has continued until late in the 1980s, when brief little short skirts reappeared, much of this newer fashion a foil to the predominant longer length, and much of it a young, frou-frou look inspired by the meteoric rise of the French flash, Christian Lacroix. While for several years, top European and American designers (Geoffrey Beene, for example as early as 1986 showed nothing but over-the knee-fashions) had occasionally included a few styles of knee-grazing skirts in collections, notably for spring/summer wear, it had been years since so many designers struck out in a new direction simultaneously. Legs, and the showing of legs, go in and out of fashion. The long skirt is more elegant: the short skirt is more fun. Both will probably survive quite happily in different markets. Skirts may go up or down, but it seems inevitable that pants will be with us for the foreseeable future. Incidentally, pants, as well, shorten and lengthen. The pedal pushers and the clam-diggers of the 1940s and 1950s are enjoying a turn in the sun once more as the 1990s approach.

As the 1970s neared the 1980s, it was a much more somber time. Government scandals, assassinations, and a decline in our economic well-being wiped out many of the excesses of the

*The total look, borrowed from men.
Fur-lined overcoats topping jackets
and slacks that owe the look and
elegance to a style that would have
been ludicrous on a woman 50
years ago.*

previous decade. We seemed to have arrived at a time of
limitations and uncertainty. These were sobering years, which
were reflected in the much more somber approach to apparel.

A growing interest in, and emphasis on, health, knowledge
about our bodies and a remarkable change in our eating habits,
also became part of our 1970 psyches. Body awareness introduced entirely new categories of functional clothing, and a
great deal of this functional clothing evolved into formal wear
and dressy fashions. This emphasis on a more natural lifestyle
has been reflected as well in hair and cosmetics. While young

*Ralph Lauren turns to the jungle and the safari for fashion inspiration. These shirts have been one of the wildest successes of the 1980s.*

women still ironed their hair into long, shining manes in the early 1970s, this hair length shortened into a smaller-headed look by the end of that decade. Cosmetics, which were bold and strident in coloration and effect, also quieted down. Eyes, as heavily outlined as an ancient Egyptian's, discarded the heavy outline and softened.

## THE INDIVIDUALISTS

Through the 1970s, there was a growing acceptance of individuality in apparel. Men, as well as women, seem to be in the process of developing singular attitudes about how they clothe themselves, in many cases totally disregarding fashion trends. While it is true that the majority of the public still marches in step with fashion as presented by the press and the creative minds of the designers, it is just as true that what was once considered the fount of all knowledge has slowly lost ground. Paris, giving ground earlier in this century to designers in New York, was assaulted further by talent appearing in Italy, London, and Japan. Actually, even these countries no longer are the only sources of fashion creativity. Inspiration comes from everywhere. As the world shrinks and people accustom themselves to more and more travel, becoming at ease with varying cultures and ideas, design turns up in the darndest places. Costume can surface in Russia, erupt in Germany, or be inspired by ethnic apparel in Africa or South America. Opening the doors to the Peoples Republic of China introduced the world to the Mao suit, and in reverse, introduced the Chinese to the joy of wearing color and decoration. Articles of apparel are made and shipped all over the world, much to the dismay of American trade unions, representing hundreds of thousands of workers in the fashion industry who are fighting to preserve their jobs from the avalanche of imports.

Fashion inspiration surrounds us. Museum exhibitions are reflected in designer collections, one of the best examples being the Yves Saint Laurent *Mondrian* collection. The theater and the dance are influential, as are the movies. Witness *Annie Hall*, which spawned hundreds of thousands of Diane Keaton clones, or a few years later, when *The Turning Point* introduced *leg-warmers* to young American women, who wore them, in hot weather as well as cold, making a fashion statement that had nothing at all to do with the ballet. Rock music has had a strong influence on the young—notably in the late 1970s and the 1980s, and although much of the rock-inspired costume is scorned by the establishment, the apparel is strong, and provokes peripheral accessories: leather, chains, heavy belts. Besides, young people simply don't care one bit about the establishment. It's their look, and they like it.

What is significant about clothing today is that generally, a softer, more conservative approach predominates. But of course, that is costume reflecting culture and society. If the 1960s and the 1970s imaged the confusion and angst of those years, so does the more somber but luxurious apparel explain the world we live in. Perhaps, however, the most significant change in 20th century fashion has been the gradual disappearance of body restriction, which is exemplified in the tremendous growth of the sportswear industry. Of all the fashion trends in one hundred years, the movement into comfort and ease has been the most profound. While women may flirt occasionally with bustles, petticoats, and tight waists, it is, after all, only a flirtation. It would take an extraordinary international upheaval to change our apparel to any permanent constriction.

Where will fashion go? Who knows. If we change, fashion will change—we wear what we are. What we do know is that the 20th century is slowly disappearing down the time stream: we are on the brink of the 21st century, close to the year A.D. 2000. What will the eyes of the future think of our clothing? As men and women become less separated by the sexual roles that have always determined costume, it may just be that they will dress more and more alike, as people did thousands of years ago. That indication is already in the wind, for runway collections often feature identical clothing for both sexes. What does it matter? After all, we can tell ourselves apart, just as the Byzantines did.

# CHAPTER SIX

# *The Great French Stars*

In the creative world, there are always some who shine with a brighter light. Just as in the firmament, some stars blaze, some glimmer. In assessing the relative merits of all the great fashion designers who have achieved fame and fortune during the past one hundred and fifty years, some seem to have stamped their image in a more powerful way on costume. In a few cases the imprint was brief: in others, there has been a lasting legacy of great taste, great innovative ideas, and original concepts of how costume and fashion should relate to life.

If one were to think of apparel in terms of flow, a flow similar to a river, it is easier to understand. Rivers are composed of one element—water, but the appearance of that element changes constantly as the river moves. At times, broad, at other times narrow: occasionally, the river will even disappear under the ground, only to erupt further downstream with violence. Sometimes brilliant and clear, sometimes opaque and murky. All kinds of peripheral life depends on the river for food and for growth. So, too, does fashion move like a body of water supporting in varying degrees allied interests. From time to time, a man-made structure will divert or change the course of the river. So, too, does this happen in fashion. And the great diverters, the great movers and shakers in the world of apparel are the stars.

These design stars capture some mood or spirit of their times, for fashion creation can only occur and be accepted if it strikes a responsive chord. There is a puzzler that asks, "if

*A Worth evening gown of the late 19th century, created in a combination of silk satin and velvet. Note the S-shape, and the sweeping train, which would have been looped over the wrist for dancing.* The Metropolitan Museum of Art, Gift of Eva Drexel Dahlgren, 1976.

there is no ear, can there be sound?'' If there is no response from the public, can costume, then, be created? By examining the stars, we understand what makes them what they are, why their names have endured, and why, in many instances, their names are still worthy of headlines, even after many years.

# CHARLES FREDERICK WORTH
## (1825–1895)

*Charles Frederick Worth*

While designer names had been before the public eye prior to the ascent of Worth (Rose Bertin, for example, dressmaker and confidante of Marie Antoinette), he is the man who truly established the French couture. Born in England in the early part of the 19th century, Worth moved to Paris before he was twenty years old where he married a pretty, young, fellow worker and began designing for her—designs that found favor with clients of the shop where they worked. Enough so, that by 1858, he was able to open his own shop (later, such shops were known as *houses*), which became the first true salon of style in Paris.

One of the most original contributions he made to the fashion world was to show designs on living models and to present a collection of gowns so that customers could select from a group. In other words, instead of being a dressmaker and creating individual styles for each client, he produced a *line*, and allowed the interested woman to pick and choose from the collection—even as women do from the modern couture. Usually, the collection was shown in black and various fabrics and trimmings could be chosen to suit the individual fancy. One of the customers that helped create his fame was the fashion plate of the time, the Empress Eugénie of France. Worth was her favorite, and as she was a woman of style and chic, what she did was avidly copied and followed in many capitols of the world. Most of the crowned heads of Europe copied her, as did women of wealth in America. Many had their entire wardrobes designed by this innovative and talented designer. By the middle of the 1860s, he was employing over one thousand people in his workrooms in Paris—an enormous number, even by today's standards.

His influence on fashion at that period in history was enormous. He boasted that he destroyed the crinoline with one sweep of his designing hand—and introduced the bustle with the other. With a flair for the dramatic, and a well-developed sense of his own importance, he maintained that fashion was equal to any of the arts, and that clothing was equal in importance to a painting.

Worth's contribution to fashion is lasting. The first use of live models to show clothing. The first presentation of an entire collection of designs, and the first true couture house in Paris. He was the originator of the couture, and while he died just before the turn of the 20th century, he left his business to his two sons, who carried on the Worth tradition for many decades. While the House of Worth has long since disappeared in Paris, it is still in existence in London and known for its perfumes, notably, *Je Reviens*. His beautiful gowns are assiduously collected by museums, and can be seen from time to time in costume galleries.

# *PAUL POIRET*
## (1879–1943)

*Paul Poiret*

Poiret (pwah-ray) was the first great star of 20th century couture. His is one of the most famous names in French fashion history, and his original concepts and designs are still used, both as reference and as a source of creative inspiration by other members of the fashion world. He served an early apprenticeship at the House of Worth, but by 1904 was able to strike out on his own.

He revolutionized fashion—not only in Paris, but throughout the sophisticated fashion world. He mirrored the excitement of that city at the beginning of this century, the city in which all the arts were centered, where theater, painting, writing and dance reigned supreme. All of these elements were splintering away from the conservative tradition that had preceded, and like his contemporaries, Poiret splintered fashion design from its heritage.

Poiret, who referred to himself first as the King of Fashion, and later as the Sultan, turned for his inspiration to the orientalia that was sweeping Europe. By 1913, his chic women were dressed in harem pants, wrapped and twisted turbans, flaunted exotically painted eyes and moved with languor and a definite slink. Her skirt was inevitably hobbled, but slit to the knee for easier movement. The gowns, narrow and slender, dropping freely from two points at the shoulder, and caught at, or above

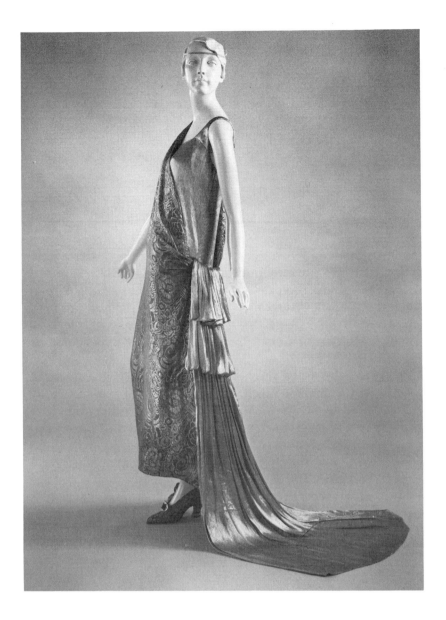

the waist, resembled in some ways classic Greek design. They were made of textiles new to the fashion world—chiffons, gauzes, and liquid lamés (known as cloths of gold), and were brilliantly colored: violets, clear greens, pinks and scarlets. He swept away the corset and rigid boning, replacing it with a lightweight rubber girdle: he invented the first brassiere, or *soutienne-gorge* (soo-tee-en gorj), in order to achieve a young, small-breasted look. It is difficult to imagine the profound influence he exerted at that time on fashion. He considered himself to be an artist of the same caliber as a painter and declared that indeed, design made as important a contribution to the world as those creative geniuses did. He was as outrageous in his private life as he was in his fashion life. He lived extravagantly, and was famous for his splendid galas and stunning costume pageants. But in those pursuits, he was also squandering his wealth.

*Evening gown by Paul Poiret, c. 1925. Cinnamon and silver lamé, the silver caught in great loops starting just below the waist.*
*Los Angeles County Museum of Art.*

His influence is unforgettable: not only did he free women from restriction and introduce them to brilliant and daring new fashion concepts, he introduced (and also scandalized) Paris to what were known then as "fashion parades" using his wife as one of the models. His women were not only elegant, but very rich. He had no interest at all in middle class or working women, considering them to be outside the pale of his costume kingdom.

The man who once reigned as King, died in poverty and obscurity in a charity hospital in 1943, forgotten for many years by the world he had once so totally dominated. Like other designers of later times, he was unable to move on. Even though he said of himself, "I do not impose my will upon fashion . . . . I am merely the first to perceive women's secret wishes" he lost this perception and fell out of favor. His designs can be seen in many museum collections, where it is possible to examine the exquisite workmanship and creativity that was present in everything he touched. His influential designs, in many instances, could easily be worn today.

## *GABRIELLE (COCO) CHANEL*
(1883–1970)

There is no question in the fashion world that the most significant designer of the 20th century would, of necessity, be Coco Chanel. Born in the 19th century, she was already a young woman at the dawn of the 20th, but all her life kept her origins clouded in as much mystery as she could, in effect, wiping out those early years. A beautiful, stunning and enigmatic woman, she was involved in one liaison after another, some of her better known affairs involving European royalty. Her friends and companions were the most avant-garde in the world of art and theater in Paris, from Cocteau to Picasso, from Stravinsky to Diaghilev. She was adored by Dali, and was a close friend of Colette, the famous novelist and writer. She was regarded by all as an equal in talent and a genius at her craft.

*Coco Chanel*

*Black silk crepe evening gown, the skirt flounced with ostrich feathers, which matched the feather cape. Chanel loved to work with black, and was famous for her "little black dresses," 1930.*

Her first designs were millinery, but by 1920, she was becoming well known for her collections of apparel as well. She hit her stride between 1920 and 1924 in a veritable frenzy of originality. Among her design innovations, all trademarks, were the use of jersey, hitherto unknown as a fashion textile, and fake jewelry, consisting of pearl ropes and colored crystal that cascaded down the front of her gowns. In 1926, she introduced the *little black dress* the first time this color had been in favor (except for mourning) since Spain of the 15th century. *Vogue* predicted it would not only be *the* dress of the decade,

*Chanel black again, a satin-backed crepe trimmed with pale eggshell crepe. Cut on the bias, the sleeves gently flared matching the skirt, 1928.*

but for the first time, used the word *Ford** in describing it. Chanel bobbed her hair, and so did most of the western world; she dared to wear pants—copied somewhat after a sailor's; she tanned her skin in the Mediterranean sun. But perhaps her most enduring legacy is the Chanel suit, a simple, cropped jacket usually bound with braid, soutache, or ribbons, open and unbuttoned, with a soft, straight, or pleated, skirt. This style was as fresh and new in 1925 as it is in the late 1980s. Copied by almost every designer in the world at one time or another, it has varied only slightly during the past sixty years, and those variations are so minute as to become insignificant.

Chanel loved simplicity, and created what was called the "poor look" as opposed to the opulence of much of the French couture. The famed Chanel shoe, black silk, patent or leather toe and beige vamp, has not varied in fifty years, except for heel height. She has been the most imitated and the most widely worn designer of this century.

At the time of the opening of hostilities in World War II, she closed her house, but even by that time, she was an extremely rich woman. She had no plans to reopen after the war, but it is said she was so competitive that the success of Dior inspired her to go back into business and give him a run for his money. She reopened in 1954, to what were generally unfavorable reviews, but within months the real world had taken her up and her designs were, once again, selling like hot cakes. It was all roses from then on. It is hard to believe that a seventy-one year old woman could reconquer the tough fashion world, but such was the case. Until her death in 1970, at the age of eighty-seven, she kept at her drawing board, turning out one rave collection after another. She was a woman of great perseverance, talent and invention, driven to perfection. Her last collection was as contemporary and influential as her first, and oddly, in many ways, not all that different. She captured the spirit of a century. Perhaps her own words sum her life up best: speaking in the third person, she said "Chanel, above all else, is a style. Fashion, you see, goes out of fashion. Style, never." The House of Chanel is still one of the most important in Paris, the collections designed by Karl Lagerfeld.

*In the fashion industry, the word *Ford* means that the style will be worn by millions—i.e., everybody's dress.

# MADELEINE VIONNET
## (1878–1975)

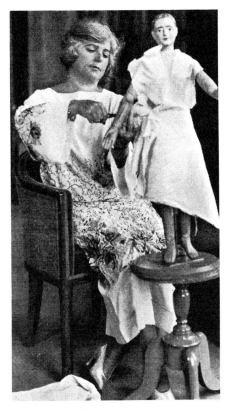

*Madeleine Vionnet*

Vionnet (vee-on-nay), another designer always known simply by her last name, worked in Paris at the same time as Chanel, and Poiret, for that matter. However, her woman moved to a different beat.

It is fascinating that she literally started her career as a child of eleven working as an apprentice, and spent her lifetime in the pursuit of fashion until 1939, when she closed her doors forever at the start of World War II. But, in the preceding two decades, she left a stamp on the fashion world that is still felt, and a stamp that is still mirrored in clothing. If the entire 20th century reflects Chanel, the late 1920s and 1930s belong to Vionnet, for that period is in her image.

Vionnet opened her house in 1919, and before it closed, it employed almost 1200 workers. It is interesting that she burst on the scene as Poiret's influence was waning, and Chanel's was increasing, but her approach to fashion was entirely different from both. More than just a designer of clothing, she epitomizes the 1930s—her obsession with the free body moving under clothing changed the direction of fashion at that time.

The short skirts of the 1920s lasted only a few seasons, and by 1927, a longer length was emerging. Vionnet's sleek, easy cuts followed the natural lines of the body, clinging and elegant. She originated the bias cut, which gave clothing the supple, fluid look so indicative of that period, and changed not only the direction of design, but the manufacturing of textiles as well. Textiles, of necessity, also developed into fluid, supple cloth. Along with the bias cut, her most famous innovation, the cowl neck and halter neckline are also attributed to her. She was the dressmaker supreme and her designs were the hallmark of the 1930s. Almost any piece from one of her collections of that period would be quite at home on Fifth Avenue today. *Vogue's* famous editor, Edna Woolman Chase once said "her design is infinitely complex . . . with a scientific purity of line . . . she is an artist in fabric as Picasso is in paint."

*Typically and beautifully Vionnet, this bias-cut silk crepe swirling loosely about the body, draped into deep, handkerchief points.*

Vionnet, a proud and egocentric woman (as seems to be true of many famous designers) said of herself, ''there's only one Madeleine Vionnet, only one.''

She founded the Centre de Documentation du Costume in Paris, which houses the records of all her collections. Represented are such innovations as argyle sweaters, pinstriped gangster suits (which Yves Saint Laurent brought back forty years later), fringes, the celebrated bias cuts, liquid crepe de chines and Art Deco embroideries. When any designer flirts with the look of the 1930s, it is in direct tribute to the artistry of this talented designer.

Her work has been featured in costume exhibits in London, at the Metropolitan Museum of Art in New York, at the Los Angeles County Museum of Art, and at the Fashion Institute of New York. Her designs are highly prized by collectors.

# ELSA SCHIAPARELLI
## (1890–1973)

Schiaparelli (Scap-ah-relli) was born to a noble Roman family, and after her marriage, moved to America. She almost accidentally became involved in fashion when an American buyer saw her at luncheon in Paris in a sweater of her own design. This was enough to launch a career that moved with flare and excitement through the 1930s. She gave fashion an entirely different slant, a direction full of whimsy, humor and great originality.

She was an original—a one of a kind. While she made formal clothes of great elegance and architectural beauty, she always added some exotic touch, unexpected and provocative . . . such as giant embroidered hands clasping a waistline. She also designed hats that were literally "out of this world" among them, some that resembled nothing so much as lamb chops with frills. Other fashions for the head included the *snood*, both the name and the design straight from the Middle Ages. A snood in its original form caught long hair in a sort of netting—and so did Mme. Schiap's. Her snood designs swept the 1940s—appearing in brilliant colors and various kinds of mesh, and were worn by women of wealth as well as college girls. She also created a line of miniature "doll hats" which caught the imagination of the fashion world.

*Elsa Schiaparelli*

Her true trademark was the range of her inventiveness—inspiration came to her from every source. The sweeping burnooses of North Africa, colors and decorations from Russia or South America, hats of newspapers like those worn by women working in fish markets. She liked to use brilliant colors, among them the most famous and most closely identified with her name, *Shocking Pink*. Her successful perfume was also known as *Shocking* and the bottle she designed for it was copied from a plaster cast of Mae West, the great movie sex-symbol of the 1930s. One of her most important contributions to fashion was the broadened shoulder, which she achieved with the use of shoulder pads, a fashion first. This square, padded shoulder, which swept the world in the late 1930s and 1940s was first shown in *Vogue* in 1932, and while it was widely adopted in America—notably by Adrian—the

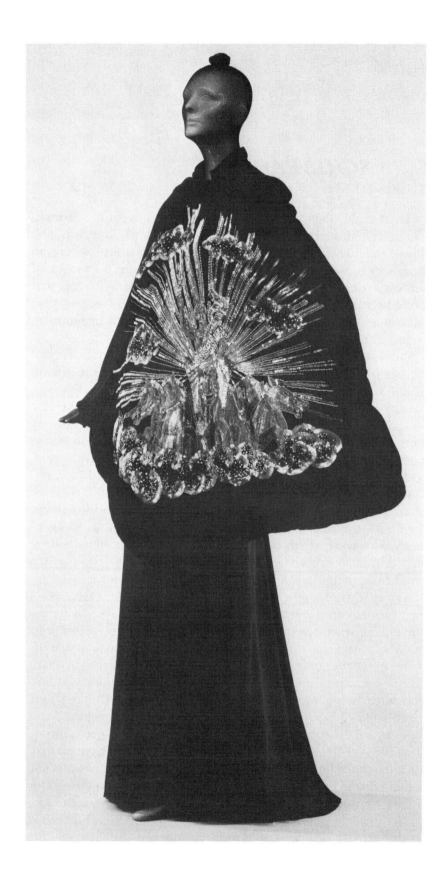

*Typical Schiaparelli, this stunning black velvet evening cape with gold embroidery inspired by the fountains at Versailles, 1938. Compare with Lagerfeld faucet dress,* page 147. The Metropolitan Museum of Art, Costume Institute, Gift of the Estate of Lady Mendl, 1955.

impetus came originally from Schiaparelli. In addition to the padding, she also achieved a broadened shoulderline with leg-o-mutton sleeves, borrowed directly from the 1890s.

For textiles, she abandoned what most designers worked with, using cellophane, straw and glass, for example. Tweeds were used for evening clothes, and other fabrics were printed with elephants, clowns, and horses. Handbags were shaped like balloons, or on occasion, lit up and played tunes when opened. Many of her fabrics were created for her by famous artists, such as Berard and Cocteau.

She is credited with opening the first boutique in 1935, the sort of shop that had never been seen before, and for that boutique, she designed totally separate collections. She didn't approve of the couture, in effect, copying itself in a secondary line.

She fled France, along with many others from the couture, when Paris was lost to the Germans, and spent the war years in America. While she returned to Paris immediately following the war and produced some collections for a brief period of time, she never regained the fame and success she had enjoyed earlier. Her designs have been featured at the Metropolitan Museum of Art in New York, and there is a permanent room dedicated to her fashions in the Philadelphia Museum of Art. She was the grandmother of Marisa and Berry Berenson of motion picture renown. Of all designers working in Paris today, Karl Lagerfeld seems to come closest to her in spirit and flare.

## CHRISTIAN DIOR
(1905–1957)

Dior (dee-or) was born in Normandy in 1905, and his family's original plans for him included a career in the diplomatic service, but by the time he was twenty-three, he had abandoned that idea, and with his parent's money had opened a small art gallery in Paris. By 1931, the money had vanished. Dior's friends in the art world taught him to sketch

*Quintessential Dior, this pouffed, tiny-waisted short ballgown, 1955. Photo by Louise Dahl-Wolfe. Staley-Wise Gallery, New York.*

and he made his first stab at designing and drawing on a freelance basis. His initial job was with Lucien Lelong, where he worked during the war years. Some of the couture operated under the German occupation, although with great difficulty, and it was with Lelong that Dior learned his craft.

In February, 1947, Dior launched the *New Look* in his first major Paris collection. He was backed by a famous textile manufacturer, Marcel Boussac, who understood the value of promotion and merchandising. Unlike most in the couture, who scrape together start-up money, Dior opened up with a staff of sixty, including key people from other houses (among them, a young Pierre Cardin). Boussac looked after the dollars, Dior looked after the fashions.

The New Look launched an entirely different look to costume, with a tiny waist, a rounded and padded hipline, and a shapely bust, usually with a low-cut neckline and a long, full skirt. To women who had lived through the war years, the femaleness of the New Look was a dazzling success, for they were weary of the severe, wartime restrictive fashions.

It is said that dresses by Dior were "constructed like buildings." They were all lined with cambric or taffeta, returning to techniques long forgotten. Dior aimed at an established, more mature clientele, but young people were attracted as well to his design revolution. All over the western world, manufacturers plunged into the production of this new style, and public acceptance was almost instantaneous. The silhouette was at first controversial, as indeed is the case with most startling fashion changes. Some saw the look as too nostalgic, with no place in the modern world. Men hated the long skirts which covered women's legs. Others declared it to be a return to the dowdiness of the preceding century. Even Schiaparelli predicted it as something which though "cleverly planned and magnificently financed . . . and . . . the greatest din of publicity ever known, would have the shortest life of any fashion in history." All to no avail. Dior's revolutionary designs sparked a whole cycle of fashion, rounded, gentle, feminine, a delight in elegance. His first success was not an accident: the "H" line in 1954, the "Y" line in 1955, and the "A" line in 1956 followed in quick succession, and met as well with instant acceptance. His great success spawned offshoots immediately. A New York House of Dior opened in 1948, followed by one in London. During his ten-year reign as King of Couture, the Dior empire grew until it covered every country in the Western world, and included furs, hosiery, jewelry, perfumes, men's wear and on and on. More than 1000 people worked at the Paris headquarters.

His sudden death in 1957 did not halt the growth of the House of Dior. Even now, so many years after his death, his

*Christian Dior*

name is synonymous with fashion throughout the world, and indeed, is one of the most recognized names in the world. He was once described as looking like a "bland, country curate made out of pink marzipan," but he was filled with a radiant vigor. His first, great New Look, with its long skirts and bouffant petticoats was an expression of freedom in the late 1940s. Each age finds its own image. The House of Dior is still of great importance, the collections being created by Marc Bohan.

*Cristobal Balenciaga*

# CRISTOBAL BALENCIAGA
## (1895–1972)

Balenciaga (bal-en-see-aga), the Spanish Basque designer who conquered Paris, was born in 1895 in a small fishing village in Spain. From the time he was a child, he was absorbed totally in fashion, and he was to spend his entire life wrapped in that pursuit to the exclusion of all else. He was an émigré from the Spanish Civil War and opened his house in Paris in 1937. However, he already claimed a reputation as a designer in Madrid, where most of the chic women were wearing his designs which even then were marked with "an odd looseness about the neck and shoulders." This is the same shape that marked a Balenciaga design at the height of his fame in the late 1950s.

This enigmatic man, who went to great lengths to avoid the press—particularly newspapers—was truly a designer's designer. It is said that every fashion creator in the world, with the exception of Chanel, copied him at one time or another. He was considered by most fashion creators to be their most profound inspiration. He dressed the wealthy, and since he felt that no woman was truly elegant until she reached the age of forty, his designs were intended to be worn by women of that age, never by the young. He gathered young talent about him, however, and launched the careers of Hubert de Givenchy (you-berr duh jee-vonch-ee), Courrèges (cur-rej) and Ungaro (un-garr-o), all of whom always referred to him as "the master."

The peak of his fame was reached in the late 1950s, when he introduced the *chemise*. This artfully curved and shaped design stood slightly away from the body at the back (reminiscent of the 18th-century chemise, or sacque), and followed the contour of the body across the front of the garment. It replaced the Dior *New Look*, which had been modifying from one year to the next.

He was one of the few who understood and could perform every function in the couturier tradition, from the original pattern to actual sewing: from how to press the garment, to embroidering a sample for the finish-workers to copy. His deepest convictions were represented in a profound respect for tradition and pure, classic lines. He literally sculpted his collections, and his vast knowledge of every phase of design produced silhouettes that were as structurally sound and as right for the times as a skyscraper.

He never lost his affinity for Spain, which was reflected in the intense color palette he worked with, scarlet, deep violets, mustard golds, hot pinks, and always, the intensity of Spanish black, often trimmed with silk braid or gold, as were the originals many centuries earlier. It was said that a woman who owned a Balenciaga was never satisfied with anything else, for the perfection of his clothing ruined forever all other talents. The sureness of his cutting and tailoring, the extraordinarily high standards of excellence that his house was famed for, the superb construction in every garment assured him a very special place in the pantheon of designers.

Chanel said of him "He alone is a couturier—he is the only one who can design, cut, put together and sew a suit or gown entirely alone," and Dior referred to him as "our master." Balenciaga said of himself, "Designing to me is an art in itself with all the arts participating. You must be an architect for your sense of measure, a sculptor for your silhouette, a painter for your palette and a musician to realize the rhythm and movement of the dress."

*Balenciaga white linen chemise, 1959. Note knee-skimming length.*
The Brooklyn Museum, Gift of Mrs. William Rand.

*Balenciaga evening gown, the
essence of the great designer: pure,
sleek, architectural in feeling.*
Copyright © 1965, The Hearst Corporation,
Harper's Bazaar.

He retired in 1968 and returned to his native Spain, where he died in 1972. One year following his death, a major retrospective of his work was shown at the Metropolitan Museum of Art, the first such exhibit honoring a single designer ever mounted by the Costume Institute of that Museum. Among the trend-setting designs shown were the seven-eighth's coat, flat-heeled shoes, the controversial chemise that swept the world in the late 1950s, and his shaped and molded evening dresses. In the late 1980s, there has been a significant revival of interest in Balenciaga as a source of design inspiration.

## YVES SAINT LAURENT
(1936–)

Yves Saint Laurent (eve san law-ron) was born in Algeria (then a French colony) in North Africa in 1936, and still carries on a love affair with that part of the world. He maintains a house in Marrakech, and African influences show up from time to time in his collections.

He seemed destined for a career in fashion from his childhood, for from the time he could use a pencil, he was busily drawing and creating fashions—then, for his toys. He arrived in Paris at seventeen, and attended the well known Ecole de la Chambre Syndicale de la Couture to study designing. Bored, however, he left, and on his own, for his own amusement, designed an entire collection. A friend, who had just seen the Dior opening was so struck by the similarity in approach, that he took the drawings to Dior who promptly hired the young man. Dior referred to Saint Laurent as his ''dauphin,'' or heir-apparent, and indeed, that prophecy came true more rapidly than was expected. Dior's unexpected death in 1957 plunged the young protégé into fame at the age of twenty-two, and his first collection for the House of Dior was a tremendous success.

A series of mishaps followed: his second collection was not favorably reviewed, he was drafted by the French army, and he suffered a total physical and emotional collapse. Unable to

*Yves Saint Laurent makes pants not only respectable but chic, 1979.*

Yves Saint Laurent (right): *The designer working with models in his atelier preparing for the 1987 collection. Left,* ethnic inspiration for the "rich peasant" look, 1976.

work for many months, his place was taken by Marc Bohan, who is still head designer for Dior.

In 1962, he opened his own house, and from that time, he has dominated the French couture. He is a man in constant motion, capable of switching gears at a moment's notice veering from one extreme to another: however, every switch has been innovative and stunning in its approach to fashion. Among the excitement he has been responsible for: the *trapeze*, the pea jacket, which appears and reappears through many of his collections, blazers, chemises inspired by Mondrian, military jackets. It is almost totally due to his influence that women are free to wear pants and pantsuits: he put the stamp of approval on them when he devoted the greater part of one collection to this fashion.

Saint Laurent is a tall, shy, bespectacled man who has at one moment proclaimed the death of the couture, and soon after, turned totally about face and produced the most exquisite designs in Paris. His plunge into ready-to-wear in 1966 with his Rive Gauche Boutiques opened the doors for other

*YSL one-piece jumpsuits, 1985.*

designers to enter that field, but there is no question that his have been the most successful. He dresses some of the most elegant women in the world, and at the same time, clothes a totally different customer through his ''prêt-à-porter'' boutiques.

A major retrospective of his work was held, again at the Metropolitan Museum of Art's Costume Institute, in 1984. The *New York Times*, January 15, 1984 noted of that current show: ''The exhibition is full, and of course one expects it would be, of beauty and spectacle, and the sort of luxurious clothes women dream of owning or wearing. It is like an all-too-brief visit to a pleasure palace . . . Another aspect that becomes clear is the roots of so much of his design derivation: the architectural shapes and cuts of Balenciaga, and to a degree, Christian Dior: the wit of the 1930s creations by Schiaparelli: the bias, sweep and drapery of Vionnet designs. There is even a slender continuing reference to the early 20th-century designs of Paul Poiret.''

He has designed for both the ballet and theater, and is one of the most licensed men in the world with interests in perfumes, cosmetics, men's wear, luggage, and so on. Actually, he is involved in over two-hundred licensing agreements, part of an empire that grosses over two billion dollars a year. There is no question but that he reigns as the epitome of the creative talent in the French couture—the reigning king of design.

# ANDRÉ COURRÈGES
## (1923–)

Courrèges, (cur-rej) like Balenciaga, was also born in the Basque region, however in the French area, not the Spanish. His early years saw him headed for a career in architecture and civil engineering, until he realized that his talents lay in another direction. He went on to study textiles and fashion design, both near his home and in Paris, where he was attracted to Balenciaga, and was engaged by him as a pattern cutter. He spent many years with "the master" and not until 1961 did he set up under his own name, along with his wife who was also an employee of Balenciaga.

He launched his fashion revolution in 1964 with a look that was totally different from the then current trend, and which totally abandoned tradition. The uncovered knee may seem tame to us now, but in 1964 when he burst on the scene in the total blaze of a completely new and different look, the world of fashion was stunned. His collections signified the innovative, avant-garde spirit of youth. His fashion sense had been sharpened by his close relationship with Balenciaga and he had thoroughly learned the master's lessons of the sculptured, clean, architectural line. As a once-to-be architect turned designer, he gave the world such unforgettable fashions as welt-seams, mid-calf boots, low slung hipster pants. He made freckles, white Mary Janes and "tough chic" the look of the late 1960s. His color palette was clean and full of verve: white whites, acid yellows, vivid greens, brilliant pinks and strong browns. Courrèges, with his ascetic scissors, cut dresses, suits and coats that were of the purest line. He was responsible, more than any other designer of that time for the brief mini. The troubled world of the late 1960s clutched at this new look with enthusiasm and the entire designing field copied him into an instant, smashing success.

Courrèges is still primarily a tailor. His clothes, even now, bear the stamp of his early studies in engineering and architecture. His cutting is skilled, and this skill gives his designs a clean, crisp line. He meant and believed that his hard-edged look would be the costume of the future; they were to be

totally functional clothing that would mask all traces of femininity. His designs had ''no give'' . . . the body was encased inside the garments almost like medieval armor, the textiles heavy and non-pliable.

As an innovator, when fashion softened, lengthened and moved on, his day in the sun was over. Weary of being copied by every manufacturer, he sold the controlling interest in his business to L'Oreal, and for some time worked only with private customers. His apparel is now sold in his own boutiques throughout the world, which carry Courrèges merchandise exclusively. In 1984, a Japanese company bought out the L'Oreal interest, and now owns sixty-five percent of Courrèges Couture.

*The definitive look of the 1960s, the welt-seamed, architectural shape, worn with the then new pantyhose and the ubiquitous white gloves.*

## PIERRE CARDIN
(1922–)

Without a doubt, the most controversial designer in Paris is Cardin (car-dan). Scorned by some and admired by others, he is a veritable whirlwind of frenetic energy, with involvement in more areas around the world than most of the rest of the French couture put together. He is a man in perpetual motion, a man whose varied interests seem to explode and swirl about him like dust in a wind storm.

Cardin presides over an empire which grosses in excess of two and a half billion dollars a year, part of which comes to him from those non-capitalistic fashion-shunning countries of Russia and China. He is very welcome in both Moscow and Beijing, and has not only set up manufacturing units in those countries to export, but ships in luxury goods for consumption, perhaps not by the masses, but certainly for the elite. To him, such trade is obvious. "After all," he points out, "half of the world lives there." In 1985, he brought a group of Chinese mannequins to Paris to show his fall designs, but that had been preceded back in the 1960s when he brought a *cabine* of Japanese to Paris for the same reason. He is close to Japan, and it is said that his is the best known fashion name in that country.

In 1946, he was working in his first job for the couturier Paquin. In quick succession, he went on to Schiaparelli, Lelong and finally Dior, where he headed the coat and suit operation. By 1950, he opened his own house, which happened to be in an attic, but just one year later, he owned his own business on the chic Faubourg Saint Honoré (foe-burg sant on-or-ray) with a work force of sixty. He is a business genius, make no mistake about that, and is said to own more real estate than anyone else in Paris. Add to that, properties in London, Rome and New York. His is one of the most licensed names in the world, with more than 640 licenses in ninety-three countries around the globe, ranging from Cadillac Eldorados to men's ties. Most argue that for a name to have license value, it must be doled out with great care, but Cardin would seem to refute that theory. He proceeds blissfully on his way, totally disregarding his detractors and rapidly adding to his empire.

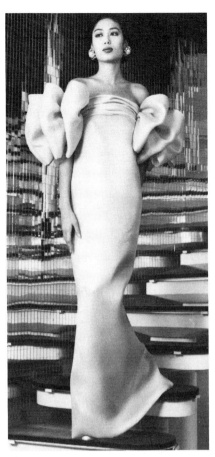

*Pierre Cardin* (left). *Sleek ballgown with extravagantly bowed bodice detail forming effect of ballooning sleeves, 1987.*

He is called the father of the "prêt" for he designed his first ready-to-wear collection in 1959, drawing inspiration from his couture collections. Within four years, a special division had to be set up to handle the business. Drummed out of the couture-corps by the Chambre Syndicale de la Couture Parisienne, the governing body of top French designers, it was only a matter of time before he was welcomed back with open arms. Another gigantic coup was his entry into men's wear in 1960. While many men derided the entire concept of smart male fashion, his creations for that division are best sellers around the world and account for sixty percent of his production.

His most recent foray into other worlds involves food and restaurants. His restlessness found a new interest in the purchase of *Maxim's*, a restaurant famous in Paris since the turn of the century. Not only did he restore it to its former glory, he started opening Maxim's in other cities: there is one in New York, Singapore and even Beijing, for example. Further spring-boarding from the Maxim's name, he has followed with Maxim's foods, china, silver and linens. Now, he proposes an international chain of Maxim's hotels, which he will control and operate himself.

He is a tall, attractive and aristocratic man, whose interests are so eclectic as to mesmerize any ordinary person. There are so many differing attitudes about him, that it is difficult to get a clear picture of the man, for he presents a different face constantly. He never stops, he is always in action, and while many of his ideas have not met with success, this has never discouraged him, nor stopped his forward motion.

Perhaps Pierre Cardin is the irrestistable force that will never meet the immovable object.

## KARL LAGERFELD
(1939–)

*Karl Lagerfeld*

German born, with a fortune in his own name, Lagerfeld has been dubbed by *Women's Wear Daily* "Kaiser Karl." He is the new big star of the Paris couture, one of the most prolific designers working in fashion. He is involved in a passionate love affair with the 18th century to the extent of wearing his hair in a tied-back ponytail and carrying (and using) a fan, à la one of the courtiers at the French Court of Louis XV.

Interestingly, his first brush with fashion fame came at the same moment as Yves Saint Laurent's—both of them won top prizes at the International Wool Secretariat contest in Paris in 1953. Both of them still in their teens at that time, both of them still shine brightly in the fashion firmament. Their paths separated, but, some say, to this day they are acutely aware of one another, and highly competitive. The King—and the Kaiser.

His first fame came as the head designer for Chloé, a firm he joined in the early 1960s and where he eventually reigned supreme for almost nineteen years. One of the most talked about and publicized seasons was his 1972 Art Deco collection, which brought him to world prominence. He left Chloé in the autumn of 1983.

Lagerfeld is undoubtedly one of the busiest designers working in Europe. He creates both the couture and the prêt-à-porter collection for Chanel: he designs the Fendi collection of furs and couture in Rome, and also designs a collection under his own name. His passion for work is not driven by necessity: in addition to inherited wealth, it is said that the House of Chanel alone pays him over one million dollars a year. He owns homes in Paris, Monte Carlo (which he prefers above all else), Rome, and an exquisite chateau outside Paris.

His fashion approach is one of great elegance and creativity. In some details his collections rival the extraordinary imagination that Schiaparelli brought to the couture. Where she turned gloves into hats, he embroiders faucets, dripping water, across the front of ball gowns. He refuses to take fashion seriously—to be serious about fashion is, to him, nonsense.

Fashion is fun. However, one has only to attend a Chanel collection of the past few years since he has taken over the designing reins, to appreciate the extent of his skill. His designs for Chanel say "Chanel" still. But, they also say Lagerfeld. Fresh, innovative, altered ever so slightly in detail, today's Chanels are still immediately recognizable for what they are in the same way they have always been: it is the attitude that is subtly different. The attitude that takes the Chanel chain tradition seriously, but has the whimsy to embroider them across the waist or the hips, or use them as straps on evening gowns.

His emergence as a major force in French fashion is no accident. A linguist (he speaks English, German, French and Italian with equal fluency), he is completely at home in almost any society in the modern world. His preference, however, is for the past. He lives, in his personal life, surrounded by an 18th-century ambience except for Monte Carlo, where he seems to be at home comfortably in a screamingly modern flat. All part of the dichotomy that is representative of his life.

There is no question about the extent of his designing talent. His innovations have included loose layering, brilliant bias cuts, and stunning and unusual beading. His discerning, and occasionally bizarre, workmanship of furs for the famous Fendi family of Rome, shearing, coloring, reversing skins, turning sables into sweatshirts, has achieved a fashion nonchalance that has revolutionized that industry. And a nonchalance about apparel that wears a slight smile. His heritage has yet to be understood: like Saint Laurent, he is a young man still with a vast future.

# CHAPTER SEVEN

# *How French Fashion Works*

Paris is over one thousand years old and throughout that long span of time, the French have had a tradition of, and an affinity for, fashion. It seems to be bred in the bone. But then the French have a long tradition of affinity for all the arts and skills that we have learned to call sophistication, the extra niceties of life that smooth the hard edge of reality. And there is no point in pretending that the French are just like us. They are not. The French are very different, and the difference probably stems from that long long steeping in a society that has always prized elegance, that has always lived with flair, that savors food, wine and music, and above all through the years, understands fashion, and the end purpose of beauty in clothing. For to the French, apparel also clothes the spirit.

For hundreds of years, the French have not only admired and respected their fashion tradition, they have supported it financially. The Hapsburg kings knew how much money the exquisite silk from the mills in Lyons brought into the tax coffers each year, and were very protective of those revenues. As was Napoleon for, as we discussed previously, in order to revive the textile industry he went to such lengths as closing fireplaces and demanding that women at his court appear constantly in new apparel, both measures designed to keep the artisans functioning at what they did best: produce the most beautiful clothing in the world.

## THE HAUTE COUTURE

The haute couture, which simply means "high sewing" (or the best sewing) really started with Charles Frederick Worth in the 19th century, and while it has lived through many trials and tribulations, some fundamental ways in which it does business remain. The couture still represents the peak of luxury, it is the laboratory where the great fashion ideas are launched, some to disappear like balloons in the air, others stamped with longevity. For many years, the couture has also lost a great deal of money, but what that amounts to is one of the best kept secrets in the world.

The couture keeps the famous names famous. The great fashion fortunes are not made by the sale of single garments to privileged individuals. The couture part of the business is a sort of "loss-leader" in Paris. Private customers represent approximately seventy-five percent of the business done in an average house, and these revenues, plus sales to manufacturers, don't begin to recover the cost of producing a collection. To present the semi-annual collection, to keep the skilled hands sewing and cutting, to buy the costly fabrics can easily cost one million dollars each season. It is reported that most houses lose up to that amount annually. The couture is the parent, the couture is the most luxurious segment of the entire fashion business. Everything is still done slowly and painfully by hand, the beading, embroideries, laces and trimmings. Each style is cut and fit individually. Until recently, it took from four to seven weeks to make one garment for a customer. That time has been shortened a little. A dress goes through fewer fittings and can be finished in as little as five to six working days, the exception being a grand entrance evening gown requiring intensive handwork.

Finally, each article of apparel is cut to individual order. The couture is still working, in that respect, as it did over one hundred years ago. It has been said that only in Paris is it possible for such a fashion system to function, for it is in Paris to this day that the trained and skilled needleworkers exist— and nowhere else in the world. The support system that makes the couture possible ranges from textile manufacturers to industrialists, from models to hand-beaders, all linked together

*The lavishness of the Paris couture is exemplified by this Lacroix swagged, pouffed, embroidered design from his couture collection, 1987. Example of the artistry available in Paris. Roger Vivier's jewelled custom shoes for a couture collection, 1960s.* Fashion Institute of Design and Merchandising, Los Angeles.

*The great Poiret at the height of his fame strolling on a Paris street with his cabine.*

with the common bond of preserving the elegance of the haute couture of France.

The couture is the apex of fashion, still the most closely watched group of designers in the world. While it is true that some of the Italian designers, Valentino and Armani as good examples, or American designers like James Galanos are equally as talented as their French counterparts, it is also certainly true that there is no collection or group of other designers extant that is on a par.

### The Chambre Syndicale

The *Chambre Syndicale de la Couture Parisienne* has a one hundred year tradition of excellence. Originally organized by Worth, it has over its many years of existence come to stand for the finest workmanship and creativity. To be chosen to become a member of this prestigious organization is an honor. A special commission of the French government in the Department of Industry makes the selection, and along with membership, certain restrictions apply. For example, a specific number of garments must be shown at each collection: a specific number of showings for private customers must be held, a certain number of employees must be involved in the production, and at least one atelier (at-ell-ee-yay, workroom) must be maintained in Paris. Designs are copyrighted and protected by law, just as in other industries where there is legal protection against plagiarism. While in most cases, the name designer of each house does the actual designing, many houses also employ assistants who work directly with the head of the house.

Twenty-four designers in Paris belong to, and are, *Le Chambre Syndicale de la Couture Parisienne.* This group makes the rules, decides who can join, and who must leave. They set the dates and coordinate the openings, see that tickets to showings are in the right hands, and generally police the various establishments. The Chambre ensures press coverage, and issues press cards to selected journalists. Buyers must also apply to the Chambre for an entrance card, although sometimes this is taken care of by resident commissioners. The French couture sets up these elaborate safeguards in an effort to keep fashion pirates out, and they have been instrumental in seeing that laws have been passed for the protection of the couture designs. The Chambre settles disputes between designers over times and hours of openings and issues and provides a calendar of these showings, with names, times and dates for the use of those attending.

### How Does the Couture Work?

How does the couture work? While the word may mean fine sewing, it has come to mean much more than that. To almost everyone in the world it means top-drawer fashion. Most of these French designers are called *couturier* (coo-toor-ee-ay) if they are men, and *couturière* (coo-toor-ee-err) if they are women. In some cases, well-established houses survive the death of the original owner-designer and go on to other triumphs, for example, Dior, Chanel, and Patou. In other words, the house itself has become the carrier of the reputation, the designer, in many cases, sublimated by the originator's name.

*Christian Lacroix working with model in his atelier, 1987.*

Collections are presented to private customers, the press and occasionally other foreign designers and manufacturers twice a year, in late January for spring and summer apparel and in July for the following fall-winter season. Private customers and the press are always admitted free, of course, although it is very difficult to get a ticket for an opening if you are not known to the house. Retailers, designers and manufacturers are charged a fee, known as a *caution*, which must be paid in advance of entrance. Sometimes the *caution* is a direct charge for entrance, at other times the caution is a promise to buy a certain number of models or paper patterns, and the caution

*Yves Saint Laurent at work in his studio. Collections often start at the drawing board.*

is applied against that purchase when the promise is kept. For this exchange, the person paying the caution has the right to reproduce what is purchased, and use the name of the designer. This amount can be extremely high. Even though the purchase of a paper pattern or *toile* (twoll, a cloth sample), is less than buying an original, when a simple day dress in a famous house costs in the vicinity of $5000, the expense of reproducing garments is obviously high.

The French couture is also fortunate because of the support it receives from the government in other ways. The fashion and needle trades have always enjoyed protection and encouragement and additionally, many of the costs of promotion, advertising and worldwide showings are defrayed by financial support.

While in a world population numbered in the billions, there are probably no more than 5000 private couture clients, these customers continue to support the haute couture. And while we have noted that it has been many years since the couture has operated at a profit, it is still the springboard for all the other money-making enterprises—notably the prêt-à-porter, the many licenses, perfumes and cosmetics.

In 1975, a new arm was established by the Chambre which included some ready-to-wear designers. This new group, which still functions under the Chambre as the parent, is known as the *Chambre Syndicale du Prêt-à-Porter des Couturiers et Createurs de Mode.* This latter group is much larger, and in addition to the members, also invites other designers to show with, and at the same time, as the Createurs. Among those invited, are Issey Miyake, Valentino, Daniel Hechter and Comme des Garçons.

## MEMBERS OF THE CHAMBRE SYNDICALE

In 1986, the members of the Chambre totaled twenty-four. They include the following famous designers:*

1. Pierre Balmain (directed by Erik Mortensen)
2. Pierre Cardin
3. Carven
4. Chanel (designed by Karl Lagerfeld)
5. Christian Dior (designed by Marc Bohan)
6. Louis Feraud
7. Givenchy
8. Mme. Grès (known originally as Alix)
9. Lecoanet Hemant
10. Christian Lacroix
11. Lanvin
12. Ted Lapidus
13. Guy Laroche
14. Serge Lepage
15. Hanae Mori (the only Japanese designer)
16. Jean Patou
17. Per Spook
18. Paco Rabanne
19. Nina Ricci
20. Yves Saint Laurent
21. Jean-Louis Scherrer
22. Torrente
23. Emanuel Ungaro
24. Philippe Venet

*Marc Bohan of Christian Dior sorting through sketches of possible designs, 1987.*

A comparable operation functions in Italy under the name *Alta-moda*, and includes such designers as Valentino, Armani, Versace, and the Fendis, much of the latter company's collections being designed by Karl Lagerfeld.

## LINE FOR LINE COPIES

During the 1950s and early 1960s, what were known as *line-for-line* copies were all the rage with many stores in America, such as Lord & Taylor and Ohrbachs (a store now disappeared from the New York retailing scene), as well as many manufacturers. The original models were shipped by air to New York, where retailers had hand-selected manufacturers standing by to make line-for-line copies. The proud boast at one time was that a line-for-line copy could be in the hands of the customers in less than a week from the day it was first shown in Paris, beating out the couture quite easily. Eventually, even the original fabric was bought in France and used: these copies were, of course, substantially higher in cost. Most of the designs purchased were shipped in what is called "in

Left: *Montgomery Ward gets into the line-for-line business. The prices ranged from $24.98 to $69.98.* Right, *Courrèges original in foreground, line-for-line copy in background, 1966.*

bond," which meant that the original garment would not itself be sold: after it was used for copying and manufacturing purposes, for fashion shows, windows, or other promotional activities, it was returned to the house in Paris. It also meant that since the garment was not meant for re-sale, no import duties were paid. Customers stampeded to buy the line-for-line copies, and by and large the garments were made with a great deal of integrity.

In addition, some of the best known and finest specialty stores throughout America bought originals with the same purpose in mind—copying. For example, Bergdorf Goodman in New York and I. Magnin in California purchased heavily from the couture. These garments were copied one by one for individual clients in the store's custom workrooms. I. Magnin maintained the last custom workroom in America, well into the 1970s, operating long after other specialty stores had abandoned the practice. Sometimes the original was sold to a favored customer (who was then responsible for the duty), but in most cases, an identical copy was created with the same love, care and numerous fittings lavished on the client by the couture in Paris.

## THE PARIS PRÊT À PORTER

Line-for-line copies diminished in importance when the couture began to experiment with ready-to-wear. Pierre Cardin, as early as 1959, presented a line for manufacture. In Paris these manufactured lines are called *prêt à porter* (pret ah portay), or ready-to-wear, but the phrase is usually shortened to *prêt*. While the wealthy still can, and do buy original models, most of the world settles very happily for the designer's name on the lower cost "prêt" line. In the 1960s top French designers slowly learned to accept the importance of secondary lines, spurred partly by Yves Saint Laurent who felt that his work should be available to all. It was at this time that his famous *Rive Gauche* collection was born, and also at this time that he announced, a little prematurely perhaps, the death of the couture.

Most of these early ready-to-wear collections were shown in the house of the creator, but gradually, as the prêt grew and garnered more and more enthusiasm from the press and the customers, the crowds of buyers mushroomed, and the designers began to understand the importance—and significance—of what they were doing: Collections were tentatively presented together. The prêt is shown in seven straight days in four giant tents set up in the courtyards of the Louvre. Buyers scurry from one tent to another, day after day, including Saturdays and Sundays, from nine in the morning often until nine at night. Whoever thinks the fashion business is glamorous and luxurious need only attend one of these weeks of total fashion fatigue to understand that only the tough survive, the weak vanish by the wayside. In addition to the couture, many other noted designers are included in the prêt: Kenzo, Sonia Rykiel, Cacharel, Montana, for example.

Another of the most important French fashion presentations is the semi-annual Salon du Prêt-à-Porter, which is literally a gigantic trade fair that brings together some twelve hundred exhibitors from all over the world, but primarily from France, and is located outside the center of Paris at a location known as the Porte de Versailles (port-duh ver-sigh). At one time, the Salon coincided with the designer showings, but currently, the exhibition is held several weeks earlier. This has caused some

*Hubert Givenchy posing in his salon with part of his all-black cabine, 1979.*

hardship, both to the buyers who are unable to cover both markets, and to the Salon which has experienced a decline in attendance. However, during the Porte de Versailles showings, Paris is packed with buyers, as many as forty thousand at one time, and the fight to get hotel reservations, a seat to a showing, and a taxi to the Porte itself where the collections are shown is monumental. Buyers from most countries in the world descend en masse, for it is not only the United States that imports these fashions. In fact, the United States is usually out-bought by other European and Latin American countries.

The Paris designer prêt was the launching pad for the wave of Japanese designers who have gained such prominence in the late 1970s and 1980s. First Kenzo burst on the scene, followed in short order by Rei Kawakubo (designing under the label of Comme des Garçons), Issey Miyake, and Yohji Yamamoto. While Kenzo in particular worked originally in a western tradition, the others tended to lean heavily on their Japanese heritage, presenting a look that was wrapped, layered, incredibly somber in color and feeling. The inspiration came from traditional Japan rather than the environs of the city of Paris that surrounded them. While there has been some western modification in their more recent collections, the premise is still Asian in feeling rather than European. Why did they come to Paris? It should be obvious. After all, to be recognized in Paris is to surf on the crest of the wave. To be accepted at the fashion center of the world is to arrive. The surge of excitement for the designers from Japan might never have happened in Tokyo . . . the movers and shakers in the industry did not search for inspiration there, but in the design ferment of Paris.

## LICENSING

The successful houses all create ready-to-wear, and, in addition, operate worldwide licensing agreements for the use of their names. Licensing is a process which involves a manufacturer being allowed to use the name of a designer. In some cases, the designer actively supervises the production of the merchandise bearing the name of the house, or creates the original, as in the case of perfume. In others, this overseer work is left to assistants. Occasionally, the designer merely edits sketches of proposed merchandise. Usually, this license fee will run from three to ten percent of the cost of the merchandise, so it is easy to see that if a line or a fragrance is successful, the money mounts quickly. Since the success of the license is dependent on the success of the couture operation, it is simple to understand why the designers continue to operate their houses at such substantial losses. The income from everything else is dependent on the couture. If Yves Saint Laurent, for example, spends two million dollars a year on couture collections, but has an income of over two billion annually, the couture cost is just a drop in the fashion bucket.

## SOURCES OF INSPIRATION

Designers absorb ideas from everything they come in contact with—museums, books, and theater—and translate bits and pieces of those ideas into the collection. In the 1920s, the discovery of King Tut's Tomb led to a worldwide love affair with all things Egyptian. A Klimt exhibit in the 1970s evoked the past in textile design. Lagerfeld, designing the Chanel collection, goes back in time to the 1920s and 1930s to rework the original spirit of Chanel, showing chains, ropes of jewelry, bound buttonholes and soutache trims, but in fresh, new ways. Yves Saint Laurent produced a famous collection based on the paintings of Mondrian, and another inspired by African costume. Designers are inspired one by another. The bubble skirt featured by Christian Lacroix in 1986 turned up in other designer collections almost immediately, but is it possible that the bubble was itself triggered by the then imminent Dior ''Forty Year Retrospective?'' No matter where these ideas come from, they are first sketched, forming the idea for a line, which can consist of up to 200 pieces.

The designer, whether creating for the prêt or the couture, is hard at work at least six months in advance of presenting any collection. Christian Lacroix, in late March, 1987, was busy spinning ideas for a prêt collection which would not be presented for at least one year. A line starts with sample cuts of fabrics, which are usually the flash-point of the designer's creativity. That is not to say that designers don't have a

Licensing means millions of dollars annually to most prominent designers. The name alone has become the powerful tool that sells vast quantities of merchandise.

*Chambre*
*Syndicale*
*du Prêt-à-Porter*
*des Couturiers*
*et des Créateurs*
*de Mode*

*Calendrier*
*des Collections*
*Automne-Hiver*
*1987-1988*

*Présentations à la Presse*

*salon international du* **prêt à porter féminin**

*Program cover of the semi-annual calendar of events for the prêt-à-porter in Paris.* Inset, *entrance to the building where the giant shows are held.*

concept in their mind before they begin: they know the direction they plan to move in. It is the fabric, though, that fills in the outline. Incidentally, it is not just the French talent who works in this manner—all designers do.

At the right hand of the designer stands the patternmaker and the head cutter who will take the sketch and make the original pattern. From this comes the first *toile*, which is nothing more nor less than a cloth garment, usually of unbleached muslin, cut and sewn from the pattern into the finished design. The toile is fit on a model and the garment is literally torn to pieces, changed and refit until both the designer, the cutter and all the assistants are totally satisfied. This is usually the most critical point in the life of a design, for once the toile meets with approval, the finished garment is produced.

Each collection is like giving birth to a baby, or so I am told by designers, with all the anguish attendant. Sometimes it isn't the beautiful baby everyone had hoped for: at other times, it is welcomed into the world with cheers and huzzahs. No creative person can please all of the people all of the time. There are disasters as well as triumphs. In the final analysis, all creators are searching for approval, either in terms of sales or in response from the press or the customer. While these two usually antagonistic forces are not always at opposite ends of the pole, it is rare that a line can be commercially successful *and* at the same time please the editors who are looking for exciting new stories for their readers. In many cases, models are designed specifically to attract the discerning eyes of those editors, with no intention at all of ever making or shipping the garment. It explains a little of the frustration of the consumer who searches in vain for something seen in a magazine or newspaper as the high spot of a recent collection. This is also true, of course, of American designers, who will occasionally, to make a fashion point, design everything in a line above the knee, or without sleeves, with no intention of ever shipping it that way.

At one time, couture collections were presented to an audience in hushed silence, broken only by the voice of a *vendeuse* (von-dooz, saleswoman) repeating the number of each garment in French, followed by English. While the couture is still somewhat quiet, the prêt has launched an entirely new system. Openings in Paris are extremely theatrical, full-fledged productions. Rock music and dancers, models swinging high above the stage in outrageous costumes and accessories are more the norm now. Most designers feel very strongly that the models themselves add enormously to the presentation. To a varying degree, designers select women who will best portray the fashion approach of their house. Pierre Cardin has used *cabines* (cab-been, the term for a group of house models) entirely made up of young Japanese or Chinese women: Givenchy for a period of time only used black models to present his collections. Whatever the selection process, the cabine is of great importance to the designer, and the final selection of models is usually left in his or her hands.

The press of the world, great fashion stores and the rich and famous still flock to the Paris openings and there seems to be a Renaissance of new interest in, and the purchase of, original models from Paris. While even the couturiers themselves sometimes bleakly predict the demise of their calling, it would seem that Paris, the thousand-year old city of lights, will support for many years to come its traditions of refinement, flare and excitement.

*Anne Klein*

*Calvin Klein*

*Ralph Lauren*

*Donna Karan*

*Perry Ellis*

# CHAPTER EIGHT

# *The All-American Team*

In alphabetical order—Perry Ellis, Donna Karan, the Kleins (no relation at all) Anne and Calvin, and Ralph Lauren.* Sometimes the design approach in their collections is so close that it is almost impossible to distinguish one from another, for they all feature classic, simple, easy apparel, touches of establishment and expensive fabrics. They are all designing *fashion*, but it is the ultimate fashion for today. It is the pinnacle of sportswear, the refinement of an approach to apparel which is relatively recent, at least from the conceptual point of view. Each one of these talents superbly reflects our times, and it is because of this reflection that they are big, big stars.

Our all-American team has totally captured the spirit of the times. It is no accident that *WWD* runs more lineage on this group of designers than on any others. These designers are heavily involved in the licensing of their names, not only for perfumes, but for other forms of manufacturing, such as home furnishings, cosmetics, lingerie, shoes, and men's and children's apparel. They count their income annually in some cases in the millions of dollars, and in our capitalistic society, money means power. They are, indeed, powers and more, powerhouses of design creativity. They are not only image-

*Designer Anne Klein died in 1974: following her death, the line bearing her name was created by a team consisting of Donna Karan and Louis Dell'Olio. Mr. Dell'Olio still heads the designing for the Anne Klein Co., and Donna Karan heads her own firm. Perry Ellis died in May 1986. His close assistants took over the creative function for the Ellis companies.

makers, but they themselves are reflected images of the most current attitudes in costume, the attitude towards clothing that started some hundreds of years ago in an effort to free women from constricting apparel. Movers and shakers of the ready-to-wear industry, they outshine for the first time, the stars of Europe. Perhaps in the sense that here in the United States of America we, as a country, are the freest, the most daring in our concepts and attitudes, our all American team is the cutting edge of future apparel.

In the 20th century, we find a rapid acceleration towards an easier approach to apparel. Clothing that is less structured, less decorative and finally, more in keeping with contemporary life. And this brings us, inevitably, to the all-American team, the designers that are celebrated, starred, sought after, in the public eye most, that move in rarefied social circles, travel in their own jets, dine at the White House, and yes, yes, are very, very rich. Where did what they do come from? Where did it start? And why is it so perfectly in mesh with our lives?

Apparel for specific sports activities really began to appear about four hundred years ago. That does not mean, of course, that in generations preceding this, no effort was ever made to adapt clothing to allow freedom of movement during various active functions. We do know that women swam, rode, hunted and participated in games of one kind or another throughout history. But women's lives until the 20th century were so constricted, their activities so supervised, that little freedom in apparel would have been possible. As we know, clothing merely reflects lives, and narrow lives surely mean little freedom in clothing.

Diana, the Roman Goddess of the Hunt, was often shown wearing loose, flowing garments with her bow and arrow. In Minoan times, both men and women danced with bulls (as they called it), a forerunner of the bullfighting so popular in Spain and Mexico. They wore very specific costumes when engaged in this sport, occasionally discarding it and performing in the nude. Tennis, as another example, was known in the 11th and 12th centuries, the game quite different from what we know, but indeed called by that name, played with rackets and balls which were made of stitched animal skin and occasionally stuffed with human hair. It is said that Mary, Queen of Scots, played golf. It certainly was a sport known during the time of Henry VIII, so it is quite possible that women golfed, for it would not have been considered too difficult or strenuous for the gentler sex. Ice skating is lost in antiquity, but there are records, once again dating from the 11th century, telling us how young people of that time fastened animal bones to their feet with leather bindings, and thus propelled themselves across the ice. The fashion plate of the 13th century, Eleanor of Aquitane, rode off to war with her husband along with other ladies of her court, dressed not only in armor, but riding astride a horse. It is probable, in actual fact, that women rode astride until some time in the 16th century, when the side saddle became popular, courtesy of another fashion plate, Catherine de Medici, Queen of France.

## *SPORTSWEAR ORIGINS*

It is, however, from about A.D. 1600 that costume for both men and women began to adapt itself to various activities, and it is only during the 20th century that totally appropriate costume has evolved for participation in sports.

In examining the origin of sportswear fashions, perhaps swimming is a good start, for it is the one sport that almost everyone enjoys. It might even be the oldest sport in the world, for in the warm Mediterranean climes where civilization was formed, it would be obvious that indulging in water activities would not only have been acceptable, but a pleasant pastime. In Greece and Rome, swimming was highly valued for therapeutic reasons, and additionally was a skill of great use for soldiers. In Minoan Crete, wall paintings show garments almost identical to our bikinis: they might indeed have been a body covering for water sport.

Let's differentiate between swimming and bathing. It is curious, actually, that the term "bathing suit" is still so commonly used, for of course it refers to a totally different activity than swimming. Bathing simply meant that the body was immersed in water. The Romans were famed for their baths, as were the peoples of the later Byzantine Empire. In Greece, the baths were great meeting halls, where philosophers, businessmen, professionals, and students met to discuss the great, and not so great, issues of the day. Not unlike one of our posh health clubs where men meet to play handball, squash, exercise, and wheel and deal. Bathing, therefore, in the past combined a double function: it cleansed the body and also provided recreational and social outlets.

Swimming is a different matter. Swimming is exercise. Swimming demands skill and involves, at differing times, both recreation and competition. During the Middle Ages, there is little evidence of women swimming, however, there are some contemporary anecdotes that assure us that women did, indeed, swim. A quote from 1538 reads, "At Zurich, the costume of young men and maidens bathing together around the statue of St. Nicolari . . . as the young girls wore bathing drawers sometimes a marriage was brought about."

By the close of the 14th century, not only was the destruction of the great pagan baths complete, but there was a growing belief that bathing spread disease. Not until the late 17th century, did a new notion take hold, that bathing was medicinal for both men and women. This created not only an entirely new industry, the spa, but started the creation of costume for "water wear." In Europe, where spas originated (and still exist) bathing in therapeutic waters was segregated by sex. In America, which followed the European custom both in the spas and the newly discovered Hot Springs, the same practice was followed. But here, bathing enjoyed a growing popularity, leading eventually to an occasional frolic in the open sea. It was indecent during the 19th century to indulge in mixed bathing, but gradually the barriers were broken down and increasingly elaborate water activities were scheduled, culminating with what were called the "bathing hours" when both men and women indulged in water activities together.

In addition to swimming, women during this same period, skated, played croquet and some tennis, and rode horseback for recreation. For most of these activities, the average woman wore everyday dress and as yet, no particular costume had evolved. This was, of course, true for most such excursions into fun away from the home. But by the late 18th century, women had adopted men's riding habits (a constant fashion practice) including a coat and vest, cravat and top hat; a long skirt, however, covered boots, breeches and hose. This is

Left, *woman's riding habit, Italy in 1780s. At that time, of course, women rode only side-saddle, but it is a definite costume for a sporting activity.* Los Angeles County Museum of Art. Right, *Ralph Lauren featured an entire collection based on formal riding apparel in 1985.*

 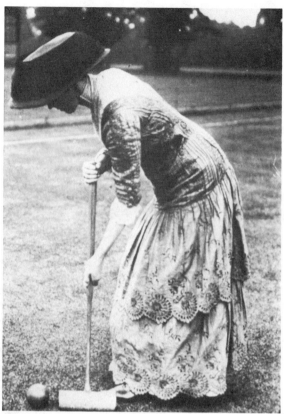

*While close to a century separates these two pictures, the woman on the left, 1988, and the woman on the right, 1910, could almost be interchangeable in their fashion approach to what the well-dressed croquet player wears for an afternoon of garden sport.*

almost the identical costume worn today for riding in formal shows and ring competitions. Riding habits are often used by fashion designers as inspiration. Ralph Lauren has created entire collections using various details prevalent in both men's and women's apparel for riding.

Swimming, as we know it, was rare in the 19th century, for indeed, the sheer weight of the costumes worn to the shore made such an activity literally impossible. Clothing for bathing was made at home (as was almost all clothing) usually from patterns, or copied from pictures in publications such as *Godey's Ladies Book*, an extremely popular women's magazine of the 19th century. The costume was worn complete with stockings and shoes, corsets and some sort of head covering, for no woman wanted to lose her pale, creamy skin. Navy blue and white, ecru, gray and olive were popular colors. By the mid-1880s, the long drawers were replaced with a shorter knickerbocker pant which was completely covered by a full skirt. At the same time, the first knitted tights, buttoned to the waist and worn under a long bathing dress arrived, an early step on the long march from restriction to freedom. These bathing tights differed from the knickerbockers in that they were hemmed, rather than gathered on an elastic band, and that they were rather like our pantyhose. While the tights were completely concealed by a one-piece, knee-length bathing dress, this marked another step towards streamlining for

*Photograph of a girl's field hockey team in the early 20th century. Note stockinged legs.*

function. As the popularity of swimming increased, the number of yards required to make a bathing dress decreased, but "bathing suits," in the original sense of the word, continued throughout the first quarter of the 20th century. While it has been almost two-thirds of a century since "bathing" has been popular, it is still this antiquated phrase that is in common use.

Photographs of East and West Coast beach scenes, in the early part of the 20th century, show women wearing costumes of close fitting knitted trunks that just covered the knees, or, when worn with stockings, came within an inch or two above the knee. This costume, sleeveless on occasion, but generally short-sleeved, with a simplified neckline and brief tunic (shades of the Roman warrior) was the functional suit of its day. Another impetus to simplify water apparel came from the entrance of women in actual swimming competitions. In 1910, a famous diver named Annette Kellerman arrived in America from Australia, and she dazzled everyone with her fancy diving exhibitions. She wore a long-sleeved, one-piece knitted swimming tight, almost exactly like a body stocking, with the exception of the sleeves. Miss Kellerman scandalized the proper ladies of that day, but it was not long before knitted swimsuits began to be seen in advertisements. Most were made of wool but, occasionally, one sees in these early ads that some were knitted of body-clinging silk. Annette Kellerman freed women, developed the first truly one-piece swimsuit and was,

The family at the beach, turn of the
century. In the group: man's striped
cotton knit; woman's ensemble,
complete with laced bathing shoes;
child's bathing suit, black hand knit
wool. At the end of the century, an
almost naked body, running free,
1987.

more than anyone else, responsible for the surge in growth of
early knitting mills into the giant swimsuit industry, the
forerunner of the entire sportswear market.

The outbreak of hostilities in Europe was to radically speed
the arrival of functional clothing. With women taking the place
of men in what had heretofore been traditional roles, costume
altered to enable them to perform these new functions with
some degree of efficiency. On the home front, women were
expected as a patriotic duty to work, and for those young
women of means, it additionally became fashionable to hold
down a job. For those who had always had to work for a living,
but only found employment in domestic service, doors swung
wide to factories, offices and service industries. Until this time,
almost all office workers were men, including secretaries,
stenographers and file clerks. The burgeoning telephone
systems as well, only used male operators. But these wartime
workplace changes were permanent. When the Allied armies
disbanded (or were de-mobbed, as the British called it) women

kept their office jobs, and for the first time, society was confronted with women as a continuing force in industry.

Costume began to reflect the struggle with less restrictive fashions, and as the 1920s arrived, the body also began to be more free. In Europe, the great Poiret had already decreed the death of the corset, and natural waistlines and busts appeared. Even ankles were peeking out from under shortening skirts.

The 1920s opened with the end of the Great War (as World War I was called) and the beginning of prohibition in the United States. Prohibition was a law which banned the selling or drinking of alcoholic beverages, and it quite literally set this country on its ear. While drinking, officially, may have been illegal, the law created quite the opposite effect than was intended. It became not only chic to break the law, but very sophisticated. By easing the attitudes towards general morality, prohibition did more to break down the social fiber of a vast part of America than any other law during this time. It introduced both the bootlegger and the so-called "Mafia" into the everyday life of the country. Speakeasies, the forbidden night-clubs, opened across the nation and were promptly filled with flappers dancing the then current rages, the shimmy, the black bottom, and the Charleston. Jazz blared and rumble-seated cars roared across the lengthening highways. Women wore short skirts, went bra-less, and for the first time put on pants and began participating in sports with a vengeance.

For the women of America, doors were opening. The right to vote had been won, no stigma was attached to working and women were emerging as individuals in their own right, not just as a masculine appendage. And of course, costume adapted to these changes—it began to simplify, become easier. Superfluous trims and decorations dwindled.

It was a period, the 1920s and the 1930s, that trousers for sports began to be worn and were found to be extremely useful. Useful, indeed. Women, who had for centuries moved mincingly, clutching at fly-away skirts, sidling through doors, gasping for breath inside cinched waists, were able to move with ease, unencumbered with rigid costume. The final stamp of approval for women in pants came from motion pictures, when stars like Marlene Dietrich and Katharine Hepburn took

*Early 1930s swimsuits: the child's suit is of wool jersey; the seated woman is wearing knitted wool, and the man is also in wool, but the tank top zips off. At this time, men who appeared "topless" on beaches were often arrested.*

to appearing publicly in trousers. Along with this embryonic sportswear development, the swimsuit industry burgeoned. Clothing was timidly introduced for tennis and golf. Beach pajamas with wide legs strolled the sands, and became quite the rage. Apparel termed "spectator sportswear" appeared, suitable fashions for sitting around watching sporting events, not intended for participating. There is no question, however, that it was the baring of the body for swimming that began to break down the taboos. When knitting mills like Jantzen of Portland, Oregon, began advertising swimsuits, the public accepted the new fashions even more rapidly. Helping accelerate the trend, movie magazines, the great communicator of the time, featured what was known as "Cheesecake" photography, and every star and starlet, wearing skimpy, body-revealing suits had a turn before the camera—even the "Great Garbo."

The advent of the flapper introduced bathing beauty contests, a phenomenon which is still very much with us. Young women across America marched row upon row in city after city vying for a crown, all parading in swimsuits. The costumes varied from the still popular ruffled silk taffetas and knits, to the more daring one piece, skirted wool tank suit, all designed by this time to specifically reveal the body. While suits were still usually worn with stockings and shoes, the stockings were rolled at the knee, a modern fashion viewed with great alarm by most proper American women.

In addition to Jantzen, other knitting mills that had turned out some swimsuits as a side line, now turned major attention to this new manufacturing possibility. By the mid 1930s these industry pioneers, including such well known names as Catalina and Cole of California, took their place as full-fledged members of the apparel industry.

In 1930, with Coco Chanel leading the way, women for the first time eagerly sought suntans, totally wiping out centuries of protecting pale skins. Helena Rubenstein was promoting an "amazing new sunburn preventive" and advised that "you smooth it on your face and body before tennis, golf, swimming or sunbathing." As more women wanted to tan and tan more and more of their bodies, manufacturers introduced low, sunback (or what were known as "California style") suits.

These had cut-out sections that exposed various portions of the midriff. Swimsuits were becoming fashionable, and consumers were encouraged to buy a new suit at least once each year. *Lastex* (a yarn made from a core of rubber covered with fabric), was invented, and this new textile process revolutionized the industry. It meant that, at last, figure control could be built into the design structure of a garment and that the body could be smoothed and molded.

Sports dresses appeared, along with the culotte, or divided skirt. Known as "bifurcated" skirts, they had appeared early in the 19th century, but were regarded with total disdain by fashionable women. In the middle of the 19th century, a woman out of her time, Amelia Bloomer, advocated for her contemporaries, a costume consisting of a short skirt over a sort of pantaloon: this, too, was greeted with ridicule, although it was certainly a costume that had been worn for many hundreds of years in the Near and Middle East. We still use her name today for "bloomers."

By the late 1930s, American designers turned to indigenous roots and used the American West as design inspiration, featuring vests, wide belts, kerchiefs around heads (a heretofore peasant style strictly), and cattle brands for printed cottons and linens. The one-piece playsuit with matching skirt

*Part of a bathing beauty parade in Long Beach in the middle 1920s. The rolled stockings would have been considered very daring. Sixty years later, a similar suit reappears. Striped one-piece maillot sports a skirt and deep, 1920s open sides.*

*The bifurcated skirt, c. 1915. Also known as a "culotte," these skirt-like pants were the predecessor to much of the functional fashions we wear.*

was the fashion of the day, and the first faded blue denim (a Western fad), made an appearance. Not willing to confine themselves purely to American sources, talented creators eyed further horizons, finding inspiration from one end of the world to the other. One prominent manufacturer of the mid-thirties, Rollins Hosiery Mills, noted that "Frankly feminine or beguilingly boyish, you'll find . . . the newest and smartest versions of casual clothes. Gay and gallant colors, new and nautical styles in shirts, shorts, slacks and sunsuits." *Vogue* Magazine, in the July 1936 issue, dedicated several pages to society women participating in sports featuring the correct costume for each activity. Sailing, riding, tennis, golf, and shooting were considered elegant methods of filling in time, and each required different clothing. Sunglasses, which had never been heard of before, became an exciting new accessory which promised to "reduce the glare of sunlight to the cool comfort of an overcast day." All of these were straws in the wind. Perhaps impending storm would be a better term.

For the second time in the 20th century, war broke out in Europe. Starting in late 1939, literally no country in Europe was spared the terror of war. In 1941, the United States joined the war on the side of the Allies, against the Axis countries (as they were known), Germany, Italy and Japan. And, once again, as men were drafted into the armed services, women worked "manning" the factories and service industries of the nation. L-85 (see Chapter 5), the wartime version of a sumptuary law added to the retreat of fashion. Clothing became almost totally functional. Women wore pants, coveralls, work gloves and protective caps—all fashions that were sooner or later to be translated into sportswear. Again, *Vogue* Magazine noted in July of 1943, that "The best dressed women in the world are . . . on scaffoldings, in turnip fields, on trucks, in assembly lines, welders and farmers and riggers and assemblers, working coast to coast." The Brooklyn Museum mounted an entire exhibit entitled "Women at War" featuring the protective apparel of the period. All of these styles, later, were to be translated into sport fashions.

What was true of women after World War I, was even more true after the end of the war in 1945. Women, bereft of masculine company for many years, toiling in factories, and deprived of all kinds of fashion inspiration, or indeed, any place to wear it, fell easy prey to a romantic and nostalgic look back to what seemed a simpler and more gentle time. This fashion reversal, *The New Look* of Christian Dior, swept the western world, but in volume fashion, the easiest, the simplest, and the least expensive way to the full-skirted, petticoated Dior silhouette, was with separates—blouses and skirts. It marked the end of the reign of the one-piece dress, and the beginning of the new order of tops and bottoms. But the one-piece dress didn't die immediately: the labels of "Anne Fogarty" and "Suzy Perette" were big, big factors in the dress market, shipping hundreds of thousands of tight-bodiced, full-skirted designs. Conversely, soft blousons topping shorts appeared, even as we see them reappear in the late 1980s. Loose middies bloomed over Bermuda and Jamaica shorts. The poncho was shown in many different lengths. The "duster" coat turned up, borrowed identically from those worn earlier in the century by motoring ladies to keep the dirt and grime of unpaved roads from their clothing. Women who were enjoying the femininity of the "New Look" were turning at the same time to the much more exuberant sport fashions, appearing in brilliant, hot colors, breaking loose totally from the more controlled designs of the predominant silhouette.

In swimsuits during this same period, there was a literal explosion of design excess. The 1950s, especially, marked a general trend by the public towards conspicuous consumption, and this reflected itself in overall fashion. American women were ruffled, laced, sequinned, embroidered, bloomered, and most of all, boned into swimwear. These styles simply reflected the tiny-waisted, high-pointed bosom look so prevalent at that time. The swimsuit of the decade, designed by Rose Marie Reid, was called "The Hourglass" for obvious reasons. The 1950s also introduced the first modest bikinis to a hostile reception in the fashion world. Bikinis also inspired hostility in the police, who, on occasion, arrested women who were showing (in their opinion) too much skin. Too much skin was considered pornographic by all the "really nice" women of the western world. The bikinis in 1950 were timid forerunners of

*The front page of* Women's Wear Daily, *April 8, 1942. It notes restrictions on garments being produced, the General Limitation Order L-85 and declares that the order is "deemed necessary. ...in public interest."*

their 1980 relatives (when strings and threads are common on beaches across Europe and the Americas), but nothing like them had been seen since ancient times. At first, few women dared to wear them: those who did were considered to be, at best, somewhat outside the pale of polite society.

At the same time, casual fashions were becoming a more significant factor as plane travel, while not yet as totally common as it is in today's jet age, opened up the world. Wardrobes of necessity became lighter, more international, took more to synthetic fibers for easy care. While women were willing to be laced and corseted into romantic designs for cocktails and evenings, they were steadily turning towards comfort during the day. Two or three interchangeable pieces created a wardrobe for a week, and what were called, for the first time, "coordinates" became the order of the day. Claire McCardell, who, without a doubt was the progenitor of the "all-American team," introduced sleek, easy, functional clothing for day and evening wear, a radical new approach to a collection. Sportswear designers were big news in the late 1940s and through the 1950s, and in retail stores across America, more and more selling space began to be turned over to these new, active departments, while the dress business continued to dwindle.

Some of the biggest fashions of the late 1950s and the early 1960s (still fashion hits a generation later), were *maillot* (my-oh) swimsuits, a return from the 1920s, sleeveless tops, tank tops, capris (tight, clinging pants that stopped short at the shin), and pedal pushers (a looser pant, also ending at the shin). Long, tight-like pants, stretched taut with a stirrup under the arch of the foot were another vogue. These pants, like men's trousers of the 18th century, also popped up in ski fashions. Skiing was just getting off the ground in America—it was until then thought of more as an European sport.

At the same time, tights, worn until this time only by dancers, were being featured in the McCardell collections, along with Capezio shoes, heretofore also worn only by dancers. Dance tights were the origin of pantyhose, for until this time, stockings (two individual legs) had been worn, fastened to the waist either with girdles or garter belts. This particular accessory had not changed much in hundreds of years: similar stockings, of one kind or another, date to ancient times. Capezio shoes were soft-toed, pliable, low-heeled and slipper-like, a whole different ball game from the spike-heeled pump of the day. The quick acceptance of these easier fashions was a further straw in the wind pointing to the incoming look and feel of fashion. Actually, the shortening skirt made shoes and hosiery much more important than they had been for some years. Both were brightening to match the more colorful, casual fashions of the late 1950s.

The general loosening of the silhouette inspired other styles. T-shirts became the all purpose top, usually of pure cotton since synthetics had yet to totally conquer the textile world. The big look in shorts at that time, Bermudas and Jamaicas, reappeared as a fashion statement in the late 1980s, although generally these items of apparel are available as classic fashions in limited distribution. Tennis dresses had been correctly tailored and pristinely white, but late in 1949, a top seeded tennis player named Gussie Moran stunned the court at Wimbledon with color and ruffles. While it offended some (and dazzled others), she was barred from further play. Tennis is played today however, in all sorts of costumes, another example of the retreat from clothing edicts and restrictions.

### AMERICAN CLASSICS

The first post-war World's Fair was held in Brussels in 1958 and for the American Pavilion, *Vogue* Magazine was commissioned to select the fashions to be shown. Among their picks of typical, all-American looks, the T-shirt dress in stripes, a maillot swimsuit with a toss-on jacket of bright yellow, a matching sweater and skirt, blue jeans with a plaid shirt, long, lean-legged leather pants, a striped wool poncho and an at-home silk pullover and pants. All perfectly geared to our life today, but trend-setting and avant-garde then. And all indicative of the growing interest by fashion designers in more function and greater and greater simplicity. As a final entry, *Vogue* showed the ubiquitous shirtwaist dress.

The two most important American classics presented were jeans and the shirtwaist. These timeless fashions never completely go out of style, but reappear constantly becoming like best friends in our lives. The jean is the most truly

*Perry Ellis creates a voluminous shirt dress, caught with a wide belt, à la the Middle Ages.*

American piece of apparel in our costume history. It is a reflection of the lifestyle of an entire nation, worn by young people, old people, teenagers, men and women. It has everything—durability, toughness, identity and a certain cachet that belies its humble origins in gold mining camps over a century ago. Invented by Levi Strauss in San Francisco during Gold Rush Days in 1850, they were designed to be work pants for miners, made of tent canvas. One hundred years plus later, they are the largest manufacturer in the world, the name itself, ''Levi'' has become generic, and the work pants have become not only that, but a uniform for millions. While designer jeans enjoyed a tremendous success in the 1970s and the 1980s, nothing has ever dented the Levi mystique. Levis have been exported everywhere in the world, and those countries where they can't be found are filled with people who will trade, buy, swap or steal, to own an authentic pair of American jeans—Levis, of course, being the ultimate.

The shirtwaist, another pure classic, was first, and notably, the look of the turn-of-the-century Gibson Girl—authentic Americana. It never went out of style, but by the 1950s, it turned up everywhere in modernized versions. No collection was complete without shirtdresses of one kind or another, and, for the first time, this simple, timeless fashion was being shown for dress-up, in silks and chiffons for evening, and allover glitter for grand balls. The 1950s fashion of the one-piece shirt dress was translated almost immediately back into the skirt and shirt that had launched the fashion at the turn of the century, and is still predominant apparel in our lives. But the revival of the shirtdress and shirt separates quickly evolved into evening separates, introducing a new merchandise category of elegant simplicity of style, now executed in brocades, velvets, shimmering lamés and laces.

By the 1960s, new sportswear adaptations arrived to shine in the sun. Pants widened slightly and lengthened, bikinis were shrinking, the hats and gloves so loved by the proper 1950s woman vanished. In the early 1950s, full, swinging skirts of felt known as *poodle skirts* were a ''hot'' fashion, but fought a losing battle to the sheath dress, the body-skimming,

20th century chiton, so loved and so worn during this decade. All this was a mild overture to what was to come, for the apparel industry was heading into the turbulent 1960s.

The eruption caused by the war in Vietnam exploded into an anti-establishment approach to apparel, and caused an almost total fashion breakdown. Blue jeans (until then, common work clothes) became part of the accepted fashion and were worn by both men and women, along with cotton T-shirts, often decorated and painted, as were the jeans. Paint was additionally resurrected as body adornment after an absence (in this particular form), of thousands of years. Flower children with elaborate painted faces walked the streets, while astronauts walked the moon. The attack on society was often expressed by attacking fashion. It was one of the significant ways, not only to separate oneself from the establishment but, to use clothing as an identity, a badge of aversion to society. It was a time of hard edges and hip. Colors and prints were bold and incandescent: more and more of the body was exposed, and skirts shot up the leg. Rudi Gernreich, a highly publicized California designer, introduced the ''no-bra'' bra, significantly reforming the structured brassiere. Gone, girdles: gone, stock-

*Left, Oscar de la Renta's pure skirt and shirt elegance. All designers revert to the classics from time to time to deliver elegant fashion, 1987. Right, Donna Karan interprets the shirtwaist dress in a luxurious, flowing evening gown, 1986.*

*Rudi Gernreich's famous topless from 1964. Rudi returned to wool jersey as fabric for many of his swimsuits. Right, a wide-strapped 1971 design.*

ings with seams. Instead, pantyhose, which at the very least, protected the modesty of the wearer. Shades of the Renaissance—once again legs were encased in brilliant tights, often meeting a brief little tunic-like top, reminiscent of the doublet. This time, however, it was the female sporting the bright leg and the brief costume.

Pants in all forms and versions became one of the uniforms of the day. Perhaps not so much because of any "unisex" drive, but because wearing pants was another expression of the rebellious spirit. Perhaps, also, because wearing pants marked another unconscious step towards clothing freedom. Paris recognized the onslaught of the terrifying young, and stamped its approval on pants by including them in all forms and shapes, even in the couture collections. Here, of course, the heroes were both Courrèges and Yves Saint Laurent, who were in the vanguard of the young look. African-inspired wildness turned up on the runways of Paris, linked plastic tunics over naked bodies (borrowed from Medieval armor) didn't draw a second look.

The topper, or "un-topper" as the case may be, was Rudi Gernreich's "topless" swimsuit, which took the naked look about as far as it could go at that time. Presented originally as part of his philosophy of the future, and with no intention of throwing down a fashion gauntlet, it became a cause célèbre. Purchased by the thousands, most of the wearers were promptly arrested and fined for indecency. Today, however, the beaches in the south of France teem with women in monokinis, or simple strings.

During this post-war era, the California market was coming of age. It was there, during the late 1930s and the 1940s that designers, already living a new lifestyle, introduced that lifestyle to the rest of the country. Patio clothing, evening pajamas, at-home apparel, pedal pushers, sit-on-the-floor comfort, jeans, all started in the West. So-called "playclothes" also originated in California. There is less difference today, however, between collections shown on the East and West coasts, partially due to the homogeneity of the fashion world. With the exception of the swimwear industry, the giants ship from New York, and the *California look*, the design touch unique to the West, and once so prevalent throughout the entire sportswear industry, has been swallowed up. But as Bernadine Morris, Fashion Editor of the *New York Times* noted, there was a period when New York and Los Angeles were the fashion capitols of the world: the end came in 1947, with Dior's New Look.

In casual wear, in the 1980s, California manufacturing represents about twenty percent of the total shipments to retailers across America and throughout the world. However, everything with a California touch has become the leading edge of new attitudes in fashion, in food, in entertaining, in language, and in lifestyles. American society more and more watches the western rim of this country. It may not be accidental that the recent craze for Japanese fashion appeared—it represented a new look at our neighbors across the Pacific, a look towards different design inspiration, different cultures, and a growing awareness of the contribution of the east to our polyglot American culture. A great deal of the so-called Japanese look, however, is a reflection of the shapeless styles and somber colors of the Dark Ages.

The swimsuit industry spearheaded the West's entry into American retailing, and other sportswear manufacturers quickly fell into step. While the California market doesn't yet give Seventh Avenue a run for its money, it does contribute a "kicky" look to apparel that helps make up for its lack of size. In large part, this may result from the relative youth of the West, and the fact that the young are always less sophisticated. Also, perhaps due to its smaller size, there is a less serious attitude about fashion in California. Sportswear designers and manufacturers in New York are huge. Witness Liz Claiborne, Evan Picone and Ellen Tracy, as prime examples. These firms ship hundreds of thousands of pieces every year, and their pared-down, classic approach to fashion fits right into the predominant apparel of our day.

In the 1950s, retailers handled sportswear merchandise quite differently. What were known as "spectator" sports departments, and "active" sportswear departments carefully delineated one sort of apparel from the other. Major traditional ready-to-wear categories were dresses, coats and suits. In the 1980s, while there is continual talk of dress "revivals," it is

*An industry ad for Dan River
denim. If there is such a thing as an
indigenous American textile, denim
would fill the bill even though this
fabric originated in France. These
are truly depictive of great
American classics.*

easy to tell, by simple measurements of the selling space on
any fashion floor, that dress departments are midgets
compared to the sportswear sections. (Actually, even in so-
called better dress and gown salons, separates and pantsuits
are to be found in increasing numbers.)

What we are talking about is a totally fresh fashion direction. The big, big volume in ready-to-wear is in this relatively
new apparel: it is what women not only prefer to buy, but
prefer to wear constantly. (In costume history, anything fifty
years old is considered new: last year's fashions are
"immediate.") We need a new terminology that is more
descriptive for modern apparel than "sportswear." It is only
that segment once known as "active wear" that really consti-
tutes sportswear in the pure sense of the word—apparel for
participating in a sport. While this category of merchandise
was relatively small until the late 1980s compared to its giant
and over-powering relative, it does represent a rapidly
expanding area in the market. Jogging clothes, exercise
leotards, ski clothing, tennis, and riding now boast entire

shops, and even chains, of their own. As women become more liberated and involved in free and active lives, these categories of merchandise will inevitably become larger in dollar volume and wardrobe importance. Once again, it would seem, the term "sportswear" may have reverted to its original definition.

So what do we live in, then, at the end of the 20th century? We live in what we still refer to by an old-fashioned term, *sportswear*. We live in separates, pants, shirts, pullovers, sweaters, jackets, and tunics. We wear all this over very little body constriction—we wear clothing over pantyhose, tights, leotards, and body stockings. The look is simple, pared down, functional. The look so brilliantly delivered to us by the all-American team.

So we come full circle. Our lives are totally different, and how we cover our bodies is totally different. During the day, women work in all the fields once specifically reserved for men: women are telephone repair persons, women fight fires and police the streets, women plumb, wire and drive buses, women are in the armed forces, women are judges in the

Left, *Donna Karan wraps and drapes silk jersey seductively about the body in her evening separates, 1985.* Right, *Calvin Klein takes the minimal look about as far as it will go, 1986.*

highest courts of the land, and yes, women run for office at the top of political tickets. And win. Even at night, out of the uniform of the day, when women want to change into a more glamorous look, more and more the change is simply into an elegant version of what is worn during the day. Skirts and jackets in cashmere and satin, pullovers of sequins and paillettes. The same ease, but with added luxe. And the all-American team is in the vanguard of this new contemporary fashion. They ride the peak of the crest of the wave. They deliver what women want, and seem to sense that want even before the woman does.

# CHAPTER NINE

# *The Great American Stars*

While the French have a long history of interest in, and affinity for, fashion, the Americans came late to the game. It was not until World War II, 1941–1945, that designers in the United States became prominent members of the designing fraternity, which until that time, had almost entirely been centered in Paris. That is not to say that *no* designers existed, or were known in this country: on the contrary, particularly in the motion picture field, creators of trend-setting apparel were not only busy at their craft, but were widely recognized by the public. In that group, certainly Adrian, Howard Greer and Irene were particularly prominent, and in the better ready-to-wear field, Hattie Carnegie, Valentina and Charles James were early stars. Millinery's most famous designer, Lilly Daché had a wide and admiring audience.

It was not until fashion information and inspiration came to a halt from Paris during the war years, however, that we find American names not only becoming recognized, but the beginnings of a truly American look. In New York on Seventh Avenue in just one short year, several new companies were set up to produce exciting, "Made-in-America" clothing. In Los Angeles, sportswear designers emerged from the obscurity of the apparel label, particularly in swimsuit manufacturing.

While in a sense, no couture exists in America as it does in

Paris, there were two American talents that emerged that carried on in the French tradition. Charles James and Mainbocher. (Mainbocher, of course, as we will see, originally designed in Paris.) Both designers worked with a devoted and private clientele, and Mainbocher, in particular, showed large collections as was done in Paris. Charles James, a brilliant and original creative genius, but a tormented and difficult man, moved back and forth from the states to Europe, working equally as well in both environments, never achieving the success of his peers, although he was highly regarded by the designing world on both sides of the ocean.

Americans tend to take heros and heroines to their hearts, and as the American stars began to shine in the New York fashion world, a love affair began with our own. In true Yankee fashion, while the industry deprecates itself as the "rag" business, we see these creative people as celebrities. Our designers are made over, petted and rewarded for their talents, are greeted like the well-known personalities they are, and by and large, tend to move about in high level social and creative circles.

Basically in this country, ready-to-wear is produced. While some of this is priced on the same astronomical levels as a gown from the couture in Paris, and might even be (for favored customers) personally cut and fit, it is simply not the same thing. By the early 1940s, collections on a large scale were being presented to the fashion press and to the buyers who were denied access to Europe. Quickly, fashion strengths developed and grew, and just as quickly, American women learned for the first time to look homeward for fashion inspiration.

There would be little controversy about the glittering designer names of our immediate past—those who were in the forefront of the American fashion revolution. Discussing current American stars is more difficult: some achieve longevity, others sparkle for a few seasons and vanish. As in most areas of contemporary life, a little distance helps distinguish the movers and shakers of the industry.

Only a few years ago, the names of Ralph Lauren and Donna Karan, for example, were unknown. Today, they rank among the first in the pantheon of the fashion Gods. The New York,

Chicago and Los Angeles fashion markets boast many brilliant talents. Some set style trends for a season, while others are continually watched for hints on what's ahead in fashion. A few design more or less outside the main fashion stream following an individual vision of apparel. While not every important contemporary designer is discussed in this chapter, it does not mean they lack importance or large followings. It *does* mean that it is extremely difficult to select from so *much* creative ability, those designers, still living, who will leave an impact on style twenty years from now. James Galanos, included among the American stars, designs more in the European tradition than the American. Indeed, it is said that he could be completely at home in any fashion capitol of the world.

Bill Blass, Geoffrey Beene, Oscar de la Renta, Mary McFadden, Pauline Trigère and Adolfo are just a few of the industry leaders: they all share the uniquely American attitude about fashion—easy sophistication and a sense of timelessness and beauty. They also are instantly recognized by the public, who follows their fame and fortune with intense scrutiny. Topnotch creators, each of them (and others) leaves an individual stamp on the fashion scene. They are part of the select.

## *GILBERT ADRIAN*
### (1903–1959)

Adrian was born in Connecticut to parents who were the owners of a fine millinery shop. Even in his early years, therefore, he was surrounded with fashion and a facility for drawing and sketching seemed to predestine him to the life of a designer. In 1921, he enrolled at the Parsons School of Art in New York, but soon became bored with the lack of challenge in his studies and moved on to Paris. Along the way, he discarded his real name, Adrian Adolph Greenburg, and decided to use just Adrian, adding his father's first name, Gilbert.

Student life in Paris in the 1920s was a free-wheeling swirl of excitement, and Adrian fell right into it. Part of the fun was parties . . . and at the huge Bal du Grand Prix, a costume ball

*An Adrian design for Joan Crawford in the movie* Letty Lynton, *1932.* Below, *the quintessential Adrian suit, drawstring waist, carefully mitered shoulder detail, Adrian trademarks.*

*Gilbert Adrian*

to which all the young and the avant-garde flocked, he caught the attention of another American, Irving Berlin. Berlin was looking for a designer for his Broadway theater productions, and, amused by Adrian's creative costume, gave him a start.

He eventually made his way to Hollywood, where he was asked to work on a Rudolf Valentino picture, and where he found total bliss. He "went Hollywood" in a grand way, renting a lavish apartment and costuming himself, for example, in a white suit under a red-lined black cape.

His success was not long in coming. By 1929, he was working for Cecil B. DeMille, designing for the great epic, *King of Kings* and his work met with acclaim. Shortly after, Louis B. Mayer hired him to head all designing for MGM, where his work made him world famous. He worked with all the movie greats, starting with Greta Garbo, and the famous slouch felt hat and belted trench coat designed for her became trademarks that were copied around the world in the 1930s, and revived fifty years later. For the film *Marie Antoinette* he designed over four thousand costumes, researching in libraries and museums in France. To him, costume went beyond its simple appearance on the screen: he believed that it set a mood or feeling that helped a performer live the role. Each garment for that picture was incredibly detailed, each section of a gown costly. In a film for Greta Garbo, *Queen Christina*, just one panel, of many, for the coronation robe cost $1,800.

For Joan Crawford, he created many trend-setting styles, including the broadened, padded shoulder, the white collar look and cascades of ruffles. For a period of time there is no question but that he was the most influential designer in America. His devoted fans went to the movies and copied what they saw. While some claimed that he was not above borrowing from other designers, he was certainly in a position to take any style and turn it into a giant success.

In 1940, as the war approached, Adrian designed a maternity garment for his wife, the star Janet Gaynor, a bright smock over a slender skirt, with the front cut out to take care of the expanding stomach. This was the forerunner of most maternity garments. It was photographed by *Vogue* Magazine and caused an instant sensation. At about the same time, discouraged by new attitudes in the industry, he decided to leave studio work and open his own ready-to-wear operation.

He was a smash. He not only became the most famous designer in America, but there was literally nothing he created that wasn't instantly copied by millions of women. He took over a restaurant in Beverly Hills and turned it into a salon, where his collections were shown to enthusiastic audiences of motion picture personalities, social leaders, and the fashion press. Ideas poured out: lean, severe suits with curved seams and mitered panels; slim dresses blazed with embroidery sparked like modern art with brilliant slashes of color; tabs of medieval splendor-dangled crests. The audiences were always in black tie, and the collections received standing ovations. No American woman was considered to have any style if she didn't own and wear, an Adrian. In addition to shipping substantial orders to most of the fine stores in this country, he had a large private clientele. If you couldn't afford the original—not to worry, millions of copies were on the racks.

Not until the end of World War II did all this vanish. When the bombshell of Dior's New Look landed, the fashion world turned its back on Adrian, who refused to accept the fact that times had changed. His reaction was bitter, and the triumphs of previous years turned to ashes. The parade simply passed him by.

He spent the last years of his life in Brazil with his actress wife and his son. At the time of his death he was busily at work designing costumes for the film *Camelot*. During his period of greatest fame, however, his clothing featuring wide horseshoe shoulders, geometric panels and slim skirts provided the look of an entire decade, the 1940s. In recent years, the *Adrian* look has strongly influenced fashion, particularly in sportswear design.

# CLAIRE McCARDELL
## (1905–1958)

**M**any consider the American designer of the century to be Claire McCardell. She best understood how women wanted to look in the 20th century, and her clothes were functional, simple and clean. She liked "buttons that buttoned and bows that tied." She was, according to Stanley Marcus (of Neiman-Marcus fame) "the master of the line, never the slave of the sequin." She is one of the few original designers this country has produced. McCardell borrowed from no one and designed from need and for function. Certainly, she was the most innovative, independent and indigenously talented of American creators. Further, she invented and developed all these wonderful things strictly within the limits of mass production, not in any couture tradition.

Born in Maryland to a well-to-do family, she, like Adrian, found herself first a student at Parsons in New York, and then in Paris. There, she was exposed to all the creative ferment of Paris in the 1920s and fell in love with the designs of Vionnet. It was the practice in the couture to sell off samples at the end of a season, some for as little as $15.00. Claire bought as many as she could afford, took them apart and put them back together again, learning construction with every stitch.

It was not her first fascination with fashion; that interest had started when she was a child playing with paper dolls, and by the time she was in high school, she was making all her own clothes. One of the enduring impressions from her school days was graph paper—a fashion detail that turned up later in her career almost as a personal trademark. She designed graph paper fabrics, stationery and eyeglass cases, to mention a few.

Her early career was spotty: her originality made it difficult to find permanent work. She said of herself later that she was a "one-day disaster," but as time went by her skills became desirable, and she went to work for a firm known as Townley, where she stayed until her untimely death.

She was a smashing success, and from her various fashion travels during these years came yet another of her most

*Claire McCardell*

*McCardell popover, the easy, wrap dress she designed early in the summer every year to use up leftover yardage in the factory. They sold by the thousands, Lord & Taylor promoted them annually with full pages in the paper and a bank of Fifth Avenue windows.* Photo by Louise Dahl-Wolfe. Fashion Institute of Technology, New York.

noteworthy additions to apparel. Tired of travelling with heavy luggage (people didn't fly to Europe at that time, they sailed) she invented an entire wardrobe that could be packed in a small suitcase, simply cut of black ribbed jersey with no trimming. The pieces worked, and though they were completely puzzling to buyers at that time, gradually achieved acceptance. It is difficult for us to understand now how separates and sportswear were handled some thirty years ago in stores. In most cases, one buyer bought skirts, another bought blouses and yet a third might stock jackets. The coordinated concept of selling had yet to be developed, and what McCardell was doing was totally innovative.

She eliminated bras and girdles: she dropped the prevalent shoulder pads for a natural line. She designed hoods, deep side pockets set into seams (even in evening clothes), she cut sleeves in one piece with the bodice, a la paper dolls and used brass hooks and other "hardware" for closings. She preferred the functional appearance of fastenings in clear view. Other inspirations included top-stitching on denim, dirndl skirts, spaghetti straps and shoestring ties which were thin bias cords with a million uses: they could wrap a high waist like her favorite Empire line, or could criss-cross down from under the bust to the waist like ancient Grecian apparel. She designed the first diaper bathing suit in the late 1930s, copied years later by Rudi Gernreich, and even later by Halston. She showed ballet slippers by Capezio with her collections creating the new genre of the soft shoe, in effect changing the whole direction of footwear. McCardell's "popovers" were probably her most versatile, famous and enduring fashion: thousands of them were sold annually. The popover was a simple wrap dress that varied in detail season by season. Again, thanks to her, we have leotards which preceded pantyhose. She used leotards, then only for the dance, in every collection. She worked in down-to-earth fabrics—jerseys, cottons, tweeds, camel's hair, mattress ticking and seersucker. Inevitably, she loved pleats, having owned Fortunys, and used them for inspiration as well.

Among the many awards and honors that came her way, was the cover of *Time* Magazine in 1955, a full-scale exhibit of her apparel in the Frank Perls Gallery in Los Angeles a smashing first, the Coty Fashion Critics Award, the Neiman-Marcus Award, and the Parson's Medal for Distinguished Achievement. By the mid 1950s she was one of the most respected and admired creators in the fashion world. She died, unexpectedly in 1958, but her designs are as fresh and modern right now, this minute, as they were over forty years ago. It can truly be said that she was the primal push of the better sportswear industry of America. She was the Chanel of America.

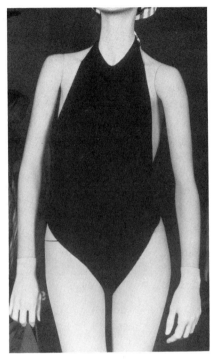

*McCardell's original diaper suit, 1937, very advanced for its time. Picked up a generation later by other sportswear designers.*

*Mainbocher*

# MAINBOCHER
## (1891–1976)

To understand the man, one must first understand the name. It was created in France by eliding his first and last names, and by changing the pronunciation from the hard, Germanic original of Main Bocher (main bocker) to the softer, more elegant, Mainbocher (man-bow-shay). This was part of the thread that ran through his life, the thread that kept him moving from rarefied Parisian circles to the crème de la crème of New York society, the thread that produced the only true couturier this country has ever known, and the thread that formed a man considered the ultimate snob of the century.

He was actually born in Chicago, but met with his first great success in Paris as the editor of *French Vogue*. He drew beautifully, had an innate, sure taste with words and his discerning eye made him an extremely capable editor in those early, heady days of Paris in the 1920s. In 1930, it is said almost on a whim, he decided to open his own house in Paris, confident that it would be a success. And it was. Surrounded by wealthy and titled friends who had known him as an editor, as well as members of the fashion press who supported him, he made an immediate impact on the fashion world. His world was a totally exclusive one, only certain reporters and editors were ever allowed to cover his collections, and that coverage had to meet his rigid specifications. He preferred women who were assured, who had a sense of personal style, who were rich and knew what they wanted, and he catered to that clientele.

The Mainbocher client supreme, probably the most influential fashion figure in the first half of the 20th century, was Wallis Simpson, later the Duchess of Windsor. (The Duke of Windsor had been Edward VIII, King of England, and his marriage to Wallis Simpson cost him his crown.) She was an early devotee of Mainbocher, and he was equally devoted to her. His most famous design for her was, of course, her wedding gown, perhaps the single most widely copied and photographed couture dress ever made. Additionally, he designed her entire trousseau. They enjoyed a sort of mutual admiration society for many years: he appreciated her extraordinary self-discipline, and she appreciated his extraordinary

talent for turning a woman into an elegant fashion plate. And yet his apparel was so understated it was the woman herself who shone. In addition to the Duchess, his clients included film stars, most of the great titles of Europe, and certainly the very rich and mannered of the world. Except for the movie stars, his clientele was reminiscent of Worth's a century earlier.

When World War II struck, he left France for New York. After all, though he seemed to epitomize French couture, he was an American. One step ahead of the Germans, he collected his mother and sister and set off for home. Without money, he was never without friends, and through their help, he re-

*The essential purity of any Mainbocher design can be easily seen in these evening costumes of wool and cashmere—understated, elegant, simple and refined.* Costume Collection, Museum of the City of New York.

opened almost immediately in New York where he reproduced, as closely as possible, the salon he had left in Paris. His return to New York as a designer of international reputation garnered enormous fashion publicity, and his views were eagerly sought on almost every subject. His list of clients read like the society pages: Gloria Vanderbilt, Mrs. William Paley, Princess de Bourbon, one of the richest women in the world, Mary Martin and Ethel Merman of stage fame. Carmel Snow, Editor in Chief of *Harper's Bazaar* and others flocked to his salon.

He was not a designer who produced a line to be manufactured. He was a couturier in the truest sense, a dressmaker for individuals. He worked within his own very restricted definition of fashion, presenting large and complete collections at elegant showings four times a year, and then cutting and fitting all the garments individually for private clients. Incidentally, it was not possible to buy at Mainbocher's salon unless you were introduced by one of those private clients. He never reproduced any of his garments for sale in other stores, although occasionally it was possible to buy something at a lesser price on the street floor of his salon, located on 57th Street just east of Fifth Avenue. He never licensed his name, he never endorsed any product, his name appeared only on the labels of his own creations. His purity of style became a yardstick against which most other Americans in the fashion industry measured themselves.

Although his fashion circle was relatively small, he was well known and copied throughout this country. Among his innovations are the famous beaded cashmeres worn as evening sweaters, bare-armed blouses for tailored suits, furs dyed in colors to match costumes and the simple, tailored dinner suit. His women wore bows flat across their heads, not hats. His shoes were always classic pumps. His jewelry was always real. The three words invariably used in describing his work are *elegant, simple, classic.* They were used to such an extent that they became clichés, but a cliché is the product of truth. It is doubtful that the world today would support a Mainbocher, but it misses a great deal in not having one around.

He closed his salon in 1971 and returned to live in Europe until his death in 1976.

# NORMAN NORELL
(1900–1972)

It is said that with Norell, you always knew where you stood: in the most beautifully cut clothes a woman could wear. Every line, from the turn of the collar to the set of the sleeve, to the placing of a pocket to the curve of a seam, rings with the music of great tailoring and the charm of perfect simplicity. Norell was the first American designer to receive the famed Coty Award, which was given to him for launching fundamental trends that set off widespread ripples. Such trends, or "Norellisms," include the blaze of the allover sequinned dress, the sweater topped evening skirt, the simply beautiful cloth coat—which was, on occasion either jewel-studded or fur-lined, the full-skirted sailor dress. He was considered to be the dean of American designers. Women collected Norells and saved them, as they would collect fine paintings or sculpture, wearing them to this day. According to Mary Lou Luther, former Fashion Editor of the *Los Angeles Times*, "His timeless formula never changed, and is understood by women everywhere . . . understated by day, drop-dead by night."

*Norman Norell*

Often called the "American Balenciaga," he was born in Indianapolis to a retailing family. He arrived in New York at the age of eighteen to study at the Parsons School, where he lasted literally no time at all, and almost immediately started designing theatrical costumes for silent movies, which were at that time filmed in New York. The great break-through came in 1929, when he was hired by Hattie Carnegie. He always gave her credit in later years for teaching him his trade. At that time, hers was probably the best known and most respected name in American fashion. She operated a custom salon, a retail store and a wholesale business which was distributed across America. In 1940, he left her and teamed up with a man named Anthony Traina. Between them they developed the famous label of Traina-Norell. Traina died in 1960, and Norell was on his own.

He researched a great deal for his design inspiration, and always travelled to Europe to select fabrics. His prices were astronomical, for he used only the finest textiles money could

*Norell always supervised every detail in his collection, personally fitting each model. Here he is fitting one of his meticulously tailored coats, 1960s. Photo by Jerome Ducrot. Fashion Institute of Technology, New York.*

buy. He liked crisp, sharp, clean fabrics, and personally selected everything that went into a garment right down to the linings and buttons. No buyer ever fooled around with a Norell—no one dared to ask for a different neckline, sleeve or collar. Further, he only made clothing in sizes six through twelve. As far as Norell was concerned, anybody larger than that didn't exist.

Starting a business in 1940 had been fortuitous. Paris was

closed as a fashion source, and it meant that for the first time someone in New York had a chance. Norell took that chance and turned it into triumph. His collections were always shown in the French manner, complete from millinery to accessories, from hairstyles to makeup, all, carefully planned and executed. Norell showed that it was possible to create outside the Paris environment and to create with great elegance and beauty in the ready-to-wear medium. In Paris, collections had been shown only for ordering by private customers. At Norell, the collections themselves were to be ordered, cut and shipped to all kinds of retailers across the country. He was the bridge across the gap that had existed between the couture and "off the rack."

He loved the look of the 1920s—the small head, the simple black dress, the color beige, relatively short skirts, plain pumps, pale stockings. He borrowed from that era in his use of jersey as the backbone fabric of his collection, and his shapes changed only slightly over the years. He loved simplicity, and even though he made some of the most romantic dresses in the world, the structure and design of each garment was clean cut. He balanced the fit of all his clothing: they were so artfully cut that it took extraordinary fashion knowledge to see what was going on. His coats stood alone, often on their own hems: they had weight and firmness. They were tactile—always beautiful for the hand to touch, and the eye to see.

How did Norell like women to look? "They can never be too simple during the day, or too elaborate at night, as far as I'm concerned." The *New York Times*, in an article printed just before his death in 1972, called him "the man who made the 'rag business' respectable." He was a man so shy and diffident that he was compared in that respect also, to Balenciaga, who was almost pathological in his aversion to the public. He was the first designer to win a Coty Award, the first American designer to have a perfume, à la the French, *Norell* (which is still one of the best sellers in the fragrance industry). He was the first living designer to have a retrospective mounted in his honor at the Metropolitan Museum of Art. It is ironic that he died the night before the gala opening.

*From the last Norell collection, cropped jacket pantsuit, 1972.* The Brooklyn Museum, Gift of Gustave Tassell.

## JAMES GALANOS
### (1925–)

*James Galanos*

Almost without exception, fashion authorities rate Galanos as the premier designer in America today. Stanley Marcus states "there is only one Galanos" for he is the epitome of elegance, style and luxury. Although everything that comes from his firm is ready-made, each garment receives the care and attention that the French couture lavishes on their designs. A Galanos is very, very costly: it would be difficult to own one without planning to part with at least $2,000 for a day dress, and upwards of $25,000 for a hand-beaded evening gown. His clients are obviously women of great wealth, taste, and intellect: his designs are unaffordable by most, and not understood by many. But for those women who can and do buy from Galanos, the purchase is regarded as an investment for a lifetime, worn year after year after year. Nancy Reagan, a Galanos fan, wore a fourteen-year old Galanos to her first State dinner in the White House. He has been called a maverick in the fashion world, totally disinterested in competition, indifferent to the press and uncaring about any form of publicity. With all that, he won his first Coty Award in 1956, and just three years later was elected to the Coty Hall of Fame.

In 1976, he was honored with a full-scale retrospective of twenty-five years of his work at the Fashion Institute of Technology in New York. Two years earlier, a retrospective fashion showing was presented at the Los Angeles County Museum of Art, with then Governor and Mrs. Ronald Reagan in attendance. Her two California inaugural gowns are in that costume collection, and her two presidential inaugural gowns reside at the Smithsonian Institution in Washington, D.C.

He is of Greek heritage and extremely proud of it. From the young age of thirteen he knew that he wanted to be a designer, and enrolled at the Traphagen School of Fashion in New York. There, not unlike some of his fellow designers, he decided that eight months was enough, and set out to establish a career for himself without benefit of formal design education. The next few years were very difficult, for he only sold an occasional sketch to a manufacturer. He went to Paris and worked briefly as an unpaid assistant in the House of Piguet, but returned to

America and tried again to find employment. New York never opened its doors to him, and eventually he found himself in California, where he lives and works to this day. The motion picture designer Jean Louis showed some of his sketches to Rosalind Russell, then a reigning movie star, and that marked the beginning of his long career. He was hired to design for one of her pictures, and elated with this success, he launched his own business. He took nine designs to New York, and returned with $400,000 in orders, a relatively large sum for the early 1950s. Remembering these lean, early years, he is generous with help to other young designers.

He runs a totally unique business. He is not only the designer, he himself chooses the fabrics—or has them made to his specifications; he supervises the manufacturing, takes his own collections to New York twice a year (never at a time

*Left, pure Galanos, a dramatic one-shouldered evening gown, painstakingly hand beaded, the designer's great skill for such extravagant decoration evident in the gradually increasing spiral of brilliants reaching the hem. Right, magnificently beaded evening gowns from the Galanos collection in 1987.*

when other designers are showing), the timing more in tune with the French than with the Americans, and finally, does his own selling. Like other fashion greats, Galanos projects a total look. He regards no detail too small for careful attention, supervising a model's makeup, hair and accessories. Most of those accessories are also designed by him: the millinery is made in his workroom, and the shoes are made by David Evins. He is rigid about a model's figure, specifying that she must be narrow across the back, slender, supple, and hips cannot exceed 33 inches in circumference.

His use of chiffon is legendary, as are his stunning and unusual beadings which are all, of course, done by hand. His favorite color, or non-color, is black. He uses printed velvets, painted laces, iridescent silks and glowing lamés. Jersey is a favorite, as are tweeds often juxtaposed with chiffon or other floating textiles.

Above all, he is a perfectionist. Nothing is left to chance, from the selection of silk for linings in the garments, to the manner in which a buttonhole is hand-bound. If there is an overall look to a Galanos collection through the years, it would have to be an attitude of spareness, of close-to-the-body design, with workmanship so skilled and superbly executed that it is almost non-existent to the eye. His only competitors are considered to be the great stars of Europe, but even in this comparison, it has been said that he is the master, they are merely next best.

## RUDI GERNREICH
(1922–1985)

Among American designers, Rudi (in his case, he was known more by his first name than his second) was an original, everything he touched was inspired by some inner vision that was his alone. Like Galanos, he lived and worked in California, and also won the Coty Hall of Fame Award, but there any comparison stops. His fashions were as original as pop art, as contemporary as cool jazz. Totally non-conforming, no stock adjectives like ''pretty'' or ''alluring'' ever needed to apply. Rudi designs were often controversial, sometimes un-understandable, but always original.

*Rudi Gernreich at work in his studio.*

In the course of his scintillating career, Rudi Gernreich became one of the best known and most notable design names in America. He and Claire McCardell shared the unusual accolade of each being selected at different times to grace the cover of *Time* Magazine. When he opened his collections, the showings were just that, *shows*, as theatrical as a Broadway opening night. His designs were often "cause célèbres"—for they usually succeeded in outraging someone or somebody. He was always ahead of the crowd, a consistent original. He may have been a household word to the general public for the uproar he created in 1964 when he designed the *topless* swimsuit, but actually, Rudi meant it to be a piece for the future not "today" apparel. To everyone's surprise, it took off. Headlines trumpeted the scandals involving the suit, the clergy railed, police arrested and daring ladies wore—the topless. It seems a little tame a generation later, but then it was not only shocking, but revolutionary. Now, topless is commonplace, at least on European beaches.

He followed a year later with another design, the "no-bra" bra, which changed women's undergarments radically, from the stiff, pointed-brassiere look still under the Dior influence, to the softened, natural bosom that remains in fashion to this day. He popularized the form-fitting maillot, and helped de-emphasize the stereotype of male, female clothing, opening another door to the unisex apparel so currently prevalent. He stood for great body freedom, comfort and function, introducing body stockings, for example, a stunner at the time, but giving fashion a free, clean, uncluttered look.

Left, *Peggy Moffat, the model who typified his design talent, and became almost as famous as the creator. While many of Rudi's designs shocked, most were functional, spirited sportswear. Right, Peggy Moffat wearing a see-through in the 1960s.*

He came to this country as a child refugee in 1938, and settled in Los Angeles. It is sure that some of his approach to fashion stemmed from his early years as a member of a famous troupe, the Lester Horton Dancers, for he worked with them for several years followed by a brief stint as an illustrator, before he became a designer. Interestingly, some of his most imaginative and creative work in later years was for the Bella Lewitzky dancers in Los Angeles, where the choreographer and the designer worked together creating dance concepts, just as artists and designers had worked in Europe. *Life* Magazine called him "America's most avant-garde designer," and it is certainly true that he had an innate sense of shifting social trends that shaped his approach to apparel.

In his later years, he moved restlessly into many peripheral fields. He worked on designs for the home, settings for dining, and even created in the food industry. His imagination was boundless: most of the time he was some place out in a future world—but that future world had an eerie way of arriving on his inventive schedule. He always claimed that the greatest influence on his life was Claire McCardell, but in addition to her sure vision of modern times, Rudi added the zing of tomorrow.

# CHAPTER TEN

# *How American Fashion Works*

If French fashion is historically marked with the touch of the individual, the fine sewing of the dressmaker, an innate sense of luxury and quality, the same fashion eyes looking at American fashion will see a different picture: a strong giant, proud of its productive capacity, roaring with energy and capable of clothing the world in the best possible sense. If one, then, were to reduce French fashion to its purest essence, haute couture, the descriptive word would be *fine*. If one were to reduce American fashion to its purest essence, the word would be *big*.

It is only recently, really since 1940 at the start of World War II, that we, in this country, have begun to develop qualities which we have always considered to be French—a mini-reverence for the designer, rather than the manufacturer, an understanding of singularity of style in place of indeterminate and indiscriminate purchasing of apparel without any particular approach or pattern. In Europe, wardrobes have always been put together rather carefully and with a great deal of thought, adding here, changing an accessory there, building one season on another, achieving a cohesive style for each individual. In this country (throw-away chic is a truly American phrase) our clothing has certainly been, particularly in the 20th century, a somewhat helter skelter affair, for the enormous productivity of American fashion manufacturers and the volume prices we have enjoyed make it possible to buy and toss and buy again. Further, Americans have more disposable income than peoples of other countries. In other words, we can not only afford to buy and toss, we rather enjoy the process.

However, this disposable wardrobe concept seems to be diminishing slowly. Our fashion sense has become more sophisticated as we as a people have become more sophisticated. In America, we are becoming somewhat more European in our tastes, and concurrently, the Europeans are beginning to pick up a few of our fashion approaches, and some of our attitudes about disposable clothing.

In America, until recently, it was the manufacturers who starred: those who made the apparel possible, who owned the factory, hired the workers, ran the business, shipped the goods and generally used a company name of indeterminate origin on the label—Catalina Swimsuits, Palm Beach Suits, Jonathan Logan Dresses, all coined names. We understand that designers are involved, and in many cases, the designer is also the manufacturer, owns the business, hires the workers, ships the goods and *does* put his or her name on the label—Donna Karan, Elizabeth Stewart, Liz Claiborne, Bill Blass. (As an aside here, most designers are "owned" by conglomerates, but the designer has great autonomy and authority over the operation that bears his or her name.)

The *prêt* in France and other ready-to-wear businesses in Europe have learned their trade from the United States. Conversely, we have learned about the tradition of dealing one on one with customers from our friends across the Atlantic. Both of us have profited from the exchange.

In the United States—as in all countries, of course—most fashion starts with the textiles. Textiles are the starting point in fashion, the manufacturers working at least five years in advance to gear up their production to meet the demands of the market in a timely way. That means it is their estimate of when the demand will not only arrive, but later on, peak. In the industry, "the market" is the term used broadly for all makers and suppliers in the apparel business. Understand that textiles operate not only with color and pattern, but with texture, surface, weight, and fiber quality. If a fashion trend is emerging, let's say, for rough-surfaced, or slick-surfaced textiles, it takes years of lead time to enable proper product development to meet the incoming demand. Fashion moves in a curve: that is, like a giant semi-circle, it slowly starts, arcs up into its peak of acceptance and gradually diminishes in importance again. Trained stylists and fashion experts understand that movement and can predict with incredible accuracy when the curve will pick up and accelerate into high gear, when it will flatten out, and when it will disappear. Only, of course, to reappear once again some years later. There is no great mystery to fashion prediction. All large producers of both raw and finished materials employ experts who work constantly in the field analyzing trends in apparel and accessories.

From textiles to you. What is the process? The designer works first with the fabric. Then turns to what has been successful in the past, repeating patterns. Perhaps a collar or skirt here, a pocket or the set of a sleeve there. Fashion evolves, it moves slowly from silhouette to silhouette, from skirt length to skirt length, from detail to detail. It has been estimated that a fashion lasts approximately seven years from inception to its end—and even at the end, it is slowly evolving into another closely related look, for very few fashions ever completely die.

An example of how fashion slowly, but progressively moves: let us start with the New Look of the late 1940s and from that point in 1947, watch as the skirts slowly shorten, as they rise from the ankle inch by inch up the leg. At the same time, see the waist gradually released from the tyranny of the Merry Widow. Follow the brassiere, softening from the up-thrust, ice-cream-coned shape to the softer, more natural bosom. By simply turning the pages of fashion magazines for a period of a few years, one can quite easily understand the transition from the artificial silhouette of Dior to the natural lines of the Balenciaga sacque. And, from Balenciaga, with the loosened jacket and waist, the gradual transformation to the mini. First, the edges grow harder, as the skirts become shorter. Decoration vanishes. Finally, as skirts reached the ultimate inanity of a "hot-pant" length and can climb no further, the only place to go is down. Costume historians maintain that fashions move to their most extreme form, beyond which there can be no further motion. Then the fashion collapses, and another takes its place. Giant hoops, towering wigs, enormous puff sleeves, and extended, foot-length bustles all reached the absurd. To accommodate such fashions, doors have been widened,

*Rudi Gernreich working with textiles on a new design in his workroom. Fabrics are rarely changed at this point in the life of a garment, but details often are.*

*Oscar de la Renta shows off two of his show-stopping evening gowns from the 1987 collection.*

carriage tops opened, chairs lost their arms, for it was impossible to sit in, or on, any armchair. In just such a way, when the mini reached its ultimate height, the fork of the legs, slowly but surely, skirts began to inch down little by little. They had to. Like the Renaissance man in doublets and tights, when his costume reached its most extreme, it gave way to a jacket and pants. The style could go no further. As the mini slowly evolved into the next look, the skirt gradually lengthened, adding more material, widening ever so modestly year after year. In 1987, we were faced once again with bubble skirts, crinoline underpinnings, frothed hats and bow-tied shoes peeking out from ankle-length dresses, or from thigh-high ruffled skirts. For fashion lives on change, but the change is seldom radical, usually gentle. The first glimpse of any new fashion trend, however, is startling. From that beginning shot, the broad trend of fashion acceptance starts the slow march to its ultimate peak and decline.

At any rate, most fashion in America has always been involved with *bigness*, whether it is a textile mill or a manufacturer. Only recently have we discovered the joy and virtue of something small—something special, the interplay of one on one. The hand-loomed fabric, the bound seams, the cutting to order, the button that won't fall off, the absolute magnificence of the zipper that stays attached on both sides of an opening, meshing its teeth together comfortably and smoothly after countless wearings, and surviving wash after wash with its meshed teeth still smiling.

So. How does all this big and small fashion work in America? Very, very well. Ounce for ounce, dollar for dollar, garment by garment, we still turn out the best apparel in the world. And turn it out and turn it out. Levi-Strauss is one of the great, shining examples of the best of America. The label stands for quality, style, longevity, and is so highly desired around the world that even in Russia or China, countries not noted for their acceptance of capitalistic fashion, people will willingly risk their very freedoms to own a pair of genuine Levis. And talk about *big*! Nobody out-bigs Levi Strauss. Recently, however, this enormous manufacturing company has recognized a new and different customer—and the jolly giant has responded with a smaller presentation, its *Americana Line* designed by Perry Ellis.

In following the process of how American fashion is created, one starts with the producer of the raw material and moves to the manufacturer of finished apparel. Over the years, the fashion manufacturers have developed the industry up and down and around Seventh Avenue on New York's west side. When *Women's Wear Daily* talks about the fashion industry, it refers to it as SA—the initials are enough for the insiders. SA stands for Seventh Avenue, and that is an overall identification for almost the entire fashion business. While the making of garments has spread into other areas of New York, as well as into the suburbs, Seventh Avenue is still the heart of the market. Giant buildings house thousands of showrooms, usually concentrated with one category of merchandise. For example, our so-called American "couture" market, which is really better to upper designer ready-to-wear, is largely housed in two buildings, 530 and 498 Seventh Avenue. Sportswear lines can be seen by the hundreds at 1400 Broadway, one block away. The fur market is primarily in lower Manhattan, and children's showrooms can be found in the cross-town streets, on 34th and 35th streets.

At the turn of the 20th century, women still made most of their clothing at home, but with the growth of retailing, this changed. The earliest American retailing giants were stores such as Macy's, Gimbels, Wanamakers, Sears, and Montgomery

*Bill Blass, top creative SA designer designs a new chemise, this one, widened through the shoulder, short and very full, 1987.*

Actual pages reproduced from an early Montgomery Ward catalogue printed in 1875. The size of these early mailers was a miniature 3-inch by 5-inch. Behind, *the facade of an early J. C. Penney store, and women shoppers lining the counter in the early twenties at Sears & Roebuck.*

Ward. They were huge monolithic operations, selling everything under one roof from groceries to beaded evening gowns to, on occasion, automobiles. These giant department and mail order stores, most of which started life as cash-and-carry operations, expanded into service and credit, making shopping even more desirable. The chicken and the egg process was in full swing—did the stores help create the market, or did the market create the stores? Probably a little of both, for in America, there is a symbiotic relationship between the maker and the merchant. But grow they both did, into gargantuan retailing and manufacturing operations. The proliferation of branch stores into new geographical areas, and the crossing of state lines to enter new markets, didn't start until after World War II in the late 1940s, and this proliferation followed the surge of population away from the central city to the outlying suburbs. However, along with the branch store and shopping malls came a new generation of retailers, discounters, closed-door membership stores, and up-scale specialty stores. The most recent growth in consumer selling has been the tremendous swing to direct mail and catalogues, which are also diverting significant volume from traditional retailers. Catalogue selling, of course, is not new to America: both Sears and Montgomery Ward have enjoyed tremendous volume from mail order business for over one hundred years. However, the

new concept of direct selling is totally different. It specializes in its merchandise selection and seeks out specific customers.

Paralleling the growth in selling to the consumer has been the growth of the market, not only in New York, but in secondary markets across America. This also has been growth that has occurred primarily since World War II. During the war, with all foreign markets eliminated, the eyes of the fashion world, of necessity, concentrated on American fashion. The store that probably did more to raise the prestige of American designers, and led the way to pride in American fashions was Lord & Taylor in New York. Lord & Taylor is still proud of its championship of American talents and skills, and continues to feature storewide American fashion presentations annually.

As the industry grew, so did the unions involved. The ILGWU (International Ladies Garment Workers Union) is the principal needle trade union, and has a membership of approximately 400,000. There has been a decline in the past few years in union membership, primarily because of a rising tide of imports from countries with lower wage scales. In the 1950s and 1960s, most of the goods bought and sold in the United States were also produced here, with the exception of a thin coat of icing from the Paris couture, and a handful of Italian and British designer imports. That has all changed. Union

*Smart New Yorkers shopping on Lower Broadway in 1905, where the elite came to see and be seen. This part of New York today bears no resemblance to these earlier days, as retailing slowly but surely moved uptown.*

*Dorothy Shaver, the first great woman retailer in America. President of Lord & Taylor, who launched promotions featuring American designers during World War II. Below, the original Lord & Taylor store, which stood at Broadway and 20th Street in New York.*

membership has dwindled almost one third, and more and more manufacturing is being done in Third World nations where labor costs are extremely low. A generation ago almost all textiles were produced in this country, but that, too, is changing. While mills in the south are still churning out yardage, the source of finer fabrics is now Europe. Our share is rapidly diminishing, so much so that Congress is passing many restrictive tariffs on textile imports to protect the remaining jobs and factories. And with the rapid growth of European ready-to-wear, further inroads are being made in American fashion markets adding to losses of American jobs. France, Italy, and London alone ship half a billion dollars worth of fashion goods annually to this country. This may not seem like a great deal when one Liz Claiborne delivers that much every year, but from where it all started from literally nothing in the early 1960s, that half-billion dollars represents tremendous past growth, with few signs of any deceleration. The one caveat—a declining dollar—may make imports too costly for further substantial increases.

In America in the various markets—principally New York, Los Angeles, Dallas, Miami, and Philadelphia—buyers buy. Buyers either work for major stores under the supervision of merchandise managers, or they buy for their own smaller shop, known generically in the trade as "mom and pop" stores. They travel to the major geographical markets to see and shop the various lines and collections which are seldom without new and fresh merchandise groupings, unlike their European counterparts. All large stores and chains own, or are part owners of, buying offices. These buying offices, usually largest in New York and Los Angeles, work with their client stores to help with merchandise assortments and buying. They seek out new resources and report on market trends. Again, in almost all cases, they have also established relationships with offices throughout Europe for the same reason—to smooth the path of the buying process.

In the better markets, just as in Europe, collections are introduced with full-scale productions, models, music and fanfare, attended not only by the retailers (buyers and merchants), but by the fashion press and more and more by fashion chums of the designer. The openings have become slightly social and not quite as business-like as they once were. On the other hand, in the more moderately priced showrooms, this sort of fashion presentation is rare. There is usually only a house model (who often doubles as a receptionist) who will show a buyer any garment on request, but there is seldom any full-scale fashion presentation. Buyers work through the racks of clothing with sales personnel from the various companies. As noted, it has become more and more common for manufacturers to continually add new items and groups to their lines, ensuring a constant flow of fresh merchandise to the retailer.

Both manufacturers and retailers rely heavily on the fashion press for sales promotion. The prominent and powerful fashion magazines, notably *Vogue* and *Harper's Bazaar*, comb the markets constantly looking for fashion excitement—and finding it. One of the problems created, however, in this search for fashion excitement, is the designer who creates apparel strictly for the press, strictly for publicity, with little or no intention of ever producing the item for shipment as it is shown. This does tend, on occasion, to "skew" the fashion stories coming from major openings, and also tends to "skew" the attitude of the consumer about incoming fashion. In the past, when a great deal of this occurred, the consumer reacted to outrageous or provocative fashion stories by closing up the pocketbook and refusing to buy anything. Another common frustration for the consumer was the futile search for the featured merchandise, which had never been cut, ordered, or delivered, but *was* to be seen on the pages of prestigious fashion magazines. Understandably, the fashion press looks for excitement, or for information that will arouse or provoke. This is no different than the evening television news, where a steady refrain of fires, murders, celebrity interviews, and tragedy greets us nightly. Those stories are deemed more apt to hold the viewer's interest. In a like manner, the fashion editor is seeking to hold the fashion consumer's interest. Most of the fashion press is exposed to so much, so much of the time, that it requires the unusual to pique their interest. After all, in the final analysis, it is the proper function of not only the fashion editor, but the fashion director of stores, the fashion consultant who deals with primary markets, or the reporter of fashion information, to tantalize, to create excite-

UNITED COLORS OF BENETTON.

ꭅ benetton

ment, to coax the consumer along. These people, of necessity, are always projecting, always ahead of the game. If they tend to exaggerate to make a point, that is their proper role. Fashion is a constant juggling act between what is, what will be, and what has been, for at any given time, all of these varieties of fashion are occurring. Trend-setters in the business have discarded what is, and are anxiously looking forward to what will be, when most of us are usually still wearing what has been.

The most important market in America is still in New York. It is the largest and most significant center of apparel in the world. New York ships over sixty-five percent of all apparel manufactured in America, approximately eight billion dollars each year, and is home to some seven thousand manufacturers. The second largest market in America is California with thirty-five hundred manufacturers, and 170,000 employees. While the bulk of the manufacturers are concentrated in Los Angeles, they are not necessarily the largest. San Francisco houses both Levi Strauss, the giant daddy of them all, and Esprit, the new kid on the block. Between these two companies, over three and a half billion dollars worth of merchandise is shipped annually.

The growth rate in the needle trade industries in California

UNITED COLORS OF BENETTON.

has been phenomenal. Certainly, one of the contributing factors to this growth has been the large influx of immigrant workers, paralleling the situation in New York in the early part of the 20th century, when wave after wave of central and eastern European immigrants arrived in New York. Just as it was then, the primary skill of many of these newly arrived peoples, now immigrating from Latin America and Asia, is often sewing, tailoring, or other needle skills. Another factor has to be the explosion of population on the west coast, creating a large, stable consumer market for goods made in their own backyard, so to speak. The California market for many years was primarily involved in active and so-called spectator sportswear; however, starting in the late 1960s, a solid and expanding group of better dress and suit makers has evolved.

Other regional markets of importance are Dallas for moderate sportswear, Philadelphia for children's wear, and Miami for resort fashions. Cities in other geographical areas have developing markets and are beginning to exert influence on certain phases of manufacturing, for example, Chicago, for better dresses and Seattle, with firms such as Eddie Bauer, which enjoys tremendous success in active outdoor wear.

Successful retailing seems to be moving towards specializa-

*Benetton, the firm that started life as an Italian knitwear company, has spread its franchised boutiques across the world. The shops, some of which are owned by the parent company, have also entered selling by catalogue.*

**HOW AMERICAN FASHION WORKS   215**

*Bloomingdale's in New York has established a gallery of boutiques for individual designers, almost an avenue of little shops. Starting from* upper left, clockwise: *down the avenue, the Chanel boutique, the Ralph Lauren shop, and the Calvin Klein shop.*

tion. It is possible that the traditional department store is like a dinosaur: the dinosaur did, and the department stores are, sharing similar difficulties in adapting to new environments. We don't really know what happened to the dinosaur except that it totally vanished. And we don't really know what will happen to the traditional department store. It may hang around for a long time yet. But there is no question that stores must learn to deal with a new consumer, who demands quicker attention and more personal service. Two of the fastest growing retailers in America have very defined, but very different, approaches to their business. One, The Limited, in 1986 ranked first in growth, earnings and profitability. The Limited stores have a specific goal as to price lines carried and categories of merchandise offered. Nordstrom, a west-coast phenomenon, ranks second in growth, and while its earnings and profitability are not quite as high, it still has achieved a very respectable position in the marketplace, continuing to grow, now eyeing the Middle West and the East. Nordstrom is loved and adored by its customers. The secret of its success? Ultimate customer service and depth in stocks.

The same pattern seems to be repeating itself in apparel manufacturing. The rapidly growing firms concentrate. Liz Claiborne has carved out an entire chunk of the American

consumer for her company, and is doing a big, big business catering to the upscale, young working woman. In a different part of the industry, Vanity Fair Lingerie has posted tremendous gains in volume and profit by slicing into the consumer pie with lines of loungewear (doubling as outside as well as inside clothing) and lingerie geared specifically towards young women. While these companies, though large by most standards, don't rate in the top apparel businesses in the United States (those rankings belong to such giants as Warnaco, Manhattan Industries, Levi Strauss, etc.), any business that brings in over half a billion dollars a year deserves our attention. And gets it.

On another level, and with a new approach, a happy marriage has taken place between Calvin Klein and Bergdorf Goodman, New York, with a special collection designed just for that Fifth Avenue store. Ralph Lauren, not content with amassing one of the biggest designer fortunes in the United States, has opened a store of his own on upper Madison Avenue

*Ralph Lauren has opened a five-floor store on upper Madison Avenue, completely renovating a private mansion to his own taste. Everything Lauren creates is in place here, from home furnishings to men's ties to women's fine accessories. Another shop has opened in Beverly Hills and more are on the drawing board.*

*Rodeo Drive in Beverly Hills, just a few hundred yards featuring almost every top fashion name in the world. A three-block stroll can open the treasure troves of the universe especially if you have an unlimited pocketbook.*

where everything he makes (one license after another) is stocked and presented in total luxury, exactly the way he wants his image to be projected. It's a smash. A must see on any trip to New York City. Perhaps some of this is following in the footsteps of the French—Yves Saint Laurent's Rive Gauche Shops, or the Courrèges boutiques which have sprung up in major cities with tremendous success. . .just two examples among many. And why not? If the French can learn from us, we can certainly pick up a few tricks from them. This may be an entirely new wave in designer-retailer cooperation, with more and more stores working with small groups of merchandise designed specifically for them and carried exclusively for their customers. These same designers are busily opening their own boutiques and shops across the country. Upper Madison Avenue in New York and Rodeo Drive Beverly Hills are possibly the trendiest locations, but most good sized cities in America can boast a sprinkling of famous designer-name shops. Not all feature only high-priced merchandise: for example, the Benetton stores, presenting bright, moderately priced sportswear currently have some 650 stores in the United States alone—and more in Europe.

In another facet of the changing retail business, it is impossible to ignore the tremendous growth in the recent past of private labels. Major stores, The Limited, Bloomingdales, The Broadway Department Stores, etc., are busily creating their own merchandise with their own labels. While in many cases, well-known manufacturers create this merchandise for the client, it is exclusive to the owner-store, and unavailable to other merchants. In some categories, the private label business has grown phenomenally, producing as much as fifty percent of the volume in the departments involved.

The proliferation of the private label business is simply another sign of the times, and like so much of what is happening, private labels are a response to customer boredom. Over the past twenty years, there has been less and less exclu-

sivity in merchandise presented to the consumer by retailers, since retailers tend to buy from the same resources. The customer has grown increasingly weary of the monotony of that presentation. Until thirty years ago, stores were almost always able to carry certain designers exclusively, either in a city, or in some cases in an entire state. This has not been true for a long time—the manufacturers lost too much business catering to this old-fashioned method of doing business. Additionally, as stores branched into suburbs, and moved across state lines, it became physically and geographically impossible to hold the line on exclusive merchandise. Most good stores carry most good labels, and this is simply good business. Unfortunately, in too many cases, the merchandise is bought identically, presented in stores identically and advertised identically. Fashion monotony sets in. One of the successful solutions therefore, has been to create merchandise for its own private label, for a store to literally become the designer and the maker. It is another part of the blurring of traditional roles of all the component parts of the American ready-to-wear industry.

It would seem that one must be a midget or a giant to survive. Huge companies are swallowing up other huge companies. The May Co. buys Associated Dry Goods, Macy's management buys itself, and then moves on to buy Bullock's, California. Apparel firms are gulped by other apparel firms and several small companies will merge together into one large one. Small companies which control and limit their sales are doing well. Conversely, so is the big company, which grows by diversifying into segments of the consumer market that have either been neglected or overlooked. When grocery chains are selling sportswear, discounters are selling designer sweaters, and young people spend a lot of time hanging out in army surplus stores putting together their own thing with little or no regard for any fashion source but the approval of their peers, it is easy to see that the way the apparel industry has operated for the past one hundred and fifty years is disappearing. But the impetus towards fashion has not changed at all—simply the mechanisms that present it.

In the fashion business, particularly the American fashion business, change is the name of the game. It is doubtful there is any other country in the world that can and does respond so quickly to the demands of the consumer. With this sensitivity to fashion change, there is no question but that both manufacturing and retailing in this country are, of necessity heading for further modifications in the way they do business. After all, when the consumer changes, fashion reflects that change. We are the catalyst of that change. We, the people, decide what will happen. If we demand better quality, we'll get it. If we want more service it will be supplied. If we want the fun of rummaging through giant bins of bargains in a discount store, the store is only too happy to oblige. As American consumers, we are forcing changes in the manner in which the fashion industry presents itself. Our lifestyles have created new categories of merchandise—running shoes, sweatsuits, sport bras, for example. Larger women, determined to get a better end of the stick in the apparel business, demanded, and whole new companies have sprung up to cater to and promote fashion for bigger sizes. And petites. There are very few big manufacturers that have not created a separate division for petite sizes—and stores have followed suit, with shops carrying only merchandise scaled to the smaller woman. These are just examples. The growing sophistication of the consumer is creating a growing sophistication in the markets, and what is offered.

What do we want from American fashion? My guess is, everything. And my further guess is that we'll get it. And that will be sooner than later.

# CHAPTER ELEVEN

# *The Story of Textiles*

All fashion starts with cloth. In this sense, leather, furs and metallics are included, for they are, after all, cloth of a kind.

Textiles are the springboard of fashion: the sibilant hiss of silk, the crisp, dry rustle of taffeta, the luxe of pure woolens with their soft, sometimes buttery, hand and the unbridled crump of pure cottons and linens all speak to us. First, they speak to the designer. One of the most fascinating experiences in the world is watching a designer working with fabrics. Eyes gleam, fingers stroke, yardage is picked up, draped, wrapped and stretched, and the creative juices begin to flow. For that is where it all begins—with textiles. Before any designer sets pencil to paper, the fabric market is worked thoroughly, and it is from the selections of these fabrics that fashion begins.

Textiles are, in themselves, fascinating. The word itself, textile, comes to us from the Latin word *texere*, which means to weave. The process of weaving is as old almost as mankind, becoming progressively more sophisticated as mankind gained knowledge. Archaeologists have discovered highly sophisticated textiles that are many thousands of years old, preserved by chance, either in the dry climates of Egypt, Peru or the Near and Middle East, or preserved in more northern climes by immersion in peat bogs or tarlike substances. Costumes and textiles have been preserved for these long periods quite intact. It is possible, then, not only to understand the method of weaving employed, but to see actual garments that were woven and worn by these ancient peoples. In most cases, they are not too different from the simple tunic shapes and wide leather belts we find so current and ''with it.''

## THE REAL THING

For many thousands of years, man depended on the real thing—and the real thing means just that—cotton, linen, silk and wool. With the abundance of synthetic and chemically produced textiles, the choice is now tremendous but there has never been anything to equal what nature sent us originally. That is not to say that some synthetics aren't wonderful: what would we do without nylon stockings? Drip-dry fabrics, and no-iron sheets have made light work of formerly back-breaking household tasks. But oh, the sheer comfort of sleeping between pure linen or cotton sheets, freshly laundered and ironed. The coolness in hot weather, the warmth in the winter, the *hand* of real textiles, their feel.

*Hand* is a word used often in the fashion industry. It refers to the surface, the heft, the quality of a textile, and of course, how it feels to the hand. . .to the touch. Fabrics, because of their very nature, all have a different hand. Silk, in differing weights, for example, feels differently and behaves differently, as do all fabrics. The designer or manufacturer assesses first the color, the pattern, the hand and the weight of the fabric, and then the designing starts.

## WOOL

In the western world, our civilization grew up with three of the four basic fibers, plus, of course, leather and fur. The earliest finds are usually of wool, for wool is probably the simplest and easiest to spin into a fiber and required no agricultural skills. Wool, of course, is simply sheep hair, and depending on where the wool comes from (cold climates, warmer temperatures) the fiber itself will change, some of it short and curly, some of it stiff and some of it long and fine. For example, wool grown in New Zealand is used almost exclusively for carpets, while the wool from Australia, a major wool-growing country, is used for apparel. Over centuries, sheep have been raised for certain qualities in the wool, which has helped produce in modern times finer fabrics. It is relatively simple to turn sheared wool into a fiber, usually by twisting different lengths into a thread. As in all fibers, the harder the twist, the stronger the thread that is pulled. Origi-

*Examples of surface interest and weaving techniques in various fabric samples.* Fashion Institute of Design and Merchandising, Textile Division, Los Angeles.

nally, the threads were twisted by hand; later, threads were pulled by a device known as a *spindle* which helped in the twisting. Eventually, the spindle was replaced by a spinning wheel, followed even later with a treadle device which enabled the spinner to use feet to help the rotating the fibers by hand.

Very few homes in early America were without spinning wheels, which can still be used for the same purpose. Most of the world (except for the wealthy) spun and made the majority of the fabrics that were then turned into apparel. Spinning wheels were invented some time around the 14th century, and it was a major step forward in textile development. All fibers are spun, in effect, to create the basic thread which, in turn, becomes the finished cloth.

## COTTON

Cotton is almost as old as wool. Fragments and scraps of cotton have been found dating back easily to 3500 B.C., preserved by the same methods. . .heat, immersion in substances which prevent destruction, etc. The word itself comes to us from the Arabic *qutun*, and it describes a material that has been known since ancient times. Just as wool needs cool weather to produce the finest fibers, cotton needs heat, so the great original cotton-growing countries were Egypt and India, now with the addition of the United States, Russia and China. It is probable that cotton was first cultivated in India and reached the countries of the Mediterranean through Arabian trade. While it was always a highly desired textile in those warm climates, cotton was not a significant fiber in western Europe until late in the 17th and early 18th centuries, when trade routes opened up in earnest to the east, and when the lighter, floatier fabrics became very fashionable because of the then current styles. The East Indian Trading Company, originally set up to import spices, added Indian cotton to its cargo, first as a trading material with primitive cultures who had no currency, and later for re-export to slave markets in Africa. It was not until 1660 that calicoes began to be accepted in England, and the brilliant, exotic prints and designs created the first boom in cotton fashions.

*ORIGIN OF TEXTILE NAMES* It is interesting the number of names for different cotton weaving techniques that have come to us from their place of origin. *Calico*, for example, from the city of Calicut, *muslin* named after the city of Mosul and *chambray*, for the city of Cambrai in France. Others include *Madras*, which describes a vividly woven, cross-barred fabric which "bleeds" or runs after washing, from the capital city (Madras) in southeast India. The word *chintz* is simply the Hindu name for cotton with a painted design. *Damask* was named for ancient Damascus, *shantung* for that province in China, and *denim*, which was first made in the French city of Nimes, or de Nimes (from Nimes), is now the all-American cloth.

## *LINEN*

Linen, or flax, is also an ancient weave, again made from a cultivated plant found in both Europe and the Middle East dating at about the same period as cotton, 3500 B.C. Egypt produced the finest linen and it was a basic fiber in their society, widely used for the costumes of the hierarchy. It was later taken up by the Greeks and Romans. A relatively tougher, stronger fiber, it requires more care in production than cotton, but it is top notch for apparel in any warm climate because of its capacity to absorb dampness and moisture. The weaving of linen in ancient Egypt was so commonplace that many tomb and wall paintings show scenes of spinning and looming, with enough detail so that the actual process can be clearly understood. A great deal of fabric has also been recovered from ancient tombs, including bundles of linen from the 14th century B.C., as well as complete garments worn at that time. The Egyptian kilt or man's skirt, pleated and stiffened, was one of the most striking examples of the textile arts of these ancient kingdoms.

Linen was used widely through the Middle Ages, but primarily for linings of garments, rather than for clothing itself. In the 1980s, it is one of the most fashionable textiles in the apparel industry.

## *SILK*

Silk has the most romantic history of the natural fibers; further, silk is the only continuous filament in the world: spun by the silkworm into a cocoon to surround it during its life cycle, the cocoon can be unwound into one long thread. If the threads are damaged by the moth leaving the cocoon the broken fibers are used for the manufacture of what is known as raw silk, a slubbed textile which will show the short, broken lengths interrupting the surface of the cloth.

Originally discovered in China, various stories abound as to its cultivation and spread into other geographical areas. Silk is believed to have been cultivated at least eight thousand years ago, and was an extremely desirable product even then, carefully and jealously guarded from the outside world. For centuries the Chinese, who discovered the secret of silk manufacture, kept a monopoly on its production, exporting only the silk thread, or finished fabric to other countries. The favorite story of how the secret left China is the romantic tale of a Chinese princess taking the eggs of the silkworms, along with the mulberry tree seeds which produced the leaves on which they live, hidden in her headdress as she left her native country to be married to a foreign ruler. True or not, it is a charming story and perhaps plausible, for by 1000 B.C., "sericulture" was known in India, Persia and other Asian countries. The Chinese monopoly had vanished.

Silk, through the ages, has been as highly regarded as gold, and in fact was often traded as a commodity on which even a higher value was placed. Silk was known to the Greeks and to the Romans as well, both of the civilizations loving the luxury and beauty of the fabric. Silk is of superior quality—it is strong, flexible and has a superb sheen, or luster. Depending on the weight of the weave, it takes on different characteristics: it can be extremely heavy, with a solid weight and heft, it can be as delicate as tissue paper, it can be woven into other fibers to produce textiles of great beauty and strength. Ancient material found in China can be dated quite easily because of the large quantities, well preserved, that have been found in burial grounds. Silk for many thousands of years was worn exclusively by royalty, or by the wealthy and titled, primarily because of its cost, but even more because it was so highly prized that in some countries, sumptuary laws made it a capital offense to own or wear silk.

By the time of the Han Dynasty in China, from approximately 200 B.C. to A.D. 200, the fabled Silk Road had been established. This was the great trading route between east and west, over which all commerce passed. Marco Polo travelled the Silk Road, and it is being restored so that travellers in the late 20th century can retrace these ancient pathways. Interestingly, the west knew nothing about the east, and vice versa. Products simply passed through many hands and many countries on the endless trading journeys. It took Marco Polo over five years to make his way to China, and just as many to return, but he brought back much information on Asia and the East. For many hundreds of years, his writings were the only source of knowledge for Europeans on these strange parts of the world.

Oriental splendor in the use of silk textiles would be difficult to describe. Not only was silk used for apparel, but it was used for palace decorations, for flags and banners of extraordinary beauty, for trappings of armies and horses. Silk was as prized as gold and jewels, and the country that controlled silk production had a powerful tool for controlling great parts of the world. The Byzantines, desperate to produce their own silk textiles, eventually developed imperial workshops which produce the most extravagant silks the world has ever known. The weavers themselves were privileged, and the right to weave was inherited. The clothing worn was rigidly proscribed, certain garments reserved for royalty, other articles of clothing allowed in proportion to importance or standing at the court. Constantinople itself, capitol of the Byzantine empire, allowed very little access to the city by foreigners. Some traders were never allowed through the gates, others were given special permission to enter by day, but they were to be outside the walls by night, where they were permitted to camp. As the power of Byzantium waned, the city-republic of Venice grew in importance, controlling the Mediterranean Sea: Venetians bought and traded in silks, and by the 11th century, had established silk mills in Europe.

Silk is still considered the most luxurious of all textiles, and while no wars are fought over it in modern times, it was the cause of great troubles and power plays throughout history.

While silk weaving passed from the east to the west early in the 14th century and Venice became the center of the weaving trade, Florence also made exquisite and finely detailed silks and silk velvets for clothing one hundred years earlier. Venice, however, with its vast shipping fleets and wealth was the most important Italian city-state in the silk industry. Weaving in the Italian cities was controlled by guilds throughout the Middle Ages as it was in most of Europe. In a sense, these guilds were the forerunners of our unions, for they formulated not only the economic status of their members, but also their social and political lives as well. Rigid work patterns were all regulated in great detail by guilds, who from time to time assumed positions of power.

From Italy, the textile arts, and particularly the weaving of silk, had passed to France by the middle of the 17th century, and by the 18th century Lyons had become the capitol of fine fabrics in the world. The first to push for establishing a center for silk weaving, was Francis I (of the Field of Cloth of Gold fame), who realized that too much good French money was disappearing to other European countries, and made up his mind to keep it at home. France, in addition to the supremacy of Lyons, claims two of the greatest textile artists ever known. The works of these artists, who also possessed superb technical skills, are still collected by museums and fragments of their creations can often be seen in textile displays: Jean Revel (born 1684) and Philippe de Lasalle (born 1723). Both of these men left a design legacy that contributed to the creation of Lyons as the center (as it still is) of the silk industry in France.

Printed cottons arriving from India, and extremely popular throughout Europe starting late in the 18th century, began to replace silks in importance, so much so that many laws were passed to keep the lightweight novelty prints out of various

*Trade ads appearing in* Women's Wear Daily, *inviting the market to see advance collections of textiles.*

*Primitive peoples still weave on the centuries-old back-strap loom, often producing rare and unusual fabrics.*

European countries. Throughout history, nations have always tried legally to protect their textile industries, which are of great economic importance. Here in America, we are witnessing similar efforts currently to protect our textile and apparel industries from foreign competition. Protective or sumptuary laws are ancient. Usually, these laws are passed in vain, thus in the 18th century, cotton gradually gained in importance. It became an even more powerful fabric when the Industrial Revolution, with its mechanized looms, arrived.

The mechanical loom radically changed the manufacture of all textiles. While looms had been used for many thousands of years, they were basically operated by hand. Now, it became possible for machinery to do the work of many thousands of those hands, and in the process bring down the cost of the fabrics. Looms are also as old as mankind. There is a picture in Egypt dating from 4400 B.C., which shows a simple loom. The purpose of a loom is to hold one set of threads evenly spaced on a structure, allowing another set to be interlaced across this first set of threads. Usually, the threads on the frame of the loom are held under tension of varying degrees, while the second set gradually produces the woven cloth. Looms are of varying degrees of sophistication, ranging from simple cross-weaving, to the powerful electrically driven mechanical monsters that can turn out thousands of yards daily.

While not every fabric in the world is woven—felt and tapa cloth, for example, are pounded—all loomed fabrics share three basic weaves.

*PLAIN WEAVE* The plain weave is the most common. It is the strongest, and it is the simplest form of lacing threads together, one thread being simply passed over and under the other. Some plain weave textiles include broadcloth, flannel, poplin, sheeting, dress linens, wool flannel, wool challis and homespun. Silk fibers are plain-woven into chiffon, shantung, taffeta and moiré, as examples.

*TWILL WEAVE* The twill weave is also widely used, and while not quite as strong as the plain weave, also has great tensile strength. Twills are formed by lacing the threads unevenly so that a raised line shows on the surface, usually on one side only, but occasionally on both sides of the fabric. Typical twill textiles include drill, some denims, gabardines, toweling, wool covert cloth, serge, tweed, whipcord, silk serges, foulards and ottomans.

*SATIN WEAVE* Satin weave has the least strength of all woven goods, and is characterized by a thread known as a "float." This means that the cross threads skip over differing numbers of threads running in the opposite direction. In other words, the "floats" (unanchored threads) lay on the surface of the cloth. Typical satin weave textiles are brocades, but other common weaves employing this technique include Jacquards, slipper satins, damask linens and cottons. Many furniture fabrics are of satin weave.

There are countless other weaves, of course, but basically they are all variations on the three techniques just listed.

While the vast majority of textiles are loomed by power, many fabric artists still work by hand making hand-loomed fabrics, which are not only of great beauty, but highly desired in this mechanical age. The power loom in a sense is nothing more or less than a hand-loom driven by machinery: the process through the ages has changed very little. The late 18th century saw most of the inventions that are still in use. In England, the *spinning jenny* and the *spinning frame*, which sped the production of threads, were invented, along with the steam-driven power loom. Steam-driven machinery was replacing water power in the weaving process. In America, Eli Whitney had produced the *cotton gin* (short for engine) which cleaned cotton seeds from the fiber, thus allowing cotton production to increase substantially—and in addition, give impetus to the rapidly growing manufacturing of textiles in the New England states. Both the growing of fibers and the looming of textiles has contributed to the remarkable growth of American industry in the past two hundred years, and both industries have made enormous contributions to apparel manufacturing in the United States.

Plain weave, simple interlaced threads.

Twill weave, uneven lacing of threads.

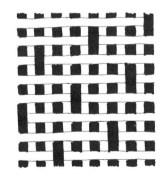

Satin weave, floating thread skips on surface.

Above left, *in May, 1940, before the start of World War II, an unprecedented store event featured nylon hosiery at $1.00 a pair. Women lined up for blocks to buy a pair of stockings, some sat down on the sidewalk to put them on* (below). *Remember, this is before pantyhose.* Above right, *models feature the latest in nylons at the 1939 World's Fair, when nylon was just being introduced.*

## MAN-MADES, OR LABORATORY TEXTILES

The story of textiles in the 20th century is totally different. This century has witnessed for the first time the addition of many new fibers and fabrics, all of them a gift to us not from nature, but from the chemistry laboratory. Man-made fibers basically copy the silkworm, for the process of producing chemical filaments is as simple as forcing man-made, rather than insect-made, liquids through fine holes. All fibers, including man-made fibers, are composed of molecules. In the most basic sense, man-made textiles copy nature by copying the molecular structure of the natural textile. Some of the most important 20th century textiles belong to certain basic families. These families of created fabrics share similar characteristics, and most of the family names are well known to us.

### RAYON

Rayon is the oldest of the man-made fibers, and is basically produced from wood. It was invented in Europe in the 19th century, as early as 1855, but its significant development was in 20th century America. Rayon was introduced as "artificial silk," and since it comes from a natural source it retains many of the properties inherent in natural fibers. It is strong and absorbent, and does not melt nor burn like some chemical fibers. It was in wide use until the early 1950s, when competition from other new textiles cut into its market share. It also suffered from a perception by the fashion industry that it was of inferior quality, and is only now beginning to enjoy a revival.

### ACETATE

Acetate fibers are created somewhat differently. Acetate is made from a chemical compound of cellulose, or the same basic material as rayon, but the fiber is created when the cellulose is formed first as a solid, and then transformed to a liquid.

As the liquid is forced through fine holes, it hardens as it hits the air and becomes a long filament. It can be woven into many different textiles, with many differing surface interests. Unlike rayon, acetate is not readily absorbent, and thus it dries quickly. It is very resilient, which means that it tends to resist wrinkling and needs little ironing. Acetates also have a soft, silken hand and drape well.

## NYLON

Nylon is a synthetic fiber made from chemicals in coal, oil, water and petroleum, as well as other ingredients. It is a complex compound, and so is its manufacture. Developed originally by Du Pont, nylon acquired its name in 1938, and by the time of America's entry into World War II had already gained wide acceptance, a great deal of it in the hosiery markets. It became unavailable to civilians until after the war, the entire production going to the armed services. The most important quality of nylon is its strength and its light weight. It, too, is very resilient, remembering its original shape. It is non-absorbent, and tends to shed dirt. It is impervious to insects, and it is difficult to weaken the fiber.

## POLYESTER

Polyester fibers are produced in a similar fashion to nylon, but depend on different chemical ingredients. The first polyester fiber was developed in England, and in 1946, Du Pont gained the exclusive right to the fiber in the United States. The fiber is also extremely resilient, and retains its shape under almost any weather conditions. Water doesn't even penetrate the surface, so it is not only water repellant, but crease retentive. It is lightweight and strong, and when heat treated will retain pleating and creasing for long periods of time.

## ACRYLICS

Acrylics are also created from a chemical compound, through a series of complicated treatments and reactions. Weaves can be lightweight or heavy, and they have a surface (known as ''loft'') that holds up through long use. Like polyesters, they can be heat-set to hold creases and pleats, they dry very quickly and do not absorb moisture, which adds to body comfort. The

*The cotton industry newsletter launches a new concept in fabrics...called True Performance, the cotton producers answer to consumer complaints about textile performance.*

best known acrylic, Orlon, is also a Du Pont fiber. Acrylics are used widely, not only in the apparel industry, but also in the home furnishings market, where their fade-resistant qualities add value to textiles. They are used most often in blended fabrics, where they add these highly desired qualities.

There are many other man-made textiles—some made from glass, some are olefin fibers, others are polyvinyl, spandex, which describes elastic textiles (notably Lastex) and metallics. Originally, stretch fibers were all of natural rubber, or *latex* but in the past forty years, latex has been replaced with the artificial *Lastex* and *Lycra*, lightweight textiles with stretch qualities used predominantly in swimsuits and undergarments.

## TEXTILE PRODUCTION

In the total process of textile production, in addition to the actual weaving, there are further steps necessary to produce finished cloth. When the fabric is first loomed, it is called gray, or greige goods. It is uncolored, full of impurities still, and very rough in texture. Before any additional work can be done, such as coloring, printing or the addition of special finishes, the fabric is first inspected and cleaned, bleached white and then formed into the proper width and length. Fabrics are usually larger at this stage than when they are finished, for there is a certain amount of shrinkage to be accounted for in the construction of the cloth. Each textile requires different treatment, but all are designed to make it ready for its final finish. For example, the finish can be texturizing, which changes the surface of the cloth, or functional, which changes the basic quality or life of the cloth. The latter includes such techniques as permanent press or soil release abilities.

From this state, it is ready for the next step which is to add color. For thousands of years, only natural dyes from nature were available, but as with fibers, there are now numerous synthetic methods of adding colors to fabrics. Once again, the chemical laboratories are the suppliers of all the new techniques. Most dyestuffs are from coal tar derivatives, and the production is highly technical, since different fabrics accept dye differently. Scientists study the nature of the various fibers to be colored, and assign the correct dye to the

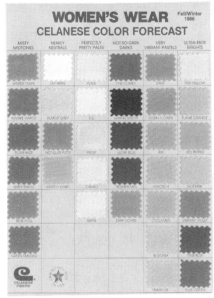

*Various marketing services predict textile futures—both in color and weave. Nigel French is forecasting in the men's wear field:* below, *Celanese Fibers provides a service to the industry predicting color trends.*

fabric. Textiles can be dyed in the yarn before weaving, or dyed by the piece, which is more common. The alternate process is printing. The development of printing is traceable to ancient Egypt, where tomb paintings dated as early as 2100 B.C., show what seem to be printed fabrics. Printing was originally done probably with the resist method, which means that parts of the textile are prevented from accepting the dye; with wood blocks, a technique which is probably of Chinese origin; and with stencil printing, also probably first used by the Chinese. By the Middle Ages, printing was being used for many woven textiles, and by the early 17th century, printed cottons imported by the East India Company were the rage in Europe. Most printing is now done with rollers, a process which is so perfected that as many as sixteen colors can be produced at the same time. Screen printing, first used in Germany and Switzerland, is also in common use.

Historically, textiles have always been considered an art form, and are highly prized possessions of most major museums. Not only have they been woven throughout time as objects of elegance and beauty, but they carried an additional mystique: they stood for wealth, power, position and authority. Weaving, from the extraordinary brocades and textured silks of Persia and China, to the mesmerizing quality of medieval tapestries which told entire histories of profound events, from the gossamer laces of Belgium and France to the embroidered, quilted satins of the Orient with their gold and silver stitching, have always been treasured. Artists are rediscovering the tactile qualities of fibers, the lure of the material itself and are producing major works of art using fibers, weavings and textiles. Contemporary textiles tend to take the material beyond its inherent form, working back in

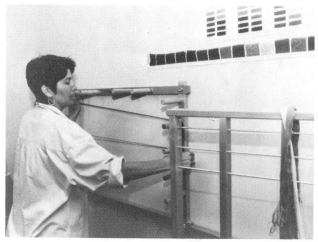

*Students at the Fashion Institute of Design and Merchandising working in a weaving laboratory. Left above, step 1 in the weaving process, measuring warp yarns.* Right above, *Step 2, threading warp yarns through the appropriate "harness" on a 6-harness loom. Left below, lifting and lowering the harness to produce a textile design, the actual process of completing a fabric. Experimenting with tapestry and pile techniques on a frame loom,* (right below), *creating surfaces suitable for wall hangings or carpet design. Fashion Institute of Design and Merchandising, Los Angeles.*

time to original techniques, and forward in time into differing spatial elements. One has only to remember Christo's "Running Fence" stretching across the green fields of Northern California into the Pacific Ocean to see textile become art, and textile changing its form into something else—mysterious and challenging. From the Peruvians of the Americas to the Egyptians and Syrians of ancient Mediterranean cultures, there are ten thousand years of textile tradition. Most of it beautiful. Most of it of great use. Much of it contributing to the continuing wonderment of man and what man can do.

# CHAPTER TWELVE

# *Summing It Up*

The fashion industry is vast. So vast, that it is estimated that one out of every seven workers in the western world is engaged in the creating, buying and selling of apparel and its close relatives. The close relatives are many: lingerie, cosmetics, jewelry, handbags, hosiery, shoes—all part of what we use to change and cover our bodies. And although our primary approach in this book has been women's apparel, infants and children also wear clothing, as do men and boys.

The same ancient origins are visible in all these related fields. Cosmetics trace their roots back to primitive societies when painting of bodies or scarring of bodies indicated varying attitudes about beauty. However, the same motivations are still at work in our use of cosmetics and other body colorings. We believe we are making ourselves more beautiful. While powder and paint are described in the Bible, and we can quite clearly see evidence of cosmetics in Egyptian tomb paintings, the products used in earlier days were quite different from our carefully controlled, government-sanctioned cosmetics. Cosmetics in the 20th century are big business, and a major profit center in retailing. The average woman spends hundreds of dollars annually on creams, polishes, blushers, lipsticks and powders. Along with cosmetics—which, incidentally during different periods of history were as commonly used by men as women—other intrinsic articles of costume also originated thousands of years ago. Jewelry, which may have started with carrying a pretty stone as a talisman, is historically a symbol of money and power. The Egyptians wore gold hoops through pierced ears, even as we do. The London punks embellished their ears with safety pins, but is this any odder than the practice of Elizabethan gentlemen who wore little threads pulled through their pierced ears, creating a rage for what were then known as "ear strings." Beauty, it is said, is in the eye of the beholder. While psychiatrists and sociologists consider this form of body adornment to belong to what is known as "self-mutilation" it would be hard to convince a young teenage girl that her pierced ears were anything but fashionable, or that they had a relationship to a not so distant practice of African tribes wearing brass coils around the neck to elongate it like a giraffe. Yet only fifty years ago, nice girls did not pierce their ears. So short a time in the past the fashion was considered to be suitable only for what were known then as "tarts."

Both men and women have turned to earrings and chains for decoration throughout history. The Greeks, Romans, Byzantine and medieval cultures wore lavish jewelry, the fashion turning from gold to silver, from pearls to gems, which were then set as polished, but not faceted, stones. This process is known as *en cabochon*, and is used from time to time for unusual designs. It was not until the 15th century that the art of cutting and faceting diamonds was invented. Most modern women (and men) have jewelry wardrobes, made possible in many cases by the invention of costume jewelry, which looks like the real thing, but of course, isn't. It is a fact, however, that when the real thing is acquired, it returns in almost every case to an ancient form. Gold formed into chains, earrings dropped from pierced ears, gems set into cloisonné or precious metals. Three-thousand-year-old jewelry is every bit as sophisticated, and in some instances, as advanced in its workmanship, as what is created and worn today.

Along with jewelry and cosmetics, hair fashions appear and disappear. One of the famous Renaissance hairstyles was known as the *coiffure à la Zazzera* which was a great cloud of frizzed hair, achieved by braiding hair tightly into tiny plaits at night, and then combing and fluffing it out in the morning. Cornrows date to the Egyptians, where this hairstyle was a favorite. In the 1930s and 1940s, women favored a medieval hairstyle (however it was borrowed from men, not women) known as a *page boy*, which was shoulder length, straight hair, curled under at the ends. Blonds have *always* had more fun, according to historians. Throughout recorded time, women have bleached their hair with often peculiar and unpleasant methods. If the dangerous bleaching techniques didn't work,

false hair was used, occasionally of silk floss. Roman women coveted blondness, and were partial to wigs made of pale hair bought by their soldier-husbands from the northern savages. Wigs, of course, have also turned up on a cyclical basis: we know that Egyptians wore them as a standard accessory, but even preceding that, other civilizations wore elaborately styled hair pieces.

Shoes haven't changed much. Sandals are almost identical copies of what ancients wore on their feet, and the classic pump hasn't varied except in detail for the past several hundred years. Shoes, traditionally worn by men, are borrowed by women: oxfords, boots, and laced shoes. This is simply part of the continual process of exchanging male and female clothing. Hats, coats, riding costumes, blazers, walking shorts, tailored shirts, pants and trousers, all have crossed the

*Returning again and again, fashion details borrowed from other times, other places. The flirty bustle, short and fun, hasn't been seen for 100 years; the wrapped, loose sports separates, long and elegant, are a nostalgic glimpse of medieval times.*

gender barrier. Both men and women accept quite easily a shoe known as a *tuxedo* pump, where even the ribbon trim is identical.

While outer accessories over time haven't changed radically—only our contemporary vision of them—it is interesting that during various historical periods the basic shape and silhouette of the body has seemed to change, representing what is currently fashionable. Because men in the past traditionally led more active lives, their apparel did not become as exaggerated in outline as women's clothing did. Details, yes, but general shape, no. While men may have worn petticoat breeches, they did not wear farthingales, for example. And while men have at varying periods, corseted their bodies, it was less for the sake of fashion than for the sake of personal vanity. It is in underclothing that we see changes from early times. While in ancient civilizations, both men and women frequently wore an extra layer of clothing under their outerwear, it was not thought of in the same way we think of underwear. It was merely an extra layer or garment, and while it served additionally to protect the body from the elements and the fine garments from soil, it basically served a different purpose.

Trousers of Byzantine origin were more often worn by women under tunics of varying lengths, but they were the forerunner of pants and trousers, both inner and outer wear. The tunic evolved into the chemise, and the trousers evolved into knickers. These garments did not basically change the shape of the body. While Grecian and Minoan women wore a sort of waist band and breast band which served as primitive body shapers, changing the body started with the Renaissance, when corsets, skirt-extenders and breast-flatteners arrived. The chic body in the 16th century was totally encased and rigid. This softened a century later, returned to rigidness, then softened again, even as our silhouettes and bodies do now. It is hard to see fashion as it is happening, but our eyes will tell us how differently our bodies are carried, how our posture changes, and how our shapes have altered during the past thirty years. We have gone from an encased, narrow waist to no waist at all. From high, pointed bosoms to the natural breast. We think nothing of girdles, padded bras, minimizer

*Mary McFadden, noted designer who often turns for inspiration to the past, created this garment as a tribute to the 18th-century woman. The pleating, even an older fashion, is of ancient Greek origin.* Fashion Institute of Design and Merchandising, Los Angeles.

bras, all designed to change the shape of the body. Perhaps not to the same extreme that bodies were altered in the past, but nevertheless, a continuing nod to current styles.

Once the fashion center of the world was Greece. Later, the Byzantines influenced civilization. Venice had its turn, only to give way to Spain at the period when Spanish power was at its peak. For a brief period of time England, under the rule of Elizabeth I captured the fashion throne, but for the past several hundred years, of course, the center of style has been Paris, giving way more recently to the powerful American industry. But gradually, over the past thirty years, fashion is spreading to other geographic areas. Once again, the Italians are making a significant contribution to apparel, and there is no question but that London has mesmerized the young.

While this book has concentrated on French and American fashion, these two countries no longer have a monopoly on fashion creativity. Not only England and Italy are teeming with

*Designers borrowing from other designers (and often from themselves): Right, Emilio Pucci from his 1965 collections. Pucci was the master of the wild and wonderful print. Left, Adrienne Vittadini bows to the master in her 1987 collection, a tribute to the Italian creator in every detail—print jersey, scoop neck and rounded sleeve.*

design excitement and brilliance in the field of apparel. What about Germany, which produces one of the most exciting sportswear lines, sold in top American and European stores, Escada? What about the marvelous leathers from Spain and the beading and embroideries from Belgium? And the exquisite linens from Ireland? Thousands of books have been written about costume, textiles and the operation of apparel industries. Library shelves are filled with brilliant discourse on French fashion, American designers and historic fashion movements. There are books which tell us in infinite detail about one single Peruvian textile, its meaning, how it was woven, and why it is significant. A lifetime can easily be spent in the study of Renaissance costume.

The objective of this book has been to supply a frame of reference as a first stepping stone to understanding fashion. To spur a sense of enchantment with the excitement of fashion history, how it ties in with all the other significant events occurring at the same time, and to point the direction to further exploration.

One thing always leads to another. To know that the Phoenicians invented glass three thousand years ago, originating beads, is a marvelous fact. But beads lead us to trade routes and explorations. Beads lead us to the eventual discovery of windows and mirrors, which in turn changed architecture. A culmination of the story of glass and its ramifications would inevitably take us to the famous Hall of Mirrors at Versailles, where Louis XIV and his scintillating court danced in the sparkle of thousands of candles. And to modern skyscrapers, towering into the sky, reflecting whole cityscapes on their mirrored exteriors. And all this is traceable to ancient Phoenicia and the discovery of glass. History threads its way through time with magic. The magic eventually brings one back to time, and then the time and dates become merged with an extra significance.

There is a great fascination to ethnic costume, which is simply clothing from another era which has become imbedded in our world like an insect in amber. While the picturesque quality and richness of detail in traditional dress is slowly vanishing, it reappears in collections modelled down runways in Paris, Italy and New York. Christian Lacroix, in the first couture collection shown from his own house, based almost all the design excitement on the traditional ethnic apparel he remembers from his childhood in the south of France. The wealth of inspiration from ethnic, or folk costume, is everywhere, in tiered, flounced skirts, in smocking and embroideries, in brief boleros and vests, that, for example, turn into brief-jacketed suits. Countries which for years tried to stamp out ethnic costume are now attempting to revive it, and other countries demand a return to original dress. In fundamental Islamic nations, as an example, the culture revives traditional values in its insistence on women covering their faces. Time can be turned back for a brief period, but over the long haul, everything moves on. In China, the government demanded rigid adherence to clothing which was identical for both men and women. This was meant to abolish both class and sex distinctions, for after all, it is in our clothing that differences in status are most quickly seen. If clothing, therefore is identical, the reasoning went, so, too, will the people wearing that clothing become identical. It worked for a while, but is disappearing rapidly as the Chinese, like other peoples in the past, are rediscovering fashion, color and the satisfaction of being an individual.

The history of costume always concerns itself with identity.

*Home on the range, these sportswear separates in denim could have been literally picked off a cowboy's back. In addition, the stone-washed rage of the late 1980s reproduces the time-worn look of true western gear.*

Apparel not only identifies peoples as belonging to specific cultures, but belonging to specific levels of society. Successful people reward themselves with the trappings of elaborate costume—furs, jewelry, expensive textiles. Just as successful people have rewarded themselves throughout time. And the reward identifies that success. Other identities are also established with apparel. Blacks in America seeking identity traced their roots to historical Africa, and adopted tribal styles of hair, jewelry and, of course, clothing. When Polish-American societies meet, they wear folk costume and celebrate with folk dances, reviving their old country antecedents. We see ethnic dress on special occasions—at parades, weddings and national days. Ethnic costume expresses a pride in tradition that exists in most of us to this day.

Costume is unique to man, and just as costume is affected by the personality of the wearer, the wearer is affected by the nature of the costume. At one time, it would have been possible to tell at a glance what remote village a traveler came from, simply by the shape of a hat, the cut of a jacket, or the color of the cross-stitching. In more subtle ways, it is still possible to recognize various cultures and places of origin by the air with which clothing is worn, and again, by the cut of the garment, or the trim. Clothing, however, is approaching one-worldliness. Instant communication via satellite television and motion pictures is the catalyst in meshing our ethnic differences. It is only in very remote areas of the world, where 20th century media has not yet penetrated, that true ethnic costume still exists.

Is it possible that this slowly merging cohesiveness in the clothing of mankind is yet another reflection of an emerging similarity in us all? Is it possible that our very apparel is trying to tell us something, to get a message through? Is clothing ahead of us? Can we believe that in the future we will indeed become one, with all the individuality we desire and enjoy, but we will share common goals, we will arrive at a common understanding of one another and achieve a community of interests that will truly make us all members of just one world?

Why not. Fashion hasn't been wrong yet.

Adler, France-Michele. *Sportsfashion*. New York: Avon Books, 1980.

*The Age of Worth*. New York: The Brooklyn Museum of Arts & Sciences, 1982.

*All-American: A Sportswear Tradition*. New York: Fashion Institute of Technology, 1985.

*An Elegant Art*. Organized by Edward Maeder, Los Angeles County Museum of Art. New York: Harry N. Abrams, Inc., 1983.

Baille, C. *Chanel Solitaire*. Translated by Barbara Bray. New York: Quadrangle/The NY Times Book Co., 1974.

Baines, Barbara. *Fashion Revivals*. New York: Drama Book Publishers, 1981.

Batterberry, Michael and Ariane. *Mirror, Mirror*. Milan, Italy: Chanticleer Press, 1977.

Black, J. Anderson, Madge Garland and Frances Kennett. *A History of Fashion*. London, England: Orbis Publishing Limited, 1980.

Bonner, Paul H. Jr. *The World in Vogue*. New York: The Viking Press, Inc.

Boucher, Francois with Yvonne Deslandres. *20,000 Years of Fashion: The History of Costume and Personal Adornment*, Expanded Edition. New York: Harry N. Abrams, Inc., 1987.

Calasibetta, Charlotte Mankey. *Essential Terms of Fashion*. New York: Fairchild Publications, 1986.

——. *Fairchild's Dictionary of Fashion*. New York: Fairchild Publications, 1988.

Charles-Roux, Edmonde. *Chanel: her life, her world and the woman behind the legend she herself created*. France: Editions Grosset & Faquelle, 1974. Distributed by Random House, New York.

Chase, Edna Woolman and Ilka Chase. *Always in Vogue*. Garden City, New York: Doubleday & Company, 1954.

Chierichetti, David. *Hollywood Costume Design*. New York: Crown Publishers, Inc., 1976.

Contini, Mila. *Fashion from Ancient Egypt to the Present Day*. Italy: Arnoldo Montadori, 1965.

Davenport, Millia. *The Book of Costume*. New York: Crown Publishers, Inc., 1976.

De Osma, Guillermo. *Mariano Fortuny: His Life and Work*. New York: Rizzoli International Publications, Inc., 1987.

Deslandres, Yves. *Poiret*. New York: Rizzoli International Publications, Inc., 1987.

Diamonstein, Barbaralee. *Fashion: The Inside Story*. New York: Rizzoli International Publications, Inc., 1985.

Dior, Christian. *Talking about Fashion*. Translated by Eugenia Sheppard. New York: G. P. Putnam's Sons, 1954.

———. *Christian Dior and I*. Translated by Antonia Fraser. New York: E.P. Dutton & Company, Inc., 1957.

———. *Dior by Dior*. Translated by Antonia Fraser. London: Weidenfeld & Nicolson, 1957. Harmmondsworth, England: Penquin Books, 1968.

Dorner, Jane. *Fashion in the Forties & Fifties*. England: Ian Allan Ltd., 1975.

———. *Fashion in the Twenties & Thirties*. England: Ian Allan Ltd., 1973.

Ewing, Elizabeth. *History of 20th Century Fashion*. New York: Charles Scribner's Sons, 1974.

*Fabulous Fashion, 1907–67*. New York: The Costume Institute, The Metropolitan Museum of Art.

*400 Years of Fashion*. Edited by Natalie Rothstein. England: Victoria & Albert Museum, 1988.

Fraser, Kennedy. *The Fashionable Mind*. Boston, Massachusetts: David R. Godine, 1985.

Frings, Gini Stephens, *Fashion from Concept to Consumer*. New Jersey: Prentice-Hall, Inc., 1982.

Geijer, Agnes. *History of Textile Arts*. New Jersey: Sotheby Parke Bernet Publications, 1979.

Giroud, Francois, *Dior*. New York: Rizzoli International Publications, 1987.

Gold, Annalee, *75 Years of Fashion*. New York: Fairchild Publications, 1975.

———. *One World of Fashion*, 4th edition. New York: Fairchild Publications, 1986.

Grayson, Martin, editor. *Encyclopedia of Textiles, Fibers and Nonwoven Fabrics*. New York: John Wiley & Sons, 1984.

Haedrich, Marcel. *Coco Chanel: Her Life, Her Secrets*. Boston, Massachusetts: Little, Brown & Co., 1971.

Hill, Margot Hamilton and Peter A. Bucknell. *The Evolution of Fashion*. London: B. T. Batsford Ltd., 1983.

Howell, Georgina. *In Vogue: Six Decades of Fashion*. London: Allen Lane, 1975.

*The Imperial Style: Fashions of the Hapsburg Era*. New York: The Metropolitan Museum of Art, 1980.

Jarnow, Jeannette A., Miriam Guerreiro and Beatrice Judelle. *Inside the Fashion Business*, 4th edition. New York: Macmillan Publishing Company, 1987.

Keenan, Brigid. *Dior in Vogue*. New York: Harmony Books, 1981.

Konig, Rene. *A La Mode*. New York: The Seabury Press, 1973.

Koren, Leonard. *New Fashion in Japan*. New York: Kodansha International, 1984.

Lambert, Eleanor. *World of Fashion: People, Places, Resources*. New York: R. R. Bowher Company, 1976.

Langner, Lawrence. *The Importance of Wearing Clothes*. New York: Hastings House, 1959.

Laver, James. *Concise History of Costume and Fashion*. New York: Harry N. Abrams, Inc., 1969.

Lavine, W. Robert. *In a Glamorous Fashion*. New York: Charles Scribner's Sons, 1980.

Leese, Elizabeth. *Costume Design in the Movies*. New York: Frederick Ungar Publishing Co., 1977.

Leymarie, Jean. *Chanel*. New York: Rizzoli International Publications, 1987.

Lynam, Ruth, editor. *Couture*. Garden City, N.Y.: Doubleday & Company, Inc., 1972.

Martin, Richard. *Fashion and Surrealism*. New York: Rizzoli International Publications, 1987.

McDowell, Colin. *McDowell's Directory of Twentieth Century Fashion*. New Jersey: Prentice-Hall, Inc., 1985.

Milbank, Caroline Rennolds. *Couture, The Great Designers*. New York: Stewart, Tabori, & Chang, Inc., 1985.

Mitford, Nancy. *The Sun King, Louis XIV at Versailles*. New York: Harper & Row, 1966.

Montgomery, Florence M. *Textiles in America, 1650–1870*. New York: W. W. Norton & Company, 1984.

Moor, Jonathan. *Perry Ellis, a Biography*. New York: St. Martin's Press, 1988.

Morris, Bernadine. *The Fashion Makers: An Inside Look at America's Leading Designers*. New York: Random House, 1978.

O'Hara, Georgina. *The Encyclopeadia of Fashion*. New York: Harry N. Abrams, Inc., 1986.

Packard, Sidney, Arthur A. Winters and Nathan Axelrod. *Fashion Buying and Merchandising*, 2nd edition. New York: Fairchild Publications, 1984.

Palacios, Alvar Gonzales. *The Age of Louis XV*. England: Hamlyn Publishing Group. Limited.

Perna, Rita. *Fashion Forecasting*. New York: Fairchild Publications, 1987.

Riley, Robert, Dale McConathy, Sally Kirkland, Bernadine Morris, and Eleni Sakes Epstein. *American Fashion: The Life and Lives of Adrian, Mainbocher, McCardell, Norell & Trigère*. Edited by Sarah Tomerlin Lee. New York: Quadrangle/The NY Times Book Co., 1975.

Russell, Douglas A. *Costume, History and Style*. New Jersey: Prentice-Hall, Inc., 1983.

Saint Laurent, Yves. *Yves Saint Laurent*. New York: Metropolitan Museum of Art, 1983.

Schiaparelli, Elsa. *Shocking Life*. New York: E. P. Dutton & Co. Inc., 1954.

Sichel, Marion. *Costume of the Classical World*. England: Batsford Academic and Education Limited, 1985.

Squire, Geoffrey. *Dress and Society*, 1560–1970. New York: Viking Press, 1974

Stegemeyer, Anne. *Who's Who in Fashion*, 2nd edition. New York: Fairchild Publications, 1988.

Tolstoy, Mary Koutouzov. *Charlemagne to Dior: The Story of French Fashion*. New York: Michael Slains, 1967.

Tortora, Phyllis and Keith Eubank. *A Survey of Historic Costume*. New York: Fairchild Publications, 1989.

Vecchio, Walter and Robert Riley. *The Fashion Makers. A Photographic Record*. New York: Crown Publishers, Inc., 1968.

Vertes, Marcel. *Art and Fashion*. New York: The Studio Publications Inc., 1944.

*"W": The Designing Life*. Staff of W, edited by Lois Perschetz. New York: Clarkson N. Potter, Inc., 1987.

Walz, Barbra. *The Fashion Makers*. New York: Random House, 1979.

White, Palmer. *Poiret*. New York: Clarkson N. Potter, Inc., 1973.

——. *Elsa Schiaparelli: Empress of Paris Fashion*. New York: Rizzoli International Publications, 1966.

Wilcox, R. Turner. *The Mode in Costume*. New York: Charles Scribner's Sons, 1958.

Wingate, Isabel. *Fairchild's Dictionary of Textiles*, 6th edition. New York: Fairchild Publications, 1979.

*The World of Balenciaga*. New York: Metropolitan Museum of Art, 1973.

Worth, Jean Philippe. *A Century of Fashion*. Translated by Ruth Scott Miller. Boston, Massachusetts: Little, Brown & Co., 1928.

Yarwood, Doreen. *The Encyclopaedia of World Costume*. London: Anchor Press, 1976.

——. *European Costume, 4000 Years of Fashion*. New York: Bonanza Books, 1982.

# A

Acetate, 230–231
Acrylics, 231–232
Adrian, Gilbert, 187–190
A-line, 111
*Altamoda*, 155
American fashion
  *See also specific American
    designers*
  The all-American team, 162–
    165
  Classics, 177–184
  Designers, and World War
    II, 108, 109
  How it works, 205–220
  Sportswear in, 165–177
Archaic costume, 21
Armor, 49, 65
Art, fashion as, 17–18

# B

Balenciaga, Cristobal, *21*, 110,
  136–139
Barbarian period, clothing
  during, 43–46, *52*
Baroque period, fashion
  during, *54*
  *See also* Louis XIV period,
    fashion during
Beau Brummell, 87
Beehive hairstyle, 113
La Belle Epoque, fashion
  during, 96–99
Benetton, *214, 215*, 218
Bikinis, *5*, 175–176
Blass, Bill, *97, 209*
Bliauts, 46–47, *48, 49*
Bloomer, Amelia, 173
Bloomer suit, *5*
Blouson, 29
Body coverings, early, 20

Body stockings, 203
Bohan, Marc, 140, *155*
Brassieres, 107, 125
  "no-bra" bra, 179, 203
Breeches, 46
  Petticoat, 69
Brooks Brothers, 111
Bustles, 90, *93, 237*
Buttons, 56
Buyers, fashion industry, 212
Byzantine fashion, 38–40

# C

Cabines, 161
  *En cabochon*, 236
Caftans, 39–40
Calico, 224
The California look, 180–181
Cardin, Pierre, 144–145, 157
Carnegie, Hattie, 197
Carolingian dress, 46–47, *52*
Cashin, Bonnie, *49*
Cavalier age, fashion during,
  *54*, 67–68
Chambray, 224
*Chambre Syndicale de la
  Couture Parisienne*, 152–
  153, 155
*Chambre Syndicale du Prêt-à-
  Porter des Couturiers et
  Createurs de Mode*, 154
Chanel, Coco (Gabrielle
  Chanel), *126*, 126–128
The Chanel suit, 104
Chemise, 47, 110, *111*, 137
Chinoiserie, 76
Chintz, 81, 224
Chiton, 28
Chopines, 60
Christian dress, early, 44–46
Claiborne, Liz, 216–217
Clavi, 38

Clerical dress, 38–39
Cloche, 104, *105*
Cocktail dress, 105
Codpiece, 51, 60
Cologne, 79–80
Color
    Use of by ancient peoples,
        29, 35–36
    Use of in textile production,
        232–233
Corsets, 103
Cosmetics
    Ancient, 24, 27, 36–37
    In the 18th century, 79
    In the 20th century, 114,
        118, 235
Costume, 242
    History of, 1–2
Cote, 47
Cotehardie, *44*, 48, 51, 56
Cotte, 48
Cotton, 223–224
    Printed, 227–228
    True Performance, *232*
Cotton gin, 229
Coty Award, 197, 200
Coty Hall of Fame, 200, 202
Courrèges, André, 112, 142–
    143
Couture, French, 104, 115,
    121–122
    *See also specific French
        couturiers*
    *Chambre Syndicale de la
        Couture Parisienne,* 152–
        153, 155
    *Chambre Syndicale du Prêt-
        à-Porter des Couturiers et
        Createurs de Mode,* 154
    Haute, 150–155
    How it works, 153–154
    Inspiration, sources of, 159–
        161
    Licensing, 158–159
    Line for line copies, 155–
        156
    Post World War II, 109–111
    And World War I, 102
Cravat (stock), 87
Crinolines, 89
The Crusades, fashion in, 49–
    52, 56

Culottes (bifurcated skirts),
    173, *174*
Cutting *en suite,* 69–70

D

Dalmatica, 38, *39*
Damask, 224
Dandy, 18th-century, *82*
Denim, *182,* 224, *241*
Department stores, 94, 107,
    209–210, 211
Designers
    American. *See* American
        fashion; *specific American
        designers*
    And the fashion press, 213
    French. *See* Couture, French;
        *specific French couturiers*
    And inspiration, sources of,
        119, 159–161, 241
    Japanese, 158
Dhoti, 21
Dior, Christian, *91,* 109, 111,
    133–136
Direct mail and catalogues,
    210–211
Directoire and Empire periods,
    fashion during, 83–91
Disposable wardrobe concept,
    205–206
Doublets, 51, 56, *57,* 59
Dresses, in contemporary
    fashion market, 181–182
Du Pont, 231, 232
Dusters, 101

E

Egyptian fashion, ancient, 22–
    24
18th-century fashion. *See*
    Revolutionary age,
    French, fashion during
Elizabethan era, fashion
    during, *60, 61,* 62–66
Ellis, Perry, *162,* 163, *177*
Embroidery, Spanish, 57
Empire periods, fashion
    during, 83–91
Esprit, 5
Eugènie, Empress, 88

# F

Fans, 76
Farthingale, 58–59
Fashion, 2–7
  *See also specific historic periods*
  American. *See* American fashion
  Centers of, in the world, 239–240
  French. *See* Couture, French
  Industry protection, 16–17
  Markets, American, 214–215
  Selection process, 6–16
  Today, 119–120
  What is fashion, 2–6
Fashion dolls (Pandoras), 80–81
Fibulae, 28
Fortuny, Mariano, 30–32
Furs, contemporary, 7

# G

Galanos, James, 200–202
Gaultier, Jean-Paul, *26*
Gernreich, Rudi, 179, 180, 202–204, *207*
Gibson girl, 92, 100
Girdles, 107
Givenchy, Hubert, *158*
"Golden Triangle" trade, 81–82
Gothic age, clothing in, 47–52, 53
Graffiti collection (Sprouse), *10*
Greek fashion, ancient, 28–32
Greige goods (gray), 232
Grès, Mme., 30
"Guardinfanta" farthingale, *58*

# H

Hair fashions, 236–237
  *see also* Wigs
  Ancient, 26, 37
  Gothic, 51
  In the 1970s, 117–118
  In the 1960s, 112–114

In the 1930s, 107
In the 1920s, 104, 105
Powdered (18th century), 72, 74
In the Renaissance, 61
Haute couture, 150–155
Hennin, double-horned, *50*
Hieratic clothing, 14–16, 35
Howe, Elias, 89

# I

Identification, clothing as, 10–12
ILGWU (International Ladies Garment Workers Union), 16, 211–212
Individuality in apparel, 118–120
Inspiration, sources of, 119, 159–161

# J

Jacobs, Marc, *44*
James, Charles, 186
Jeans, 177–178. *See also* Levi Strauss' Levis
Jewelry, 235–236
  Ancient, 20–21, 24, 37

# K

Kalasiris, 23
Kamali, Norma, *18*
Karan, Donna, *162, 163, 179, 183*
Klein, Anne, *162*, 163
Klein, Calvin, *37, 162, 163, 183*, 217
Knickers, 105

# L

Lace, 59
Lacroix, Christian, 7, *79, 85, 91, 97*, 116, *151, 153*, 241
Lagerfeld, Karl, *15, 93, 98*, 128, 146–148
Lastex, 173, 232
Latex, 232

Lauren, Ralph, *11, 118, 162, 167,* 217–218
L-85 law, 108, 174
Leotards, 193
Levi Strauss's Levis, 178, 209
Licensing, 144, 158–159, 163
The Limited, 216
Line for line copies, 155–156
Linen (flax), 23, 224–225
The little black dress, 127
Looms
  Mechanical, 228
  Power, 229
Lord and Taylor, 211, *212*
Louis XIV period, fashion during, *55,* 68–70
Lycra, 232

# M

McCardell, Claire, 176, 191–193
McFadden, Mary, *31, 239*
Madras, 224
Maillot, 176, 203
Mainbocher, *79,* 186, 194–196
Mantua, *75, 84*
Marie Antoinette, 76, 77
Markets, American fashion, 214–215
Mary Jane shoes, 114
Maternity garments, forerunner of, 190
de Medici, Catherine, 62
Men's fashion
  In the 18th and 19th centuries, 86–87
  In the Louis XIV period, 69–70
  In the 1960s, 114
  In the 20th century, 105
  In the Victorian era, 92
Midi (maxi) skirts, 115
Miniskirts, 112, *113,* 114, 115
Minoan fashion, 25–27
Missoni, *45*
Models, fashion, 161
Muslin, 224

# N

Needles, steel, 57

The New Look (Dior's), *91,* 134, 135
The 1970s, fashion during, 115–118
The 1960s, fashion during, 112–115
The 1930s, fashion during, 106–107, 171, 172, 173
The 1920s, fashion during, 104–105, 171
Nordstrom, 216
Norell, Norman, 197–199
Nylon, 111, 231

# O

Orientalia, in 20th-century fashion, *40*
Orlon, 232

# P

Panier, 72, 76
Pants, 238–239
  Ancient, 38
  In 18th-century France, 86
  Women in, 106, 115–116, *117, 139,* 140, 171–172, 180
  Yves Saint Laurent's influence on, *139,* 140
Pantyhose, 114, 176, 180
Patching, 76
Peplos, 28–29, *30*
Peplum, 29
Plaids, ancient, 46
Playclothes, 180
Pleating, 30, 32
Poiret, Paul, 102, 103, 124–126, *152*
Polyester, 231
Pompadour, Marquise de, 76, 77
Popover (McCardell's), *192,* 193
Poulaines, 50
Prehistoric clothing, 20–21
The press, fashion, 212–213
  *See also Harper's Bazaar; Vogue*
Prêt-à-Porter (prêt), 140, 145, 154, 157–158, 161

Princess line, 39
Printing, textiles, 233
Private labels, 218–219
Protection, clothing as, 7–8
Psychological clothing, 9–10
Pucci, Emilio, *114, 240*
Puffing, 65
Pumps, 64
Puritan and Pilgrim fashion, 67

# R

Rabanne, Paco, *47*
Rayon, 101, 230
Ready made garments. *See*
    Ready-to-wear
Ready-to-wear, ready-to-wear
    industry, 90, 212
    American, 100, 107, 164,
        186, 199
    Contemporary, 182
    French, 115, 140, 145, 154,
        206. *See also* Prêt-à-Porter
Redingote, 81
Religious or superstitious
    clothing selection, 8–9
Renaissance
    Early, fashion during, *53*,
        56–59
    High, fashion during, *54*,
        62–66
    Late, fashion during, 60–62
de la Renta, Oscar, *179, 208*
Retailing industry
    *See also* Department stores;
        Direct mail and catalogues
    And the consumer, 219, 220
    And designer-retailer
        cooperation, 211, 217,
        218
    And private labels, 218–219
    Specialization and, 215
Revolutionary age, French,
    fashion during
    In the court, 71–82
    Directoire and Empire
        periods, 83–91
*Rive Gauche* collection, 157
Robe, 56
Roman fashion, 33–37
Ruffs, 59

# S

Sacque, 72, *73, 78*, 110
Saint Laurent, Yves, *80*, 111,
    139–140, *154*, 157
Saris, *20*, 21, *36*
Scalloping (dagging), 56
Schenti, 23
Schiaparelli, Elsa, 131–133
"S" curve, *92, 98*, 99
Seventh Avenue (SA), 209
Sexual attraction, clothing for,
    12–14
Shamask, Ronaldus, *40, 45*
Shantung, 224
Shaver, Dorothy, *212*
Shirtwaist dress, 92, *100*, 178
Shoes, 237–238
    Ancient, *19*, 24
    Capezio, 176, 177, 193
    Chanel, 128
    In the 18th century, 83–84
    Gothic, 50–51
    Greek-inspired, *34*
    The Louis pump, 69
    In the Renaissance, 59, 60–
        61, 64
    In the 20th century, *34*,
        105, 107, 110
Silk, 36, 225–228
Skirts
    Bifurcated. *See* Culottes
    Length of, 103, 104, 112,
        113, 114, 115, 116
    Men in, *26, 27*
    Extenders, *89, 90*
Slashing, 65
Sleeves, fake, 50, 61
Snood, *107*, 131
Soutienne-gorge. *See* Brassieres
Spanish fashion in the early
    Renaissance, 57–59
Spindle, 223
Spinning frame, 229
Spinning jenny, 229
Spinning wheel, 223
Sportswear, 164–177
Stockings
    Nylon, *230*, 231
    Silk knitted, 65
Stola, 35
Suits, 70

Sumptuary laws, 16, 50, 61, 66, 82
Surcoat, 48, 49
Swimsuits, swimsuit industry, *23, 170, 171*, 172, *173*, 175–176, 181
    Diaper, 193
    Maillot, 176, 203
    Topless, 180, 203

## T

Tea dress, 99
Textiles, textile industry, 221, *223*
    *See also specific textiles*
    And American fashion industry, 206–207
    Ancient, 1, 23, 39
    English, in the 18th century, 81
    French, during the Empire, 86
    Hand, 222
    Imports, into U.S., 212
    Man-made, 111, 230
    Production of, 232–234
    In the Renaissance, 56–57
Togas, 33–35
Toile, 160
The "trapeze," *110*, 111
Triana, Anthony, 197
Trousers. *See* Pants
Trunk hose, *57*, 59
T-shirts, 177
Tunicas, 35
20th century, fashion during, 164
    *See also specific 20th century decades*
    La Belle Epoque, 96–99
    Early, 100–102
    And the World Wars, 102–103

## U

Undergarments, 66
Unions. *See* ILGWU
Unisex apparel, 25, 56, *87*, 203

## V

Victorian era, fashion during, *25*, 92–94
Vionnet, Madeleine, 106, 129–130
Vittadini, Adrienne, *240*
Vivier, Roger, *151*
*Vogue*, 174, 177, 213

## W

Watteau gown. *See* Sacque
Weaving, weaves, 228–229
Wigs
    Egyptian, *24*
    Powdered, 69, 72, 74
Wimple, 51
Windsor, Duchess of, *79*, 194–195
Women, women's fashion
    In the Louis XIV period, 70
    In the Renaissance, 61–62
    In the Victorian era, 92
    After World War I, 171–172
Wool, 23, 222–223
World War I, functional clothing and, 170
World War II
    Apparel controls during, 108–109
    Couture during, 107–108
Worth, Charles Frederick, *25*, 88–91, *122*, 123–124, 150